VIRAL LOOP

VIRAL LOOP

From Facebook to Twitter,
How Today's Smartest
Businesses Grow Themselves

Adam L. Penenberg

HYPERION

NEW YORK

Copyright © 2009 Adam L. Penenberg

All rights reserved. No part of this book may be used or reproduced in any manner whatsoever without the written permission of the Publisher. Printed in the United States of America. For information address Hyperion, 114 Fifth Avenue, New York, New York, 10011.

Library of Congress Cataloging-in-Publication Data is available upon request.

ISBN: 978-1-4013-2349-3

Hyperion books are available for special promotions and premiums. For details contact the HarperCollins Special Markets Department in the New York office at 212-207-7528, fax 212-207-7222, or e-mail spsales@ harpercollins.com.

FIRST EDITION

10 9 8 7 6 5 4 3 2 1

SUSTAINABLE FORESTRY INITIATIVE
Certified Fiber Sourcing
www.sfiprogram.org

THIS LABEL APPLIES TO TEXT STOCK

We try to produce the most beautiful books possible, and we are also extremely concerned about the impact of our manufacturing process on the forests of the world and the environment as a whole. Accordingly, we've made sure that all of the paper we use has been certified as coming from forests that are managed to insure the protection of the people and wildlife dependent upon them.

To the Penengirls,
Charlotte, Lila, and Sophie

CONTENTS

II

Viral Marketing

III

Viral Networks

VIRAL LOOP

An Insanely Viral Scheme

How the Guys from Hot or Not Rode a Simple Idea to a Fortune

Two Heinekens into a lazy Tuesday afternoon, James Hong, a twenty-seven-year-old dot-com refugee from Mountain View, California, was listening to his roommate, Jim Young, a Berkeley graduate student in electrical engineering, wax on about a woman he had spotted at a party the previous weekend. Young, also twenty-seven, insisted she was a "perfect 10." Hong didn't believe him. He knew his roommate had a thing for "goth," while Hong's own tastes were more Abercrombie & Fitch. What the world needed, they agreed, was a metric to reliably rate someone's looks.

The two out-of-pocket entrepreneurs weren't just in a frat-like buzz obsessing over women who likely wouldn't give them a second look. This exchange was the logical outgrowth of a broader discussion they had been having about Web services, something that had long been on Hong's mind. At the time, October 2000, Web services focused on business-to-business applications, but Hong wondered about a consumer play—a product that would appeal to regular people. A year earlier, he and Young had toyed with the idea of creating a dating site with collaborative filtering to better cluster people: users would scan a series of pictures, then express an opinion as to how attractive the person was. This, they reasoned, could increase the efficiency of dating, although it didn't end up spawning an actual business. Now he and his roommate were ginning up more ideas for a start-up.

Young's "perfect ten" comment got Hong thinking. What if you could rate someone's looks by opening it up to a vote? Most people believed they were above average, which was, statistically speaking, impossible. Hong, an athletic extrovert with a buzz cut and zingy wit, rated himself a 7. And his skinny partner with the modish, foppish hair? About the same, but who really knew? In the way the value of a house or used car was whatever someone was willing to pay—that is, whatever the market would bear—a person's attractiveness could be based on whatever a large community of people judged it to be. For it to work, all they would need were pictures and a grid from 1 to 10 for site visitors to click on. Then they would crunch the aggregate data and spit out the results. Hong didn't know many people who had a whiteboard in their living room, but he and Young did, and they quickly drew up plans. Burned out on his dissertation, Young figured it could be an entertaining diversion and suggested they build a simple website instead of a vastly more complicated Web service.

Hong scoured the Web for candid shots—he wanted real people, not *Sports Illustrated* swimsuit models—while Young got cracking on the digital infrastructure, cobbling it together with Linux code. A couple of days later, while visiting his parents, Hong was tinkering with the site when in walked his father, a Taiwanese-born engineer who wore pocket protectors and had given him a slide rule for his thirteenth birthday. If he found out what his unemployed son was working on, he would shake his head and mutter that he was wasting his education. Hong told him it was all Young's idea.

Peering over his son's shoulder, his father looked at the photo on the screen. "Oh, she's hot. She's an eight," he said. Hong could scarcely believe his ears. He was half convinced his father had engaged in sex only three times in his life—when he, his brother, and his sister were conceived. Without prompting, his father clicked on another photo. "Not so hot," he clucked. Then *click.* . . . *Click, click, click,* until he pored through the entire cache of photos—forty in all.

His father was hooked. Because of the way Hong and his partner designed the site, a user couldn't find out the poll results until he voted and the next page loaded. They purposely placed the aggregate score on the left side over a smaller version of the picture while the next picture, significantly larger, sat front and center. The idea was to train a user's eyes to flow from the middle to the left. Because there was always one more photo to be judged, a user would feel compelled to cast another vote. It was like the old Lay's potato chip ad: "Betcha can't eat just one." The interface demanded engagement, and this in turn made it sticky. If a site retained a visitor's interest, it had the potential to be popular and spread by powerful word-of-mouth endorsement.

When his father was out of earshot, Hong phoned his roommate. "Dude, we have to launch this thing right now!"

[GOING VIRAL . . .]

On Monday, October 9, 2000, Am I Hot or Not went live, not that anyone but its two founders knew about it. Hong emailed forty-two friends (partly, he said, because forty-two was the answer to "life, the universe and everything" in the cult sci-fi classic *The Hitchhiker's Guide to the Galaxy*). "Here's a website that Jim and I made—be nice," he wrote and inserted a link to their own pictures. Soon after, visitors pinged the site, quickly spreading well beyond Hong's forty-two friends. It didn't take an epidemiologist to recognize a viral spread in the making. To test it, Hong slipped on a pair of Rollerblades and skated across the street to an office park where Tellme, a software call center and services provider, was located. He glided over to an office worker in the parking lot.

"Hey, have you seen this website where you can rate people if they are hot or not?" Hong asked.

He hadn't. Hong told him and bladed home. Inside ten minutes Tellme's IP address appeared in the site logs. Hong monitored the man's activities as he clicked through the photos. Suddenly more Tellme IP addresses popped up. Clearly the man had shared the link with coworkers, who then passed it to others. A drizzle turned into a full-blown storm, with the hits coming in fast and furious from all over the country. Traffic swarmed their borrowed server; the site slowed to a crawl. It took half a minute for each page to load.

Hong was hosting the site on his brother's machine, which sat in a data center. The more bandwidth they consumed, the more they would have to pay. Hong knew this would quickly become unsustainable. By the end of the first day thirty-seven thousand unique visitors had found their way to the site and two hundred people had uploaded photos. On day two, they broke one hundred thousand in addition to the mass of returning visitors from the first day. At the current run rate, Hong estimated that Am I Hot or Not would cost $150,000 in bandwidth in their first year. The more successful they were, the more likely they could go bankrupt. Hong, a self-described pop culture junkie with an MBA from Berkeley, was broke, $60,000 in debt, and living rent-free in his roommate's parents' house. He had no idea how the site would make money and frankly didn't care. All he knew was that he had stumbled into an insanely viral scheme, but he had to figure out how to keep it going before the levees gave way and it drowned in its own popularity.

It would only get worse before it could get better. Salon.com was planning an article for the following day. The reporter contacted Hong after a friend had emailed her the link with the comment, "I think this is quite viral." Hong begged her to push the story back a few days until he could solve their bandwidth woes. She refused. (Slow news day, she explained.) In her essay, she called Hong and Young's brainchild "nothing more than a virtual meat market," "indescribably horrible . . . and yet utterly addictive," "fashion police with a twist," a site that "manages to throw the whole idealistic notion of 'beauty comes from within' right out the window in about three seconds flat." She uploaded a five-year-old photo of herself, claiming unconvincingly that she didn't want to know how she would fare. Her mix of opprobrium and self-loathing found a hungry audience. Readers slammed Am I Hot or Not's server. Now Hong and Young were fielding two viral storms.

[TOO BIG, TOO FAST]

Survival depended on solving their scaling problem. Step one was to confront the colossal amount of bandwidth the photos soaked up. Around midnight, while commiserating with Young at the drive-thru of an In-N-Out Burger, Hong had an idea. "We don't need to host the pictures," he said. "We'll let Yahoo do it!" Based on his analysis of the server logs, Hong believed twenty-five new pictures a day would be enough to attract fresh traffic to the site—eventually people got bored and moved on. They would effectively cap the number of new pictures. While they were at it, they would direct users to post their photos on Yahoo GeoCities and submit the URLs (the Web addresses) to Am I Hot or Not. By 3:30 a.m. Hong and Young had transferred their entire collection to Yahoo.

Then they addressed the next challenge: offloading the site from their clotted server and out of the data center. At 4:00 a.m. they drove to Berkeley where Young had an office. They pulled the plug and reinstalled the site on a cheap 400-megahertz Celeron PC that Hong had gotten free for opening an eTrade account. So no one would turn it off, he popped the top off a case of pushpins and mounted it over the PC's power switch. Then they secreted it under Young's desk, stashed in a corner and buried by books. To the uninitiated it looked like a pile of stuff with an Ethernet cable poking out.

It was five in the morning and Am I Hot or Not had been down for two hours. They wondered if the outage might have killed it. As soon as they switched it back on, they got their answer. *Bam bam bam*, IP addresses pounded into their logs. Three hours later Young's adviser, the dean of the Berkeley engineering department, informed them the university's information technology department was up in arms. Their single PC was weighing down the entire network. Amused by their plight, the professor promised to cover for them, but they had twenty-four hours to set up shop elsewhere.

Beg, borrow, steal, whatever it took. Hong searched for a new home, settling on Rackspace, a Web-hosting firm. Although he and Young had no money, they were getting heaps of press. The *Guardian*, the *New York Times*, and news outlets from around the world found Am I Hot or Not irresistible. Hong cultivated the media because he knew their concept would be easy to steal. The more stories, the more spikes in traffic, the harder it would be to dislodge them when the inevitable copycat arrived on the scene. He cold-called the head of Rackspace business development to propose a trade. "I know you guys want to go public and it's great to get your name out," Hong said. "Your whole value proposition is that you can help companies scale by outsourcing. If you can help us, we will have all these upcoming interviews, and we can be a poster child for you." The Rackspace executive agreed, and every day that week Hong called to request more machines. By its eighth day the site was fielding 1.8 million page views per day, and both Hong and Young, who had slept eight hours over those eight days, were literally shaking.

[SHOW ME THE MONEY]

Now that Hong and Young had, for the time being, solved the site's scaling challenges, they needed to figure out how to monetize it. With the kind of traffic they attracted—within six weeks of launch the site had 3 million page views a day and posted more than three thousand photos—advertising made the most sense. These were the days predating automated ad servers like Google AdSense, which meant they had to enlist an online advertising network. But a number of users had been uploading nude photos, while pornographers were tricking users into passing on their emails so they could spam them. Hong knew that they couldn't attract advertisers if there was objectionable material, so he and Young came up with the motto "Fun, Clean and Real," and issued basic rules: no celebrities, minors, models, or porn; no group photos, ads, or anything with contact information such as email addresses or phone numbers.

They created a community monitoring system: users could click a link under an inappropriate picture and, based on an algorithm, anything that was tagged too often was deleted. Ready to approach ad networks, Hong emailed the founder of DoubleClick, who replied that when he visited the site, the first picture he encountered was of a naked woman. What we need, Hong told Young, was a more intensive moderation system: someone to approve the photos before they posted. Originally he appointed his parents, who were retired and had plenty of free time. After a few days he asked how it was going.

"Oh, it's very interesting," his father replied. "Mom saw a picture of a guy and a girl and another girl and they were doing . . ."

"Dude," Hong told his partner, "my parents can't do this anymore. They're looking at porn all day."

They turned to their community to act as moderators. Each applicant was required to pen an essay. Those chosen to moderate were instructed to reject inappropriate pictures, ads, or anything with someone's contact information. With hundreds of users trolling the site, they could filter what was posted. After this went into effect, it didn't take long to land an advertising network. Although the click-through rates were low—on the order of 0.2 percent—the immense number of page views still made it a money-making proposition. Within two months they had counted 7 million page views a day and had collected 130,000 photos. By year's end, three months after the site's launch, they had broken into Nielsen's Top 25 advertising domains on the Web and had generated $100,000 in advertising revenue.

But they were nowhere near Easy Street. Hong received a cease-and-desist letter after Howard Stern, on his radio show, mistakenly called their site Am I Hot, the name of a far racier site pushing skin and cleavage. Hong had done his due diligence and looked for similar-sounding domains before launch. It wasn't his fault Stern had made a mistake, but he wanted to avoid a battle over the name. He agreed to change it to Hot or Not, and they promised to redirect traffic to the new domain for three months. Hong made good use of all the press coverage to rebrand the site, and traffic barely hiccuped. In the meantime, he chopped their overhead. He approached Ofoto about an affiliate deal, telling an executive how he had dispatched people to Yahoo to upload photos. Hong could just as easily send them to Ofoto, and by hosting them, Ofoto would have the lead in offering additional services. The agreement he struck meant that Hong had moved something from costing money to making it free to actually generating a profit.

[REVENUE STREAMS]

Just when things seemed to be humming along, the Web ad market stumbled, a victim of the dot-com bust, and advertising rates dropped. "Can we charge for anything?" Hong wondered. The answer was staring him right in the face. After they had launched the community monitoring system to stamp out pornography, they received emails from users complaining that they could no longer meet people through the site. Since it made sense to stoke the community, Hong and Young set up Meet Me, which allowed active users to commingle online. It was a hedge against porn operators, since a member could no longer simply post an ad and wait for email to roll in. A user had to engage in the community.

In April 2001, they instituted a $6 per month fee to join Meet Me, fig-
uring it was cheap enough to qualify as an impulse buy. In its first month
it generated $25,000 in revenue; by year's end it had brought in $600,000.
Their success spurred them to work even harder; most nights neither got
much sleep. They turned it into a race: could Hong bring in people faster
than Young's system could handle? Hong's job was to create a bottleneck
and Young's was to clear it. That first half-year felt like it lasted a day.
Practically every waking moment they considered ways to make the site
run faster and better. They were featured in *People*, *Time*, and *Newsweek*
and by the end of the year they were on *Entertainment Weekly*'s It List.
They were profiled in the *New Yorker*. Hong became the first in his MBA
class to make it into the *Wall Street Journal*.

There were the inevitable copycats: Bangable—which needs no
description—RateMyFace.com, and a number of parodies, including a site
that ranked monkeys. None, however, could rival Hot or Not's popularity.
There was something ingeniously simple and intuitive about Hong and
Young's formula that others couldn't replicate. The site grew so big so fast,
and continued to attract visitors at an exponential rate, that it had achieved
a point of nondisplacement. No one could knock them off their pedestal.

Besides money and fame, the site offered fringe benefits. It vastly improved their dating lives, for one. Now Hong could afford a Porsche and
a posh condo and dated women way out of his league. The site also added
to his encyclopedic knowledge of American pop culture. At times he felt
like an amateur sociologist. Initially his photo rated a 3.8, once plummet-
ing to 2.6 after a particularly unfortunate haircut, while Young averaged
3.5. That changed after they inserted a "Meet the guys that run Hot or
Not" link on the home page and their scores rose. It figured, Hong thought.
The more successful the site, the more money they made, the more famous they became, the hotter they got.

When Hong dug into the logs, he learned that two-thirds of visitors to
the site were men and only two out of a hundred bothered to post a photo.
Most logged on from work and stayed for an average of forty-five minutes
a session. The largest demographic segment was eighteen- to twenty-four-
year-olds, followed by twenty-four- to thirty-year-olds, and 15 percent
were under eighteen. Most men voted strictly for the ladies. So did
women. (Hong found that surprising, although virtually every woman

he spoke to said it made perfect sense.) A guy holding a puppy scored higher than one who didn't. A bikini-clad female almost always scored a 9. The best-looking, as voted by their audience, hailed from warm-weather states, with women from Florida, California, and Hawaii populating the site's top 10 lists, probably because they were more comfortable baring skin than their cold-weather counterparts.

It took a while for Hong and Young to realize that they had a viable business, even after Lycos offered $2 million (they turned it down flat) and venture capitalists expressed interest. There was nothing inherently viral about Hot or Not. It was simply compelling enough to induce people to spread the word. Like any fad, Hong believed it would lose steam and their gravy train would run out of track. Young could then return to grad school to complete his dissertation, "Design and Specification of Heterogeneous Systems," and Hong would move on to other ventures, both richer and wiser. But in their first full year, they pulled in $600,000 in almost pure profit, and their revenue doubled each and every year that followed. By 2004, the site generated more than $4 million annually, which the two partners split in the form of dividends. In July 2006, the site tallied its 13 billionth vote and was the third most popular dating site on the Internet.

Two years later Hong and Young sold Hot or Not for $20 million.

Viral President

Positive Feedback Loop, Spreadable Concepts,
and the Three Categories of Viral Expansion Loops

As James Hong and Jim Young demonstrated, it's possible to build a multi-million- or even billion-dollar business from scratch, simply by designing a product the right way. No advertising or marketing budget, no need for a sales force, and venture capitalists will kill for the chance to throw money at you.

This may sound too good to be true, like some dodgy get-rich-quick scheme from a late-night cable TV infomercial or the latest spam come-on to hit your in-box, but some of the most iconic Web 2.0 companies— Hotmail, eBay, PayPal, MySpace, YouTube, Facebook, relative newcomers like Digg, LinkedIn, Twitter, and Flickr, as well as hundreds of widget makers navigating the emerging "social media" economy—fit this description. The trick is they created something people *really* want, so much so that their customers happily spread their product for them through their own social networks of friends, family, colleagues, and peers. That's one of the beautiful things about Web 2.0: you can nurture a business like never before and achieve almost cosmic valuations in record time.

These companies are powered by something called a "viral expansion loop," which is accomplished by incorporating virality into the functionality of a product. In plain English, it means a company grows because each new user begets more users. Just by using a product they spread it. After all, what's the sense of being on Facebook if none of your friends are, or using Flickr if you can't share your photos? Why post an item for sale on eBay if no one is around to bid on it, or use PayPal if no one accepts it? It's not quite enough to click through a cache of photos on Hot or

Not and vote on people's relative attractiveness unless you can share the experience—and that's precisely what happened.

Within ninety minutes of Hong and Young's brainchild hitting the Web, the number of users doubled every two hours. On day two, they doubled every hour, breaking one hundred thousand users. For every ten visitors, two or three were—without prompting—passing the link to others, with the pattern replicating itself en masse. That's because in large numbers, human behavior is largely predictable. We seek to pass on interesting or funny memes or products to our personal social networks, whether they are included in our email address books, part of our collection of friends on Facebook, visitors to our blog, followers on Twitter, or participants on discussion threads.

Viral-loop businesses seek to take advantage of this trait.

[POSITIVE-FEEDBACK LOOP]

While a negative-feedback loop can create a vicious circle and drive investors to dump stocks, further pushing down the market, leading to more bad news and inducing others to sell, and so on, a viral expansion loop is the opposite, a type of positive-feedback loop, a virtuous circle. The result is a type of alchemy that, done right, leads to a self-replicating, *Borg*-like growth. Put another way, a viral expansion loop is like compounding interest on a bank account: one user becomes two, then four, eight, to a million and more. Not unlike taking a penny and doubling it every day for a month: by the end of a week you'd have 64 cents; within two weeks, you have $83.92; by day thirty, about $5.4 million. Viral loops have emerged as perhaps the most significant business accelerants to hit Silicon Valley since the search engine.

Venture funds have been gravitating to companies with viral loops baked into their business models, inspired, no doubt, by the success of Peter Thiel, whose $500,000 investment in Facebook is worth, depending on how you value the company, anywhere between $300 million to $750 million (on paper, at least). Sequoia Capital's Roelof Botha, an early YouTube backer, has also placed his bets on viral loops. Social-network creator Ning raised $104 million in venture capital while widget maker Slide, which creates photo slideshow tools, attracted $50 million from Fidelity Investments and T. Rowe Price, giving it a $500 million valuation. Fred Wilson, managing partner at Union Square Ventures, joked that he's considered changing his firm's name to Viral Ventures, since almost two-thirds of the $20 million his firm invests annually goes to viral-loop companies such as Twitter, the microblogging outfit.

Although the word "viral" has been co-opted from epidemiology to explain how things spread from user to user over the Internet, there is a stark difference between virality online and what is found in nature. Most people do not spread viruses intentionally—it is a natural by-product of being human. Over the Web, however, users enthusiastically disseminate ideas, information, opinions, links to blogs, photos, videos, and Web services. (The exception is when a user downloads a computer virus; as in the real world, nobody wants to spread that.) It's perhaps surprising that something so profound, powerful, and potentially profitable as a viral loop has remained under the radar for so long. Entrepreneur Andrew Chen, a former advertising executive who worked with MySpace, hi5, and other social sites, has a simple explanation: this critical insight "is worth a lot of money," and the few people who understand it "are all doing their own companies."

Chen views viral loops as "the *most* advanced direct-marketing strategy being developed in the world right now." And make no mistake: viral expansion loops *are* about marketing, just not in the traditional sense. "Nothing can be truly viral unless it is good," venture capitalist Wilson says. "You can create a crappy application, build viral hooks in it, but if it's bad nobody will follow the viral channel and the company will go out of business." But if you make something people really want, your customers will make your business grow for you. Just by using a product users are, in essence, offering a testimonial.

Viral business models are not entirely new. Tupperware, for example, where each party attendee is a potential salesperson, has elements of virality etched into its marketing formula. So does Amway's multilevel marketing strategy to sell personal-care products, jewelry, and household goods. MCI's Friends and Family campaign from the early 1990s offered customers inducements to spread the product. And what are chain letters and pyramid schemes but a permutation on viral loops with irritating (and often nefarious) intent?

Virality is, however, better suited to the frictionless environment of the Internet, where enough clicks can project a message to millions of people.

[VIRAL PRESIDENT]

Viral strategies aren't strictly for businesses. They are also seeping into other arenas—like politics. And no one was more successful in imprinting a viral loop into a campaign than Barack Obama. "One of my fundamental beliefs from my days as a community organizer is that real change comes from the bottom up," Obama said in a statement. "And there's no more powerful tool for grassroots organizing than the Internet." Because an organization can reach only so many people, it must turn to loyal followers to widen the pool. As with all things viral, connecting to others outside the initial cluster of supporters depends on the quality of referrals. Friends, family, and colleagues are far more credible than any advertisement a marketer could dream up. This was what drove the campaign's online strategy. The Web was especially helpful in organizing supporters in caucus states like Iowa, which gave Obama his first big victory. And this approach was arguably the difference between beating Hillary Clinton, the heavy favorite, in the primaries and coming in second.

A pivotal moment came when the campaign hired Chris Hughes, a twenty-four-year-old founder of Facebook. With the informal title "online organizing guru," Hughes retrofitted grassroots campaigning to Web 2.0 by weaving together social networks and the mobile Internet into a central platform of Obama's presidential campaign. The linchpin was My .BarackObama (MyBo, for short), which functioned as a lively online community and social network, registering 1.5 million volunteers. There users created profiles, complete with personal descriptions, friend lists, and blogs; joined one of the twenty-seven thousand groups that formed; raised money and organized meetings and get-togethers—all through a Facebook-like interface. The site had a search function, enabling like-minded people to find each other; a page offering tools to create a personal fundraising page ("You set your own goal, you do the outreach, and you get the credit for the results"); a blog; and a forum that drove even more traffic to the site.

Leading up to the election, MyBo members organized more than two hundred thousand campaign events. This didn't just energize Obama's base of support; it generated loads of cash. Over the span of two years, the campaign brought in $750 million from 4 million donors; nine out of ten donations were for less than $100—and half were for $25 or less. The campaign achieved this by democratizing its fundraising. Instead of turning to wealthy Americans, who could be seen as leveraging their privilege into power, Obama's campaign tapped the little guy, spreading donations across millions of Americans—giving each donor a stake in his campaign's success. It accomplished this largely without fundraisers, which until the advent of Obama's viral money machine, were viewed as unsavory necessities for any candidate running for office. But not only do such fundraisers sap the candidate's time, which could be better spent campaigning and making a case for being elected, they give the appearance that rich, influential donors expect political favors in return for cold, hard cash.

In February 2008, Obama's campaign raised $55 million online without its candidate attending a single fundraiser. What's more, while the law allowed large donors to contribute $2,300 for the 2008 primaries and the same for the general election, smaller donors were tapped repeatedly, forging ongoing connections with the candidate. "Since most have not donated anything like the maximum amount, [Obama] doesn't just have a list of names to thank; he has a huge list of names to ask for more," political blogger Andrew Sullivan pointed out. In one sense, the smaller the donations, the more the campaign was able to invest in its supporters, who could be counted on to raise money, knock on doors, and spread campaign memes.

[SPREADABLE CONCEPTS]

Here, in broad brushstrokes, are the viral strategies the campaign embraced:

1. A short, clear positioning statement: Unlike Hillary Clinton touting her "experience" or John McCain bragging that "I have the record and the scars to prove it," Obama's two core messages were "Change" and "Yes, we can." A call to arms, these taglines offered supporters a clear rallying cry, while Clinton's and McCain's messages were more nebulous and top-down (that is, elect me because I'm more experienced). Obama's campaign galvanized its supporters, who in turn virally extended his message.

2. Multiplier effects: During the campaign, Will.i.am, frontman for the Black Eyed Peas, created a musical mash-up based on Obama's phrase "Yes, we can" that included celebrities like Scarlett Johansson and Kareem Abdul-Jabbar. After the rapper uploaded it to YouTube, its virality didn't go unnoticed. The campaign quickly embedded a link to the clip on its website. "After nearly a year on the campaign trail, I've seen a lot of things that have touched me deeply, but I had to share this with you," Michelle Obama wrote in an email to supporters. "Sharing this video, which was created by supporters, is one more way to help start a conversation with your friends, family, co-workers, and anyone else who will be voting soon about the issues important to them in this election." In the end, the video was viewed 20 million times. Another music video—"I Got a Crush . . . on Obama," by a woman who called herself Obama Girl—was downloaded more than 13 million times, while comedian Sarah Silverman produced one that took a humorous look at convincing seniors in Florida to vote for Obama. Promoting the creativity of its supporters helped the campaign extend its message.

3. The long tail: If Obama had asked for $100 million in the weeks leading up to the election, he probably wouldn't have gotten it. Instead he told people to donate whatever they could—a few bucks even— and then he was able to return to them over and over. In other words, small is the new big. Gopal Shenoy, a blogger and software product manager, extended the strategy to the private sector: "Don't walk away thinking that you can only talk to one customer, you can only attend one trade show, you can only make one customer happy," he wrote.

"What if everyone in your team talked to one customer a week, made one customer happy, helped the salesperson close one more deal. How better off would you be?"

Other Obama campaign viral tactics ran the gamut. A simple word-of-mouth approach revolved around volunteers mentioning one positive thing about their candidate any time they were asked for the time. The mobile arm of the campaign could text 3 million volunteers with schedules, speeches, and video links while a viral tell-a-friend mechanism made it simple to forward the site to another person's phone. To attend Obama rallies, participants were required to provide an email address and cell phone numbers. Within hours the campaign was already asking for donations and referrals to other friends, urging them to form "affinity groups" to further spread the network. The campaign took full advantage of You-Tube, posting Obama's speeches, events, and advertisements on its own channel that could be spread user-to-user or through links embedded on blogs. A viral tell-a-friend mechanism made it possible to forward information to another person's phone.

Barack Obama's campaign wasn't the first to unleash the power of the Web on politics. Howard Dean did this in 2004, but he wasn't able to translate his fundraising prowess and eager support base into primary votes and victories. Joe Trippi, the campaign's strategist, compared his team to "the Wright brothers," while Obama's "skipped Boeing, Mercury, Gemini—they're Apollo 11, only four years later."

Viral schemes are not only applicable to politics and businesses. They are a natural for nonprofit organizations. On Facebook, the number-one most popular social application isn't a game or a mobile app. It's Causes, which lets users promote a favorite charity and induce friends in their network to contribute. The mission of another organization, JustGive, is to connect people with the charities and causes they care most about. The idea is simple. If twenty-five people make a donation and each person convinces twenty-five others to donate, there is the potential for an exponential increase in both donors and donations.

In the spring of 2009, Razorfish, a digital agency owned by Microsoft, combined viral commerce and charity with a television-web promotion for All detergent. In a thirty-second commercial near the end of an episode of

Donald Trump's *Celebrity Apprentice*, contestants Joan and Melissa Rivers asked viewers to visit All's website to view a couple of videos. Joan Rivers appeared in "Guess That Stain," based on a fictitious game show, while daughter Melissa starred in "Laundry Fairy." Every time a user shared one of the videos with a friend, All promised to donate 50 cents to the favorite charities of Joan and Melissa Rivers.

All of this is a far cry from the traditional direct-mail solicitation, which can cost a nongovernment organization hundreds of thousands of dollars for high-quality paper stock, personalized laser printing, postage, and a comprehensive list of addresses. Viral fundraising runs on a fraction of the cost and relies on volunteers to raise funds on behalf of a charity or cause.

[VIRAL LOOP, VIRAL NETWORK, DOUBLE VIRAL LOOP]

There are three categories of viral expansion loops: viral loops, viral networks, and double viral loops, the last a hybrid of the first two. To create a simple viral loop is relatively straightforward. In 1996, Hotmail placed a link in the body of every message, offering the recipient the ability to set up his or her own webmail account; within thirty months Hotmail went from zero to 30 million members. YouTube deployed a viral mechanism by allowing people to embed video links in their blogs or MySpace pages: the more people who saw it, the more links were embedded, and soon millions of users were funneled directly to YouTube. Also in this category are the scads of widget makers creating digital bling on Facebook, MySpace, and elsewhere: the infamous "hatching egg," glitzy slideshow creation tools distributed by Slide and RockYou, the online Scrabble game Scrabulous, horoscopes, calendars, and so forth. But it's on viral networks like eBay, Facebook, MySpace, Twitter, and LinkedIn that scale and power really snowball, providing an ecosystem in which other businesses can thrive.

"The viral adoption model" is the "cheapest way to grow an audience," declares Union Square Ventures' Wilson. And the bigger a viral network gets, the faster it germinates. Once this phantasmagorical growth kicks in, it is possible to predict its rate with astonishing accuracy, because it spreads at an even rate and eventually tips to a point of nondisplacement. Then it continues to add users even if it does nothing.

Viral Loop is a short history of this paradigm-busting phenomenon. The book tells the story of viral referral companies like Tupperware and Hotmail, and of the Mosaic browser, which transformed the Internet from a playground for geeks into a mass-market phenomenon. It explores Ning, which deploys a double viral loop, and deconstructs viral marketing to get at the concept of "collective curation"—when the audience decides what's good and passes it on to others. *Viral Loop* looks at the underlying economic forces leading to ubiquitous broadband, which has increased the pace and reach of virality, and shows what happens to a business that becomes too viral and outstrips its ability to keep pace with exponential demand. Then there's stackability, when one viral business is overlaid on another, and social networking, which is redefining how we as humans connect with one another. Finally there is the search for the new ad unit— the heart of any moneymaking scheme in this new Web world of interconnectedness and interoperability.

Over the last decade and a half some of the world's most successful businesses started from scratch and then rode a viral loop. Never before in human history has there been the potential to create wealth this fast, on this scale, and starting with so little. Here's how they did it.

I

VIRAL
BUSINESSES

1

Tupperware and Ponzi Schemes— the Original Viral Models

Party Plans, Referral Networks, and Sizzlemanship

Half a century before anyone heard of Facebook or MySpace, and Silicon Valley was famous for prunes, Tupperware, the kitschy plastic food-storage-container company, was tapping into vast social networks of women to generate a massive viral loop. It all began in the midst of the Great Depression, when Earl Silas Tupper was inventing all sorts of trivial contrivances—from the sublime to the outright kooky. There was the nondrip ice-cream cone, the fish-powered boat, plastic eye shields for dyeing eyebrows, fake fingernails in red, blue, gold, and pearl, plastic garter hooks to hold up stockings, "Sure-Stay Hairpins," and a "corset with muscles" to give women faux flat tummies. A tree surgeon until he declared bankruptcy in 1936, Tupper created the "Knee-Action" Agricultural Harrow and the Gypsy Gun, a pump that sprayed creosote to rid trees of gypsy moth eggs. He designed a medical device for the nonsurgical removal of the appendix "thru the anal opening" and an instrument he claimed would kick off "menstruation in women who have delayed monthlies or who are pregnant." Somehow he found time to produce flour sifters, dish rack pans, knitting needles, a tampon case, a portable necktie rack, a self-standing toothpaste-and-shaving-cream dispenser with self-closing cap, and the "Kamoflage comb," which was a combination nail file and comb dressed up as a fountain pen. None of these sold particularly well, and if it weren't for a greasy, smelly, rubbery chunk of black polyethylene "slag," the name Tupper would have faded away.

During World War II, that slag, a by-product of smelting, was cheap and plentiful, while resin—the core ingredient of most plastics at the time—was scarce and expensive. The U.S. and British militaries used polyethylene in radar installations and to insulate cables. Tupper, who worked at a plastics factory in Leominster, Massachusetts, creating prototypes for DuPont and sealing gas masks with plastic filler, figured he could make something out of it. One day in 1942, he discovered something quite remarkable. When stripped to its essence, this malodorous chunk of petroleum waste emerged as beautifully translucent material unlike any plastic of its day: it was unbreakable, flexible not brittle, and it didn't chip or retain odors (even vinegar or onions). It handled extreme heat and cold, and when squeezed, it sprang back to its original shape.

Back then, American consumers were wary of synthetics. Plastic buttons cracked, tortoiseshell eyeglasses warped when laid too close to the radiator, Christmas toys broke out of the box, combs' teeth snapped, shower curtains putrefied into sticky clumps, and mixing bowls smelled like oil refineries and split, shattered, or peeled. The public's view was well expressed in *The Plastics Inventor*, a 1944 Disney cartoon starring Donald Duck, who bakes a plane from melted plastic and takes it out for a test spin. It works perfectly . . . until it rains and the plane turns into a gooey mess.

Tupper christened his discovery "Poly-T: Material of the Future" and by the end of the war, his factory churned out a steady stream of plastic merchandise. He was fielding orders from American Thermos Bottle Company for 7 million nesting cups, from Camel for three hundred thousand cigarette cases, and from Canada Dry for fifty thousand bowls to offer with its soft drinks. *Time* magazine estimated his annual revenue at $5 million. The Museum of Modern Art in New York included two of his bowls in a special exhibit of useful objects. *House Beautiful* dubbed his designs "Fine Art for 39 cents."

Poly-T should have been ideal for food storage, except Tupper didn't have a lid to fit his thin-lipped containers. Before the 1940s, most American families had iceboxes; then came electric refrigerators, putting the ice-making industry out of business. To retard spoilage, consumers stretched shower caps over leftovers, which left an unpleasant aftertaste, or wrapped them in tin foil. It took a while, but Tupper, modeling his airtight seal after the inverted rim of a paint can, filed a patent application for an "Open Mouth Container and Nonsnap type of closure" on June 2, 1947, and Tupperware was born.

By 1949, Tupper's fourteen-piece "Millionaire's Line," composed of bowls and tumblers, was available at Bloomingdales, Gimbels, and Detroit's J. L. Hudson, at the time the tallest department store in the world. Despite a national media campaign that included newspaper ads, magazine articles, and prominent department store displays, sales of his eponymous tubs were disappointing. Consumers didn't know what to make of the "Wonderbowl" in pastel shades of blue, pink, and pearly white. They fumbled with creating an airtight seal to "lock in freshness," and some, complaining the tops didn't fit, even returned them, according to Bob Kealing, author of *Tupperware Unsealed*. A lot has happened since the late 1940s, when Tupper's business was in danger of being tossed out like a Chinese take-out carton, to today, when 90 percent of American homes own at least one piece of Tupperware and the company reports billions in revenue.

[PATIO PARTIES]

Tupperware's unlikely savior was Brownie Wise, a single mother from Dearborn, Michigan, who worked as a distributor for Stanley Home Products, a direct seller of detergents, mops, household cleaners, and floor waxes. In 1948, shortly after Tupper introduced his product to stores, Gary McDonald, a young salesman working for Wise, was browsing J. L. Hudson when he realized these plastic containers would be ideal for home demonstration. He could see that customers didn't buy them until someone demonstrated how to put the tops on, then explained that they were for food storage and that leftovers wouldn't spoil. You could even toss a sealed bowl in the air and not a drop of salad dressing would spill. "Yank it, bang it, jump on it," they said. What's more, the product had no natural competitors other than zippered "grease-proof, stain-proof and mildew-proof" plastic bags, which were sold three bags for $1.98 at hardware stores, compared to the three-piece Wonder Bowl set, retailing at $1.39.

McDonald brought a sample to Wise, who at first didn't know what to make of it. She had never seen a bowl you could squeeze, and she had a hell of a time getting the lid on, accidentally knocking it off the table. To her surprise, it bounced instead of breaking, which would become one of her marketing mottos. After spending a couple of days trying to figure out the magical vacuum seal, she realized "you had to burp it like a baby." Wise added Tupper's wares to her product line.

The thirty-four-year-old Wise had gotten her start with Stanley Home Products when a salesman knocked on her door and botched his sales patter. *I could do better than that,* she thought. Because her secretary job at Bendix Aviation Corporation barely covered her ailing son's medical expenses, she moonlighted evenings and weekends. Within a year she became one of Stanley's top earners and quit her secretarial job. The secret of her success: "patio parties," where she peddled household wonders like the ashtray with a brain, Atomite ("the cleaner with ATOMIC like action"), and truckloads of Tupperware.

In the years leading up to and following World War II, there was a gradual shift toward modernity. Technology had been screaming forward for more than fifty years—the invention of electricity, the automobile, the airplane, the light bulb, the telegraph and telephone—there was even talk of flying to the moon, and the United States was ready to reap the benefits. Colonizing space was a theme of comic books and radio shows like *Flash Gordon.* In 1938 Orson Welles's radio broadcast of *War of the Worlds,* based on H. G. Wells's sci-fi novel, set off panic as rumors of a Martian invasion swept through some communities, multiplied by the sheer force of word-of-mouth distortions. The theme of the 1939 World's Fair was "The World of Tomorrow." It featured a special exhibit called Futurama, which envisioned Earth twenty years ahead. In the span of two decades—from the 1930s to the 1950s—airplanes like the Lockheed Vega, which Amelia Earhart crashed into a watery grave, went from being constructed of little more than wood, glue, and baling wire to sleek steel jets; television was replacing radio as America's favorite entertainment choice; the acoustic big band swing era gave way to electric rock 'n' roll; medical advancements yielded a cure for polio; and psychologist B. F. Skinner postulated that people could be conditioned into creating social utopia. Earl S. Tupper's "Poly-T: Material of the Future" fit in perfectly.

By 1949, Wise dispensed with other products in the Stanley line and established "Poly-T parties." Many of her dealers grossed $100 a gathering and Wise distributed $1,500 of Tupperware a week (worth almost $14,000 today). Within a decade, Wise and her army of Tupperware ladies would move tens of millions of dollars' worth of merchandise every year via the Tupperware home party, the greatest viral network of its day. It worked like this: a new dealer relied on her social network of sympathetic friends, neighbors, and relatives to schedule a gathering. The party hostess invited women from her social circle to attend—a form of word-of-mouth virality. Meanwhile, the dealer hit up other friends to host parties, with each hostess tapping her particular social network, and the pool of buyers grew with each additional social circle. What's more, the dealer identified hostesses with the right attributes to join in selling Tupperware.

In Laurie Kahn-Leavitt's PBS documentary *Tupperware*, Lavon Weber, who hailed from a small rural community, recalled that a neighbor living half a mile away offered to get her started in Hugoton, Kansas, "and we dated two or three parties there that day. And then my mother said she'd have a party, and some of my sister-in-laws [too]. I'd go to church and people would say, 'I hear you're selling something,' and I said yes. 'Well, I'll have a party for you.'" Multiply this by thousands of women, and that offers a glimpse of its rabbit-like growth.

[REFERRAL MODEL]

Tupperware as a business grew in multiple ways. Both the pool of buyers and the number of parties increased exponentially, each forged via social networking, while the number of sellers also expanded virally. More parties not only begat more buyers; they begat more sellers, who begat more buyers, and so on. The more Tupperware sold, the more people would sell Tupperware products. It was like having thousands of salespeople on commission instead of a few dozen working the phones at corporate headquarters. "Three people must gain" at every party, Wise wrote: the dealer through sales of Tupperware "and the booking of future parties"; the hostess, who acts as a subdealer "and upon whose hospitality and initiative, the success of the party plan depends"; and the guests, who "enjoy a sociable get-together." This viral marketing plan made perfect use of a part-time labor force of able-bodied, sociable, stay-at-home women. The seller earned a commission, the hostess basked in her role as queen bee,

and attendees played party games, received gift bags, gossiped about husbands, kids, and neighbors, and had a small stake in helping one of their
own sustain a business. Meanwhile, partygoers brought home a product
that, at the time, had cachet. It was a win-win-win for everybody.

The first home party in the United States can be traced to the 1920s
and was introduced by WearEver Aluminum Cooking Products, which
found it an efficient strategy for reaching women in sparsely populated
rural areas where there were few stores. Cultural historian Alison J. Clarke,
author of *Tupperware: The Promise of Plastic in 1950s America*, posits that
direct-selling schemes blossomed during the Depression because mass unemployment allowed a displaced workforce to pursue casual labor with
"minimal capital outlay, formal skills or professional qualifications." A
door-to-door salesman from Maine working for Stanley Home Products stumbled on the concept in the 1930s when he knocked on the door
of a minister's wife while she entertained potential donors to the church.
She told him to return another day, but before he left she proposed a
deal: in exchange for a cut of sales that she would donate to the church,
she would gather her group again and the salesman could demonstrate
his wares.

It acted as a powerful referral from a trusted source and solved his biggest problem: access. The public held door-to-door salesmen in low esteem.
Itinerant sellers were known to harass housewives, dump second-rate
merchandise, and move on, and the sleazy traveling salesman became an
archetype. In Flannery O'Connor's short story "Good Country People," a
peripatetic Bible salesman trolling the South seduces a woman and runs
off with her artificial leg. The public outrage over pressurized sales tactics, with shifty men knocking on the doors of unsuspecting women, led
local governments to pass so-called Green ordinances, named for Green
River, Wyoming, the first city to enact it, which banned door-to-door solicitation. These salesmen were the equivalent of the spam that deluges
email in-boxes today or the telemarketers who ring up at dinnertime to
pitch a product, service, or cause over the phone. (They, too, invited regulation, namely the CAN-SPAM Act of 2003 and the Federal Trade Commission's National Do Not Call Registry.)

By inviting customers to his home, the Stanley salesman avoided all of
this. Instead of trudging to individual households, a time-consuming

proposition since he couldn't be assured the person answering the door would be welcoming, potential customers came to him with purses open. This intent to buy opened up a whole new value proposition. With home parties, "the buying spirit is contagious," Brownie Wise wrote in a training manual. "It is a proven fact that you will sell more to a group of 15 women as a group than you will sell to them individually."

Soon the Stanley salesman from Maine was reporting impressive sales figures, and it didn't take long for word to spread within the company. Other Stanley sellers across the country approached local groups to inquire about demonstrating their products. After they hit up most of the organizations, they turned to their wives to organize parties, with the hostesses receiving either a cash commission or a gift. This selling strategy helped push Stanley Home Products sales from $3 million in 1940 to $50 million ten years later.

Meanwhile, as Tupperware sat idly on store shelves from coast to coast, Brownie Wise in 1949 ordered $152,149.13 of Tupperware, which in today's dollars would be $1.4 million.

[PONZI SCHEMERS]

WearEver, Stanley, and Tupperware weren't the first to tap viral expansion loops, but they may have been the earliest to promote legitimate businesses. Get-rich-quick pyramid schemes based on the "rob Peter to pay Paul" principle had long relied on word-of-mouth virality to expand the pool of money at breakneck speed. Organizers attracted large numbers of participants with the promise of sky-high returns on their investment—sometimes offering to double a person's money in as little as ten days. In the nineteenth century schemers bilked investors who thought they were financing silverfox fur farms, an experimental engine that used water for fuel, technology that could extract gold from the sea, and bonds covering exotic products in even more exotic locales. Their fast-talking operators, relying on the same "splash, cash, and dash" formula, paid off as promised to the first people to contribute. These lucky early investors inevitably told their friends and family, who also invested. They too were bought off, and suddenly thousands of people were throwing money at the operators until the whole pyramid came crashing down when the operators couldn't continue to pay back investors. By then they were usually gone but not forgotten.

The biggest viral schemer of all was Charles Ponzi, an Italian immigrant who registered a business in Boston called the Security Exchange Company in December 1919. He claimed to have figured out a system to reap 400 percent profits by engaging in arbitrage with international postage relay coupons. These functioned like promissory notes that could be used by a recipient in one country to pay postage to another, since stamps could not be used to mail letters across borders. Because the same coupon could be purchased in Italy for a fraction of what it cost in the United States, Ponzi surmised he could pocket the difference. He printed certificates promising investors 50 percent interest on their money in three months, which he later shortened to forty-five days. But he never bought more than a handful of coupons.

Instead, the penniless Ponzi used them to justify his swindle. A month and a half after starting, he redeemed his first certificates. When early adopters got back their money plus 50 percent, they spread the word. Like any con man, Ponzi knew that greed was an effective viral mechanism—not that he would have described it that way. The average investment was $100, but many invested far more than that. People mortgaged their homes and cashed in their life savings to get in on the action, while those who redeemed their certificates simply plowed their proceeds back into the company. Eager investors packed the sidewalks outside his office, and Ponzi hired off-duty police to keep order.

Although money was going out to pay back those with certificates, it was coming in even faster. By February 1920, Ponzi had accumulated $5,000; a month later he banked $30,000. He quickened the pace of virality by hiring agents on commission, who spread out across New England to preach Ponzi's sermon. The more money that came in, the more lavish Ponzi's lifestyle became. He purchased a twenty-room mansion with a swimming pool and a $12,000 automobile with a chauffeur and wore only hand-tailored silk suits. On May 1 he had $420,000, and by July he had amassed millions, all the product of a viral expansion loop, with each investor yielding two, three, or more investors.

It all came to a head in August 1920, when Ponzi was arrested on charges of larceny after an auditor estimated that he owed $7 million yet had less than half that in the bank. Even then he was pulling in $250,000 a day, which would have meant his revenues would have topped $91 million in its first year of operation—almost $1 billion in current dollars— before it crashed and burned.

[A DIFFERENT KIND OF WORKFORCE]

Earl Tupper's company would end up surpassing Ponzi at his scheme-iest, and do it legitimately. In late 1949, as a drumbeat of orders came in to Tupperware headquarters from Stanley Home dealers, he dispatched Victor Collamore, a company executive, to Detroit to meet with Wise and Gary McDonald, the salesman who first introduced her to Tupperware. "Just what in the hell are you guys doing to sell the amount of Tupperware you're doing?" Collamore asked. "You're selling more Tupperware than the J. L. Hudson department store by far, and that's the biggest department store in the world."

Impressed by what he heard, Collamore hired Wise to act as a distributor for Tupperware and directed her to build a sales team to cover the entire state of Florida. She jumped at the chance, especially after Stanley founder Frank Stanley Beveridge told her she would never land an executive position in the company because it was "no place for a woman." In the late 1940s the glass ceiling was knee high. Women made up a third of the nation's workforce but only 5 percent of them held professional positions. The majority trudged through low-pay, mostly dead-end jobs— stocking shelves in retail stores or working as cashiers, earning dismal wages as secretaries (as Wise had), teaching school, working man-sized shifts at factories, or simply staying at home.

Cultural and demographic shifts created an ideal environment for Tupperware's ascent. As the 1940s swept into the 1950s and a painful recession gave way to a burgeoning economy, a diaspora ensued. Nineteenth-century pioneers had traveled westward to settle a vast, inhospitable continent, and a century later postwar baby boomers moved to suburbia; more than 80 percent of U.S. population growth in the 1950s occurred there. And they had money, with an average family income of $6,500, not quite double the national average.

With these new homes came a desire to stock them with blenders, stoves, ovens, vacuum cleaners, and other appliances. In 1950, 9 percent of American households had television; by 1959, 86 percent did (almost 44 million homes). About 1.7 million washing machines were sold in 1950; by 1960, 2.6 million. Lawn and porch furniture sales tripled to $145 million over the same period. By the middle of the decade the United States had, for the very first time, more white-collar than blue-collar workers. And, of course, there were the kids. Between 1948 and 1953 more babies were born stateside than had come into the world over the previous thirty years. Dr. Benjamin Spock's *Common Sense Book of Baby and Child Care*, first published in 1946, became a perennial bestseller and instructed a whole generation of baby boomer parents, while cloth diaper sales went from $32 million in 1947 to $50 million a decade later (disposables didn't hit the market until the 1960s). Toy sales shot up from $84 million in 1940 to $1.6 billion in 1960, a twenty-fold increase. Into this thriving consumerism stepped Tupperware, a brand that combined status and frugality with family values. "Get rid of your shower caps!" Brownie Wise urged. "Turn your leftovers into makeovers!"

Shortly after relocating to Florida, Wise encountered problems. Patio party dealers from Michigan who moved with her found that territory they had been promised was already covered by preexisting Tupperware sellers intent on protecting their turf. The same thing was occurring in other states, with the company's original network of dealers fending off these interlopers, undercutting them on price, offering fatter commissions, trying to blackball them in their communities, and even threatening to run them out of town. Although a young company, Tupperware was faced with the cannibalization of its existing business, a challenge confronting many on the precipice of change—today, for example, newspapers in the age of the Internet, film and camera companies such as Kodak and Polaroid, the music and movie industries. It hobbled Wise's push to populate Florida with handpicked distributors, and led to six months of infighting, until finally the company shaved her territory into a 650-mile swath from Miami to Savannah, Georgia, that she could run any way she saw fit. Despite all this, Wise booked more than $14,000 in sales in her first two months.

[GROWING PAINS]

But then Wise confronted another issue that can vex fast-growing companies: scaling. Wise's network of dealers, who operated in six fast-growing
sunny cities in Florida, sold so much Tupperware the factory couldn't
keep up. Earl Tupper was fanatical about quality, and every polyethylene
pellet that arrived at the plant was tossed in a jar and heated to 180 degrees along with a saltine cracker. Hours later, if the cracker retained even
the slightest whiff of plastic, the entire car of polyethylene was rejected.
This quality control extended to the manufacturing, too, with samples
checked at every machine during every shift. Were bowls leak-proof, were
there any irregularities, were the colors precise? A high percentage of
Tupperware fresh from the factory floor didn't meet Tupper's exacting
standards, with whole rooms stuffed with barrels of rejected Tupperware
destined to be razed, re-liquefied, and re-formed.

Several of Wise's orders were delayed, with customers wondering if
they would ever receive what they had paid for. The display cases she ordered for her sellers didn't arrive, nor did stationery. Dealers in Fort Lau-
derdale and Hollywood, Florida, were forced to either drive to the Miami
airport to pick up errantly shipped orders or pay to have them redirected.
December 1950, in particular, lacked holiday spirit, with dealers unable to
get Tupperware to their customers in time for Christmas. This also meant
her twenty dealers didn't receive their commissions, which Wise covered
out of her own pocket. Her frantic calls to the company went unanswered,
and Wise briefly considered quitting. After another delayed shipment, she
made a fateful decision.

As Charles Fishman, one of the last journalists to interview Brownie
Wise, recounted in the *Orlando Sentinel* in 1987, she picked up the phone
and called long distance to the Tupper Corporation, demanding to speak
with Mr. Tupper. She didn't even know if there was such a person—she
just assumed there was. Suddenly his voice came over the crackling line.

"This is Brownie Wise!" she shouted. "In Miami!"

"I know who you are," Earl Tupper said.

She told him her order was late. *Again.* "I wonder if you know how
serious a problem that is?"

Tupper knew how much Brownie Wise contributed to the company's bottom line. While many direct sellers distributed Tupperware, no one approached her sales volume. After getting off the phone, he straightened out her orders, then called back, asking if she would visit the factory in Massachusetts for a meeting.

"I'm busy," she retorted. He would have to come to her.

There they were, two pig-headed savants bickering over who would do the traveling. Eventually they agreed on a summit in Long Island with other top freelance sellers. There they convinced Tupper to distribute Tupperware exclusively through the home party plan, and in May 1951 he pulled his merchandise from all stores.

[SOCIAL NETWORKING AND "SIZZLEMANSHIP"]

It was a bold gamble, but Wise had shown what was possible when you combined the power of social networking with "sizzlemanship"—a word Wise had invented. Within a year, Tupperware distributors brought in wholesale orders of $2.2 million, and Earl Tupper rewarded her with a new Cadillac. In 1953, Wise was overseeing a network of three thousand dealers, managers, and distributors, with sales growing 115 percent. By 1955, sales volume hit $30 million and Wise's network of sellers had grown to twenty thousand. Wise became the first woman to grace the cover of *Business Week*, accompanied by her quote: "If we build the people, they'll build the business." Meanwhile the Tupperware party seeped into the public consciousness. Producers from *I Love Lucy* approached the company with an idea: Lucy would host a Tupperware party with the usual disastrous consequences. Wise turned them down flat. "Oh, no!" she cried. "I won't allow it. It won't help us." She was afraid Ricky Ricardo might end up with a bowl of spaghetti on his head.

For seven years, Wise was the effervescent face of the company while the tart-tongued Tupper toiled in relative obscurity. That was fine by him—at least in the beginning. They were polar opposites. Wise was a people person, a hands-on manager who kept a typewriter on her bedside table in case she thought of a memo to write in the middle of the night. She organized frenetic sales conferences in Florida called "jubilees," where "some 600 women dug dementedly in an acre plot for buried prizes," as *Business Week* described it, and sang, "I've got that Tupperware feeling deep in my heart." For prizes Wise gave away cars, diamond rings, mink stoles, and TV sets. She cajoled, encouraged, and enlightened her growing sales force, all the more amazing because she had no formal education in running a business.

As for Tupper, he never had much use for people, preferring the sanctity of his laboratory. The first time he attended a jubilee, he watched from the back of the auditorium, then snuck outside. When Wise caught up to him, he confessed that just the thought of her up there in front of so many people made him sick. Like Wise, he was demanding, a perfectionist who painted his factory floors white to illuminate any dust. While she became a celebrity engaging in glitzy displays of razzmatazz, he remained a solitary figure in the background, personally designing and overseeing the manufacture of every product. Together they made up far more than the sum of their parts, and like many legendary companies, owed their rise to their opposing personalities. Steve Wozniak built the Apple personal computer, but it took Steve Jobs to market it. At Microsoft Paul Allen was instrumental in pushing for new products and technological innovation, while Bill Gates had the greater business vision. And Earl Tupper was just another kooky inventor until Brownie Wise came along.

By 1958, after eight years together, Tupper tired of Wise receiving the lion's share of credit and abruptly fired her with a year's salary as severance, expunging all references to her in the company's literature. Shortly after, he sold the company for $16 million to Justin Dart of Rexall Drug Company, divorced his wife, and bought an island in Central America, eventually skipping off to Costa Rica, where he gave up his U.S. citizenship to avoid paying taxes.

[MOVING BEYOND SATURATION]

Tupperware prospered well into the 1970s, revenue doubling every year, achieving half a billion dollars in sales in 1976. Along the way it hit a point of nondisplacement—competitors couldn't knock it off its pedestal even with comparable products. Eventually, though, like all viral companies, it reached a point of saturation and began a steady decline. Tupper's patents expired and competitors like Rubbermaid entered the fray, but the predominant reason was socioeconomic. Women had entered the workforce and weren't around to host or attend parties, which disrupted the vast social network that had driven sales for more than a generation. The company struggled into the 1990s, losing $22 million in the United States in 1992. Then a former senior manager at Avon, E. V. "Rick" Goings, took the company's reins.

As his name implies, Goings is a fast-talker who could sell dial-up Internet access to an AOL customer service rep. He has been experimenting with viral strategies in the offline world for almost forty years, believing that products that require a customer education are best suited to direct selling. (Direct selling involves person-to-person contact or home parties like Tupperware's, while direct marketing is simply catalog sales.) If you are unloading blue jeans, he says, direct selling probably isn't for you, since everyone knows what jeans are and what they are used for. If you are peddling something in a new product niche, say, gourmet food that must be tasted to be believed, direct selling could be an apt strategy. Then it's all about what Goings calls "FNR": friends, neighbors, and relatives, "who go out and tell their friends, neighbors and relatives, and so on and so on." It works as a marketing strategy because it offers the product credibility. "In a world of friends I'm not going to tell you about something unless I think it is for your own good."

While attending classes part-time at the University of Virginia, Goings started his first viral business, a smoke detector distributorship in 1970. Because forty years ago no one knew what a fire alarm was (or was even aware of the need for one), Goings opted for a direct-sales approach. He recruited college students to create fire safety crusades in their communities to induce people to buy smoke and heat detectors. Because he offered sky-high commissions (each smoke alarm retailed for $100, and each distributor pocketed $60), it didn't take long for Goings to set up three hundred locations across the United States. The key portion of each sales pitch involved a short film explaining that most fire victims die between 10:00 p.m. and 6:00 a.m., usually from smoke inhalation.

"Customer education was extremely important because most people didn't even know they had a problem," he says. With the group primed to act, the representative would take orders, then ask, "If you knew the cure to cancer, who would you tell?" He would request from each attendee a list of ten FNRs with whom he would like to share the filmstrip. Then the presentations spread virally, with each purchaser doubling as a highly credible referral—someone who had your best interests at heart.

For eight years Goings earned a low six-figure income, until federal law mandated smoke alarms and Sears came out with First Alert, which it promoted in a national advertising campaign. Goings sold his interest in the business for a few million dollars, getting out before the price of smoke alarms fell from $100 to as little as $5. He took a job at Avon and eventually moved to Tupperware. Aware that cultural changes in the United States made a referral model a hard sell, he turned the company's attention overseas. Within a few years Tupperware's home party social-networking model was exploding across Latin America and Asia, where women, like their American counterparts thirty years earlier, were expected to stay home and raise the children. By 1996, it had earned 95 percent of its profit abroad on sales of more than $1 billion, and was spun off as an independent company.

Since then Tupperware has grown into a global concern, with $2.2 billion in revenue, encompassing cosmetics, kitchen tools, small household appliances, and toys. After an ill-fated attempt to once again sell Tupperware in retail stores like Target, it returned to its classic party plan roots. Today Tupperware's viral loop continues unabated. Somewhere in the world a party occurred just in the time it took you to read this sentence. Almost 120 million people in one hundred countries will attend a product demonstration this year. And all of this was accomplished without the benefit of the Internet, which makes up less than 2 percent of sales.

But the frictionless Web would prove to be a potent force for businesses that followed Tupperware's viral-loop example. And they would expand further and faster than anything Brownie Wise could have ever imagined.

2

The First Online Viral Expansion Loop

Mosaic, Netscape, Network Effects, and the Spark that Touched Off the Internet Boom

Two years after British academic Tim Berners-Lee unveiled the protocols that made possible the World Wide Web, enabling users to embed hypertext links into documents and connect them to others anywhere in the world, the "information superhighway" was little more than a pothole-strewn country road. The Web of the early 1990s comprised less than 1 percent of Internet traffic, and with only a handful of websites in existence, there wasn't a whole lot to see. Getting around was a chore even for the savviest computer user, which was how Berners-Lee liked it. He saw the Web as a text-based academic utopia for the intellectual elite. Images, he believed, would only make the content impure. Worse, it might attract hoi polloi, who were apt to publish their own magazines or diaries online decorated with photos of their cats. This, he feared, would dumb down the Web to the lowest common denominator. If someone needed a chart, a graph, or pictures to accompany a research paper, Berners-Lee figured he could upload them to a file transfer protocol (FTP) site.

Software lagged a decade behind hardware, with application fiefdoms holding sway over a small, captive computer population. Gopher helped users locate documents, FTP let them download and transmit them, and Telnet hooked them up to other computers. Those who had taken the plunge online connected to one another through communities like the Well in San Francisco, signed up for newsgroups, and frequented chat rooms, many devoted to sex and fetishes. To navigate the Internet required a working knowledge of the Unix operating system and a communications protocol called TCP/IP. The Web wasn't searchable; you had to know the addresses of the few sites out there you could visit. Then you had to type arcane commands and addresses like "$ find / -type l -print | perl -nle '-e || print';" (a command to find links that point to nothing). The schism between the pros and the rest was further exacerbated by the prevailing computer systems of the time. Geeks spoke Unix, a staple of college networks, while the public tooled around on Macs and Windows machines. Despite its grandiose name and intentions, the World Wide Web wasn't very web-like.

That's precisely what Marc Andreessen, a twenty-one-year-old computer science student at the University of Illinois in Urbana-Champaign, aimed to change. Raised in rural Wisconsin—his father was a seed salesman and his mother was a shipping clerk at Lands End, the mailbox-stuffing catalog retailer—Andreessen figured he would spend his life with computers even before he had actually touched one. When he was ten, he checked out a computer book from the local library and taught himself Basic (a programming language). At eleven he coded his first application: a virtual calculator to assist him with his math homework, until the janitor shut off power for the night, wiping out his handiwork. Soon after, his parents plunked down $595 for a Commodore 64, which he plugged into his television, storing files on a cassette tape recorder. He quickly learned that hardware had constraints but with software he was only limited by his imagination. Anything was possible, yet nothing was doable if the program didn't function.

Andreessen enrolled in college to study electrical engineering, thinking it would pay better, but ended up in computer science because it required less work. Working part-time for $6.85 an hour creating 3-D graphics programs at the National Center for Supercomputing Applications (NCSA), Andreessen burned through hours in chat rooms and roaming around the Web, frustrated with how hard it was to navigate. Berners-Lee's browser, introduced in February 1991, ran solely on NeXT machines, which made up a fraction of the world's computers, and displayed text one line at a time like a teletype machine. Other browsers followed, all with shortcomings. Erwise, released by students at the Helsinki University of Technology in April 1992, was the first to work on non-NeXT machines, but development stalled when the students graduated and moved on to other projects. Worse, it was coded in Finnish.

Viola originated at Berkeley and incorporated style sheets and tables, plus a bookmark function so users could track where they had been and which sites were their favorites, but it was notoriously hard to install. MidasWWW, developed at the Stanford Linear Accelerator Center, only worked on Unix and Vax computers while MacWWW was the first designed expressly for Macintosh.

He decided to fashion his own browser, one that would meld Telnet, Gopher, and FTP into one program and secret it behind an attractive, easy-to-master graphic interface. This would build on Berners-Lee's work, which had created a standard for the Web, key to the Internet's evolution. Europe of the eighteenth century didn't move from separate agrarian and cottage industry–based economies to massive industrialization until countries agreed on standardized weights and measures. In pre-Revolutionary America, each colony minted coins and issued its own paper money, which slowed the march to commerce. Eli Whitney reaped a fortune by inventing interchangeable parts for muskets in the 1790s, making machinery reparable and more efficient. Berners-Lee's standards had the potential for a similar impact on digital communication, except on their own they weren't far-reaching enough. As with cross-border trade in seventeenth-century Europe, surfing the Web was inefficient, time-consuming, and largely restricted to those fluent in the medium of exchange (in this case, arcane computer systems).

That's where Andreessen came in. He wanted to democratize the Internet so that anyone with a computer and a modem could sally forth online. Then users need not be fluent in Unix, Linux, Perl, or DOS. The Web would be open to all, and, if it followed the dictates of history, would grow far beyond the cloistered academic community. It would truly become a World Wide Web.

Until 1866, when the transatlantic cable was laid, the quickest way to send news internationally was to stash carrier pigeons on ocean-skimming ships and release them near shore. In the early twentieth century, stock exchange runners called "pad shovers" rushed from one broker's office to the next, shouting the latest prices, which were transmitted by telegraph and published in the next day's newspapers while pneumatic tube networks fueled by compressed air conveyed small but urgent packages like mail, stock purchases, or money over short distances. Then came the telephone, radio, TV. Yet it wasn't until the Internet that instantaneous visual and audio communication without regard to geography was possible. Anyone and everyone would be interconnected, and this would have a profound impact on . . . everything. The idea boggled Andreessen's mind.

But he needed help. At first, Eric Bina, a full-time programmer at NCSA, told him he was too busy. Andreessen persisted, sketching out an almost mystical vision for the World Wide Web, a place where people could access information in a completely different way. He egged his colleague on, realizing the best way to convince Bina to do anything was to tell him how impossible it would be. They were ideal foils. While Andreessen had a voracious appetite and a cosmic view of the world, Bina was short, shy, and wiry, the kind of guy who peered down at a desk and saw molecules. Andreessen was a natural risk taker, "evangelical" compared to the "apprehensive" Bina. George Gilder described them thus: Andreessen was "expansive" and "prodigal with bandwidth"; Bina was "bitwise" and "focused."

[MOSAIC]

After receiving approval for the project, the two started coding in late 1992. Andreessen wanted it to process images, but Bina, like Berners-Lee, was concerned that people would abuse it, and since graphics files were much larger than text, he feared they could bog down entire networks. Andreessen, the antithesis of the pie-in-the-sky academic, argued it was about time someone brought some color to the Web. He believed that most users, the ones with whom he communicated in chat rooms and forums, would love having pictures, and this would attract others to the Web. Bina gave in. Sketching out their browser's characteristics, they agreed it had to be reliable, easy to use (reminiscent of the pull-down tabs in Apple's operating system), and extremely forgiving. Unlike other browsers, if there were errors in a page's HTML code, theirs would still access the content. It would also enable users to create personal Web pages, which would encourage people to create online identities.

Andreessen's timing was born of luck, being at the right place at the right time. NCSA's supercomputing program originated in the mid-1980s because the government believed it was crucial to provide scientists with a powerful computing infrastructure. Around 1990, however, the nation's supercomputing centers began to shut down their mammoth Crays. The centers simply couldn't afford to keep them running, especially with the advent of cost-efficient microprocessors. Because it cost $500,000 to re-move a single supercomputer from the premises and scientists preferred crunching data at their desks on a DEC Alpha workstation or Silicon Graphics machine, they just sat there, dead. At this pace of innovation vast computing power would be available to almost anyone in just a few years, and that would profoundly alter the technological landscape. Computers would go mass-market and users would need a simple, intuitive tool to navigate the Internet.

For the next six weeks, Andreessen and Bina ensconced themselves in the basement of the school's Oil Chemistry Building, pounding out code from dawn to dusk to dawn again, once for four days straight, Andrees-sen subsisting on Pepperidge Farm cookies and milk and Bina on Moun-tain Dew and Skittles. Each worked on the parts that most interested him, so much so it didn't feel like work. Working in the C programming language, Bina compiled the actual rendering engine that displayed the content, and Andreessen designed the interface—the look and feel of the browser—as well as the network backend. They christened it Mosaic af-ter Andreessen laid out the graphics as a mosaic of icons for users to point to and click on. Their Unix version was a lithe nine thousand lines of code, a fraction of the size of Microsoft's Windows 3.1, the prevalent oper-ating system of the time, which weighed in at 3 million lines. After a dozen friends tested it for bugs, Andreessen unveiled it to the world.

On the morning of January 23, 1993, he posted a message to several online bulletin boards, which read, in part:

By the power vested in me by nobody in particular, alpha/beta version of 0.5 of NCSA's Motif-based information systems and World Wide Web browser, X Mosaic, is hereby released.
Cheers,
Marc

X Mosaic (they later dropped the *X*) was the Internet's first smash hit, with enthusiastic early adopters conjuring a powerful word-of-mouth marketing campaign. Even the Web king himself, Tim Berners-Lee, found Mosaic "brilliant," "exciting," and "full of features," promising to advertise it inside the community. Andreessen was overwhelmed by the kudos and queries pouring into his email box. It was a chore just to keep up with the correspondence—people with technical questions, suggestions for more advanced features, bug test results. Companies inquired about licensing the browser or hoped to commercialize it. Just when he thought things were calming down, a new wave would roll in. Within six months of its release, the Unix version of Mosaic, by Andreessen's count, had one hundred thousand users.

Even before finishing Mosaic, Andreessen and Bina had rounded up five NCSA colleagues to code versions for Windows, Mac, and software to run a Web server. Crack programmers all, a friendly competition developed. Not only hell-bent on speed, they added additional features like a cursor that changed shape over hot links to make them easier to see. During Thanksgiving week 1994, on the first day Mosaic was available for PCs, the NCSA server overloaded and crashed. By the time Andreessen graduated in December, more than a million people were surfing the Web with Mosaic in Unix, Windows, and Mac flavors.

[NETWORK EFFECTS]

Andreessen had uncorked a "network effect," a term first used to describe the spread of the telephone in the early years of the twentieth century. Simply put, the more people who own a telephone, the more valuable an added line is to each person already on the network. The potential number of connections grows exponentially in relation to the number of people on the network.

With two people there are two communications paths:

1.	User #1	→	User #2
2.	User #2	→	User #1

With three, there are six potential paths:

1.	User #1	→	User #2
2.	User #2	→	User #1
3.	User #2	→	User #3
4.	User #3	→	User #2
5.	User #1	→	User #3
6.	User #3	→	User #1

A network with five members yields twenty possible connections, while twenty results in 380 potential connections. Thousands of users result in hundreds of millions of connections. Millions of users . . . well, you get the idea.

Mosaic forged a positive-feedback loop: the more people who discovered Andreessen's browser, the more who spread it, and this unleashed an ancillary virality stream expressed in the growing online population and the number of websites. The more who downloaded Mosaic, the more websites they created. This attracted additional users, who built more webpages. The greater the online population, the greater the utility of being there—both for those already there and for those entering for the first time. The release of separate Macintosh and Windows versions spiked the virality, as the general public began to pierce this once impenetrable academic sphere.

In 1992, 4.5 million people were plugged into the Internet and there were perhaps fifty websites. By the end of 1993, 1 million people had downloaded Mosaic, there were 6 million total users, and 623 websites. Within a year the online population jumped to 13 million with 10,000 websites. Web traffic shot up more than 300 percent, with users creating their own home pages, uploading photos, and setting up chat rooms. Today's Web, with more than 1.5 billion users worldwide and almost 200 million websites, owes its existence to three men: Paul Baran of the Rand Corporation, who conceived the Internet; Tim Berners-Lee, creator of the World Wide Web; and Marc Andreessen, who figured out how to navigate it. In essence, Baran provided the land, Berners-Lee built the roads, and Andreessen manufactured the vehicles (see Figs. 1 and 2).

NUMBER OF INTERNET USERS, 1992-2007

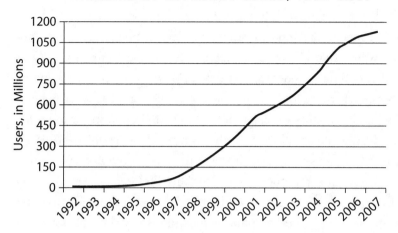

FIG. 1. Number of Internet users increased exponentially between 1992 and 2007.

NUMBER OF WEBSITES, 1992-2007

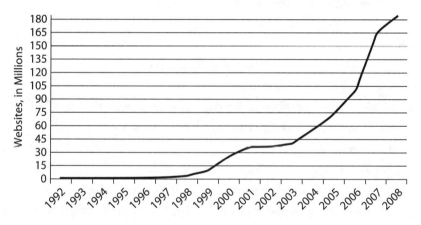

FIG. 2. Growth of websites increased exponentially in tandem with increase in growth of Internet users.

In a few years Andreessen would know precisely what to do. In 1993, however, there were no clear paths for capitalizing on a free Web browser, and start-up companies didn't exactly sprout up in Illinois cornfields. What's more, since Mosaic was coded under the aegis of NCSA, it didn't belong to him. The supercomputing center was not shy about trumpeting its ownership. Just as Andreessen was set to graduate in December 1993, a *New York Times* article on the front page of the business section called

Mosaic "a map to the buried treasures of the Information Age" that was being hailed as the "first 'killer app' of network computing," and listed companies, including Digital Equipment Corporation, Xerox, and Novell, that were exploring ways to exploit it for online commerce. NCSA director Larry Smarr, quoted as saying that Mosaic was "the first window into cyberspace," received the lion's share of credit, complete with a photograph, while its creators weren't even mentioned. To add insult to injury, NCSA, which inked a million-dollar licensing deal for Andreessen's handiwork, asked him to stay on full-time as a manager—but not on Mosaic.

Andreessen didn't bother to pick up his diploma before skipping town. Later he would claim he wished he had never studied computer science and instead had taken philosophy and history courses. Trying to forget all about Mosaic, Andreessen relocated to Silicon Valley, where he took a job at a small company specializing in artificial intelligence and defense consulting.

He wouldn't last three months.

[MOSAIC KILLER]

Across the Valley another technology visionary was feeling used and abused. James H. Clark, a year shy of fifty, was packing up his office, about to depart Silicon Graphics, the company he had cofounded a dozen years earlier. Clark had divined a method to coax supercomputer performance out of networked desktops and in the process transformed three-dimensional computer graphics, reinventing the way everything from cars to jets, buildings to suspension bridges and Hollywood films were made, producing the special effects for movies like Steven Spielberg's *Jurassic Park*.

When he first set out on his own, however, Clark was a neophyte in the ways of business. To get SGI off the ground he sold a 40 percent stake to Glenn Mueller of the Mayfield Fund for $800,000, giving his company a laughably low valuation of $2 million. Less than a year later Clark went back for more, trading away another slice of SGI for $17 million. A third round required him and his engineers to dilute their equity even further. At the same time the company sustained a growth rate of more than

40 percent a year, with revenue jumping from millions to billions. When it went public in 1986, its stock leapfrogged from $3 to $30 a share.

Although Clark was chairman, SGI's chief executive officer, Ed McCracken, who was brought in by the company's venture capital backers, ran operations. By 1994, cut off from influence, Clark walked away with a severance of $15 million, a fraction of what Ed McCracken and other executives were worth. Red with rancor, Clark plotted his nemeses' come-uppance, wanting more than anything to start a new venture that would make SGI look like a mere garage hobby. He couldn't do it alone, though. On his last day, he asked Bill Foss, a young SGI colleague who often func-tioned as Clark's jack-of-all-digital-trades, if he could recommend any brilliant software engineers. Foss tossed out the first name that came to mind.

Clark had never heard of Marc Andreessen. Preoccupied with his dealings with McCracken and SGI's board, he hadn't been paying atten-tion to the browser craze sweeping the tech world. Foss downloaded Mo-saic on Clark's computer and told him, "You'll figure it out." Walking out of the room, he watched Clark squint at the screen, tentatively clicking around. A few minutes later Clark came upon Andreessen's home page, where the former University of Illinois programmer had posted his re-sumé. Clark marveled at the browser's simplicity, and it crossed his mind that the first time he was using Mosaic was to contact its creator.

He typed a now famous email:

Marc,
You may not know me, but I'm the founder and former
chairman of Silicon Graphics. As you may have read in the
press lately, I'm leaving SGI. I plan to form a new company.
I would like to discuss the possibility of you joining me.
Jim Clark

Then he went back to packing. On the other side of the ether, it took Andreessen all of ten minutes to reply. He knew who Clark was. In col-lege he had whiled away many happy hours on SGI machines. The next morning they met at seven thirty for breakfast in Palo Alto to plot their future—except they had no idea what they wanted to do. All Clark knew was whatever it was, he wanted to do it with Andreessen. Beneath the façade of the gloriously grimy, bleary-eyed twenty-two-year-old was vast experience in programming on a bevy of machines and a vision that jibed with Clark's. Both searched for ways to simplify technology to make it attuned to the needs of a mass market. Both believed others had cheated them by wresting away control of their creations, and in the process skimming vast sums of wealth off their sweat and inspiration. Both were capable of seeing the big picture and burned with a desire for sweet revenge. Clark wondered about building on the browser, but Andreessen was firm: "I'm finished with all that Mosaic shit," he said.

[THE NAVIGATOR]

Over the next few months they explored ideas. Clark's first plan involved interactive television, but with no hardware, there was no market for software. The second involved an online gaming network for the Nintendo 64, but there was too much risk in being dependent on one manufacturer; this became especially clear after the game console shipped late. Also, sufficient numbers of gamers weren't yet online, although it was clear the Web and Mosaic-enabled Internet were becoming part of people's everyday lives. Clark saw that in the near future the law of large numbers would take hold. If he and Andreessen could figure out a way to make a little money off enough users, they could have themselves a very healthy business. But how? Churning with his signature impatience, Clark was tired of talk without action.

One night in March 1994, after dinner and a second bottle of burgundy at Clark's house, Andreessen changed his mind, suggesting they create a "Mosaic killer." The university was making a business out of the idea that he had conceived and coded with his friends. All they would need to do was release a better version of the browser and let it take over. Andreessen was sure he could line up the original Mosaic team to come onboard.

He emailed his former comrades in code, telling them to pack their bags because he and Jim Clark—*the* Jim Clark—were coming to town. In the months since Andreessen had taken off for sunny California, life for his friends, who had taken to calling management at NCSA the "Politburo," had become downright gloomy. Before Mosaic, NCSA administrators couldn't have picked out the young programmers in a police lineup. Now they were called to meetings with forty people, and everyone, it seemed, outranked them. They didn't need much convincing to join Andreessen.

Clark incorporated Mosaic Communications in Mountain View, California, committing $3 million, about 20 percent of his net worth, and renting office space. The programmers separated into three teams—one each for Unix, Mac, and Windows—and got down to work. One of the key differences between Mosaic and the new browser was the kind of equipment it would run on. With Mosaic, both its creators and most of its users raced around on powerful computers whose information traveled over thick pipes, high-speed T1 and T3 lines paid for by government, universities, and corporations. To become a mass-market product, the new browser would have to course over phone lines and into PCs with sluggish 14.4 modems, which Clark likened to "soda straws." Speed and economy would be crucial, and each team competed to see who could come up with the fastest program, using a stopwatch to clock which version downloaded a page the fastest. No matter which was slowest, they all slaughtered NCSA's Mosaic.

They lost track of the hours as they sat transfixed by their screens, sitting around in T-shirts and underwear and arguing about everything from politics to sports. In other words, it was a typical Silicon Valley tech start-up. Andreessen was anointed "vice president of thinking up stuff" and practically never left the building, exhorting his engineers to press on. Summer seeped into fall, and the company continued to expand not only its personnel but the number of products it would offer—server and security software, an e-commerce application, and, of course, the browser, which was the linchpin.

The big debate was over pricing. The head of marketing hailed from Apple and proposed charging $99 for the browser, but Andreessen wanted to give it away so it would spread virally and create a huge installed base. "Ubiquity," he argued, was key to jump-starting the company and wiping Mosaic off the face of the Web. For inspiration he turned to Microsoft, the dominatrix of the desktop, which had leveraged an early lead in the DOS and Windows operating systems into PC hegemony. This coaxed application vendors to create applications for Microsoft's operating system and ignore the rest, which, starved of compatible software, faded away. Andreessen saw it as a simple equation: market share today equals revenue later; without market share, you don't generate revenue, but whoever achieves and hangs on to it wins.

It didn't bother him that the conventional wisdom of the time was that nobody could make money off the Internet. Somebody sold the first train, the first telephone, the first car, he argued. A network has to begin somewhere. Only then would formidable business opportunities ensue. He was sure the same would happen with the Web, which had achieved a self-sustaining momentum that was quickly turning into a self-fulfilling prophecy. In the end, Andreessen came up with "free but not free." They would give away the browser to students and educators and charge everyone else $39 (then $49 a year later). Even then, they offered a ninety-day free trial, which was never enforced, so businesses would primarily be the ones to pay.

The engineers pressed on, and the browser was shaping up to be a significant improvement over the original Mosaic. Not only was theirs ten times faster (according to in-house tests), more secure, and less prone to crashes, users could create far more complicated page layouts and encrypt credit card numbers, which was necessary for commerce to bloom on the Web. All of this would serve to juice its virality. In the way that including pictures was key to the original Mosaic's success by transforming a gray world of text into a multicolor extravaganza, fostering individuality and expression for users' webpages encouraged webizens to tag their sites with buttons that said, "Best viewed with Netscape" along with a link to download.

["THE SPARK THAT TOUCHED OFF THE INTERNET BOOM"]

Late on October 13, 1994, engineers posted the beta version of the browser online. A few stomach-churning minutes later someone in Japan downloaded it. A trickle became a stream, then a geyser. Someone jerry-rigged an alarm system to keep track—a bell for Macs, a moo for PCs, an explosion to indicate Unix. This quickly turned into a drinking game, with mooing drowning out the rest as the PC version pulled away. At the same time, their archrival Mosaic continued to spread, accounting for 60 percent of all Web traffic, and the university was licensing it to companies for $100,000, with Fujitsu and SpyGlass basing their own applications on it.

But NCSA didn't stop there. It retained lawyers who claimed that Andreessen and Clark were infringing on its intellectual property, implying that Andreessen had stolen the software he himself had created, and demanded a 50 cent per copy royalty for every download. Clark hired a forensic software expert to comb through the code to compare it to the original Mosaic. After the expert found "no similarity in form, only function" between the two, Clark rejected their demands. It was becoming clear, however, that naming the company Mosaic Communications Corp. was a liability, and battling over it only diverted their attention away from the big prize: an IPO. The last thing Clark's young company could afford was a lawsuit hanging over its head. He offered to drop Mosaic from the name and pay NCSA $3 million or fifty thousand shares of stock. NCSA took the money and settled.

Two months later, the newly named Netscape Corporation officially released Version 1.0 of the Navigator browser. Around midnight on December 15, 1994, the engineers gathered once again, this time rigging servers so a cannon fired every time a browser was downloaded. At first, virtually all of the activity occurred in Japan and Australia, since it was during their business hours. Within a few hours, ten thousand copies of the browser had been downloaded. With virtually no advertising or marketing, more than 6 million copies of Netscape Navigator were in use by spring 1995, and 10 million by the summer. The "browser," as John Cassidy, author of *Dot.Con: How America Lost Its Mind and Money in the Internet Era*, quipped, "was spreading like one of the filthy jokes that Clark liked to tell"—at a time when only 45 percent of Americans had even heard of the World Wide Web.

As Netscape's market share rose, Mosaic's plummeted to 5 percent. Businesses showered Netscape with licensing requests and purchases of server software, and by March 1995 the company generated $7 million in revenue. With newly installed CEO Jim Barksdale, a former executive at AT&T, handling day-to-day operations, Clark pushed the next step on his agenda: an initial public offering. Conventional wisdom dictated that a company needed to have three-quarters of robust revenue growth before going public, but Clark, who viewed an IPO as a media event, was in a hurry. SpyGlass, which licensed Mosaic's code for its browser, filed paperwork to go public in May 1995, which prompted Clark to initiate June's board meeting with a suggestion that Netscape follow suit. John Doerr was all for it. "Put the puck on the ice!" he said. But Barksdale thought it might be too early. While deliberating, they agreed the big risk was Microsoft, which planned to bundle a browser in its next Windows operating system upgrade. To fight Microsoft would take ample resources. They would either need to go public or go back for more venture capital, which would further dilute their shares. They decided on the IPO.

On August 9, 1995, interest was so keen on Netscape's first day of trading that Charles Schwab reset its phone welcome greeting: "Welcome to Charles Schwab. If you're interested in the Netscape IPO, press 1." Morgan Stanley added an additional line to handle the intense call volume. There was so much demand the stock—initially priced at $28—opened late so the market could set a price, which it eventually did: $71 a share. After peaking at $75 it would end the day at $58. Almost instantly, Clark and Andreessen had created dozens of millionaires. Each of the original Mosaic coders from Illinois cleared several million. Clark's stake was worth more than $663 million that first day. Andreessen, who had worked late the night before, rolled out of bed, logged in to check the stock, then learning he owned $70 million in stock, promptly went back to sleep. "It's probably a Midwestern kind of thing," he said later.

Editors at *Fortune* would look back in time and call Netscape's IPO "the spark that touched off the Internet boom." They weren't alone. The Netscape IPO was largely credited with instigating the mania in technology. A sixteen-month-old company with picayune revenues and few products was suddenly worth close to a billion dollars. It stunned bankers, stock analysts, and the media.

[DISRUPTING NETSCAPE'S VIRALITY]

A year earlier, when Mosaic was first taking off, Bill Gates noted that the Web was free and couldn't see any way Microsoft could make money on

it. He changed his mind by the time Netscape Navigator squashed Mosaic and grabbed 75 percent of the browser market. In a memo titled
"The Internet Tidal Wave" that Gates sent his executive staff and their
direct reports a month before Netscape made the decision to go public, he
said the Web was the "most important single development" since the IBM
PC. "I have gone through several stages of increasing my views of its im-
portance. Now I assign the Internet the highest level." In fact, he called it
"critical to every part" of Microsoft's business. What spooked him was
that after ten hours of browsing, Gates hadn't come across a single Microsoft file on a website—no Microsoft Word, no nothing. He vowed to take
on the company's newest competitor: Netscape. "We have to match and
beat their offerings," he wrote. But that didn't mean Microsoft would give
away the browser, a suggestion one of his subordinates made weeks later
at a company retreat. "What do you think we are," Gates asked, "com-
munists?"

In November Netscape's stock was topping out at $171 per share.
When Goldman Sachs downgraded Microsoft stock because of concerns
over the impact of the Internet on the software maker's future, Gates
rolled into action. He licensed the Mosaic browser from SpyGlass, which
had also recently gone public, and made the creation of Microsoft's own
browser a priority, throwing a battalion of programmers at it. The irony
wasn't lost on Andreessen, who had conceived and coded both browsers,
noting he would be competing against himself. In August 1995, with
Netscape enjoying an 80 percent share of the browser market, Microsoft
released Internet Explorer. Although it was greeted with a collective
yawn, hammered by critics, and didn't make a dent in Netscape's advantage, the so-called browser wars had begun.

With Netscape riding high and revenue flying to $346 million in 1996,
Andreessen appeared on the cover of *Time* on a throne and with bare
feet. Meanwhile Microsoft kept chipping away, releasing Internet Explorer 3.0 a year after it first entered the browser market. Microsoft often
took three tries before it got something right, which was true of Windows and true of the new browser. But Microsoft hadn't simply closed the
technology gap. Gates did an about-face, deciding to give away the browser
and bundling it with every new computer that ran Windows. Any PC
maker that didn't offer Explorer as the default browser on every machine

would lose their license to run Windows. A computer without an operating system was like a man without a brain. Years later a federal court would rule against this monopolistic behavior in a case that eventually settled. Too late. The damage was done.

Six months after Internet Explorer 3.0 hit the Web, Microsoft's market share jumped 10 percent up to 22 percent, increasing to 32 percent in the next six months. While Explorer climbed, Netscape sank and its revenues slipped—the company had $132 million in operating losses that year. By the time AOL bought Netscape in 1998 for $4 billion in stock (worth $10 billion by the time the deal closed), Internet Explorer had a 50 percent market share and Netscape was en route to flaming out.

Andreessen had achieved two viral loops in the span of a few years, but Gates found a hole in his strategy. With everything depending on spreading the browser, Gates simply disrupted Netscape's virality, "choking off Netscape's air supply," software publisher Tim O'Reilly once said. Studies have shown that it is very difficult to induce people to switch browsers once they have selected one, so by pushing Explorer as the default option on PCs, Gates made his the de facto standard.

But Netscape was hardly the ultimate dot-com flop. Not only did all those associated with Netscape walk away with riches—Clark made billions, Andreessen hundreds of millions, and his engineers tens of millions—the browser wars of the 1990s resulted in a higher purpose. By the end of the decade, about 400 million people were on the Internet, virtually all using either Netscape or Internet Explorer that ran on code that Andreessen conceived and created.

By seeding the Internet with navigation tools, Mosaic and Netscape made possible today's Web—and there was no turning back.

3

The Spreadable Product as New Business Paradigm

Viral Plain, Ning's Double Viral Loop,
Your Digital Self, and Crushing Crushlink

To understand how a viral expansion loop works, there's no better place to begin than with Marc Andreessen's latest company, Ning, located in Silicon Valley a couple of blocks from Facebook and a few clicks down the road from Google. The company has been growing automagically from the moment it launched its "Social Networks for Everything"—a free platform for do-it-yourself social networks—in February 2007. Within four months there were 60,000 Ning nets, and by six months, 80,000. At year's end there were 150,000, and roughly 325,000 of them eighteen months into its run, increasing by about 2,000 a day. As of April 2009, Ning counted almost 29 million users (adding 2 million a month), more than 1.3 million social networks (with 3,500 new groups being formed each day) and 2.7 billion page views the previous month. By the end of 2009 it estimates it will have more than 60 million members and close to 3 million groups. About 40 percent of Ning networks originate outside the United States, and members from almost two hundred countries have signed up, with the service already available in several languages, including Chinese, Japanese, Spanish, and Dutch. At this rate, within a few years Ning will host millions of social networks with tens of millions of members serving up billions of page views daily.

On its social networks, users post comments, questions, photos, and videos and topics run from parenting to Pez dispensers, movies to motorcycles to motherhood, TV shows to customized cars to Thai kickboxing. There are groups for horse enthusiasts, gamers, and gays, health, information technology, ska music, and urban living. (A few dealing with marijuana and stoner culture have been, perhaps not surprisingly, forgotten.) Over a two-month period almost one hundred thousand people joined the official fan site for *The Twilight Saga*, a vampire-themed book series cum hit movie. Another popular social net that belongs to hip-hop mogul 50 Cent boasts hundreds of thousands of members (and is growing every day).

Chris "Broadway" Romero, creative director of ThisIs50.com and a producer at his G Unit Records, describes it as "an entertainment industry news/rumor/editorial blog in the vein of tmz.com, combined with unparalleled access and interaction with the celebrity." Romero uses the site to cast parts for music videos and film projects, and one day hopes to release music and video directly to the public, bypassing record companies completely. To Romero, it's nothing less than "a new entertainment platform, period." A single Ning group can, in theory, serve as an artist-owned and -managed foundation for an entire business; and collectively, the networks represent an ever-expanding commercial universe. Indeed, even within networks viral growth dynamics persist. When a group registers 150 users, it also reaches a point of nondisplacement, continuing to grow even if organizers do nothing to promote it.

That's because someone setting up a social network has no choice but to invite friends, family, colleagues, and like-minded strangers to sign up, and each new member brings others with him. That pushes Ning's "viral coefficient"—the number of additional members each person brings in—way above 1. That's key, because if the virality coefficient is 1, the start-up will grow, but at a linear rate, eventually topping out. Above 1, it achieves exponential growth. The table, created by Jeremy Liew, a venture capitalist with Lightspeed Venture Partners, an investor in RockYou, illustrates the difference a tiny increase in the viral coefficient can make, showing relative growth rates based on a viral coefficient of .6, .9, and 1.2. Liew started with a base of ten members and defined time as the period it takes for a member to invite others, which he estimated could be anywhere from two and eight weeks. Starting with 10 members and a viral coefficient of .6, you flatten out at 25 people, a gain of 15 users. At .9, you end up with 75 new members and growth slows dramatically. With a viral coefficient of 1.2, however, those same 10 people yield 1,271 additional users (see Table 1). Expressed in a line graph, a viral coefficient of 1.2 takes on the form of an exponential curve (Fig. 3).

VIRAL COEFFICIENT

TIME	.6	.9	1.2
0	10	10	10
1	16	19	22
2	20	27	36
3	22	34	54
4	23	41	74
5	24	47	99
6	25	52	129
7	25	57	165
8	25	61	208
9	25	65	260
10	25	69	322
11	25	72	396
12	25	75	485
13	25	77	592
14	25	79	720
15	25	81	874
16	25	83	1,059
17	25	85	1,281

TABLE 1. Relative growth rates for three different viral coefficients

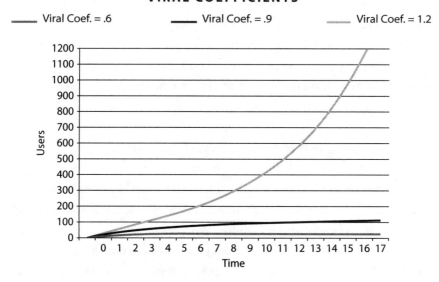

FIG. 3. Growth rates for viral coefficients of .6, .9, and 1.2.

With Ning, Andreessen estimates the viral coefficient is a whopping 2.0: each person who signs up is worth, on average, two people (compounded daily). The next day she brings in four members; on day 3, eight; within a week, 128 people, each worth double her weight in virtual clones. The curve is almost twice as steep as the one that represents a viral coefficient of 1.2, and that is how Ning has been able to double in size roughly every five months. "It's the power of compounding, predictable growth rates," Gina Bianchini, Ning's cofounder and a former Goldman Sachs investment banker, says.

When Ning veers from its projected growth pattern, it's usually because of a performance issue. Perhaps pages aren't downloading fast enough—even milliseconds can affect virality—or there is a change in the size or shape of user pages, all of which can put downward pressure on the viral coefficient. At one point Ning slipped and Bianchini's engineers tracked it back to a new sign-up system, which required registrants to retype passwords (for security purposes). They changed it back and Ning's viral coefficient popped back to 2.0. In January 2009, Ning shut down its red light district, finding that adult-themed networks didn't generate enough advertising or premium services to cover their costs—plus its ad partners were leery of porn. These kinds of networks also resulted in a disproportionately high number of Digital Millenium Copyright Act notices. What's more, the more legal adult networks there were on Ning, the more illegal ones posting kiddie porn popped up, which required contacting the FBI. While Ning initially lost 20 percent of its page views from blacklisting porn-themed social networks, traffic bounced back within five weeks, and Ning was back on track, growing faster than ever.

[ANATOMY OF A START-UP]

A thirty-five-year-old northern California native, Bianchini met Andreessen after receiving her MBA from Stanford and launching a software start-up that tracked and measured advertising. Andreessen sat on the board of the company, which went under in the dot-com crash; he and Bianchini dated for a spell before becoming friends. Andreessen, of course, had built Netscape and off-loaded it to AOL for $4.2 billion in 1999. Even before he

sold his next company, Opsware, an automated network and server company, to Hewlett-Packard for $1.6 billion, he had begun casting about for his
next billion-dollar act. One thing he knew, it wouldn't be a Web business.

Still smarting over the end of the bubble, when the NASDAQ lost
four-fifths of its value from its peak in March 2000, Andreessen believed
the Web was closed for business. But Bianchini, who was consulting for
Michael Ovitz, saw things differently. As Warren Buffett put it, "Get
greedy when others are fearful and fearful when others are greedy." Bianchini had been hearing about a bevy of smart start-ups she dubbed "garage viral businesses" that were thriving while Rome burned. There was
Craigslist, PayPal, Hot or Not, Crushlink—a million-dollar email dating
scheme started by two Harvard physics students—and Birthday Alarm,
which generated $3 million a year in revenue by automatically reminding
users of important dates. And, of course, Google, which was en route to a
$100 billion market cap, and a young start-up from Los Angeles called
MySpace, which launched in 2003 and was showing great promise. Bianchini believed it was the perfect time to start a new viral venture.

Slowly Andreessen began to see the light. He realized the entire sector
was underfunded, since all anyone seemed to hear was bad news. Bianchini provided data that showed there was a five-year gap in Internet
investment, and it dawned on him that whoever got to market early would
have a tremendous advantage. Then twenty to twenty-five media companies would go shopping when they realized they were in danger of falling
behind. When he thought about what was working on the Internet, he
came up with eBay, PayPal, MySpace, and sites that enhanced social be-
haviors like blogging, photo sharing, and reviews. He wondered about
combining all of them into a single platform that could grow virally. Over
brunch with Bianchini, Andreessen suggested they focus on creating social networking platforms, and Ning ("peace" in Chinese), seeded initially
with $1 million of his own money, was born.

They make an exquisitely odd pair: he is the gangly six-foot, four-inch
former coder with the huge egg-shaped head, famous for having posed
barefoot on a throne for the cover of *Time*; she is the petite, feminine jock,
a former field hockey standout at Stanford, a woman from working-class
roots anointed a "Web 2.0 Hottie" by Valleywag (a fact she concedes only
reluctantly). He's the grand visionary, the company chairman whose speech

unfurls in sheets of sound and who peppers his emails with smiley face emoticons, because he learned long ago that his droll sense of humor did not travel well over the asynchronous Web; she's the effervescent CEO, a social networker at heart who prefers roaming Ning's hallways to the isolation of working at home. He once won Customer of the Year at Hobee's, a local restaurant chain, for eating there every day for a year; she waitressed at a Hobee's in high school.

In the early days, not everyone knew what to make of Ning. The company spent three years designing and building the site's underlying platform; a year into that process, it released a couple dozen social applications to begin testing and refining what they had made. Those simple applications led Michael Arrington to post an entry on his TechCrunch blog entitled "Ning RIP?": "The reality of Ning is that it has lost whatever coolness it had, no one uses it, and Ning is going to have a very hard time getting people's attention." But Arrington did an about-face eighteen months later, after Andreessen and Bianchini attracted one hundred thousand online groups in about six months. "Everyone wants a social network of their own, and Ning is here to give them one," Arrington wrote. "The company sure has come a long way since I pronounced it dead in early 2006. Sometimes I like it when I'm wrong."

[DOUBLE VIRAL LOOP]

Significantly, viral loop companies are a form of organizational technology. In the way that Google doesn't own the Internet (it just seems that way) but simply helps you find what's out there, Bebo, Facebook, Friendster, Flickr, MySpace, and YouTube don't create content—their audience does. To Skype or not to Skype may be the question, but what if no one were on the other end to answer? Would you "tweet" if no one else were on Twitter? PayPal is a quasi bank for online transactions; it doesn't mint money. These viral loop companies provide an environment that is, in theory, almost infinitely scalable, relying on the wisdom of crowds to create or aggregate masses of material to fill it. The more people, the more content; the more powerful the lure for those sitting on the sidelines, the more value the company has.

There is also a multiplier effect, because the bigger the viral network, the faster it grows. (Double 10,000 users in a month and you get 20,000; double 50 million and you get 100 million.) Some of the biggest names on the Internet rode this viral wave to stratospheric heights until ultimately hitting saturation. EBay went from online garage sale to megasite because sellers attracted buyers who attracted more sellers and buyers. Google has pursued a similar strategy outside of search: under every set of ads it serves up sits a link to its AdSense program, which encourages more web-site owners to join (and in Google's case, joining leads to cold hard cash, which amplifies the viral effect).

The same mechanisms are at work with the spread of any network, whether it is the telephone, fax, cell phone, instant messaging, email, or Skype. Each additional user is worth more than any individual user. Eventually almost everyone joins such a network, the way that everyone has a telephone or an email address, because the value to being on it is so huge as a result of everyone else being on it. Nicholas Economides, a pro-fessor of economics at New York University's Stern School of Business, characterizes it as "a network effect": "The more connections you have, the more nodes, the more people, the more valuable it will be," he says.

What's more, viral networks can be stacked. PayPal came into being because buyers and sellers on eBay needed a way to complete transactions online, since most sellers without traditional storefronts couldn't process credit cards. YouTube took off by piggybacking on the success of MySpace, becoming the go-to site for video posters and watchers alike. Flickr grew in tandem with the entire blogosphere. Google's Gadget Ads was spun off as a mini viral network to serve ads on the tens of thousands of widgets, which themselves were layered over MySpace, Facebook, Bebo, and the rest.

This stackability will only increase as the walls between social net-works and websites crumble, hastened by the creation of OpenSocial, which provides a common programming standard so that applications can run across multiple websites. Ning, Google, LinkedIn, Yahoo, and My-Space are members; the coalition has taken the Facebook platform con-cept and applied it to the entire Web, meaning that a widget that works on one site will work on all the others. Think of it as the cyber equivalent of introducing standard railroad gauge during the Industrial Revolution, which helped spur American economic development coast to coast.

What separates Ning from other viral networks, however, is that it benefits from what Andreessen calls a "double viral loop." It spreads two ways because every network creator is a user and every user is a potential network creator. Say someone sets up an Angelina Jolie network with ten members, which grows as each person draws in others. An adoption site breaks off, a Jon Voight hate group rises up, a Brad Pitt love club forms, a Lara Croft nostalgia net appears, spawning a legion of anime spinoffs. Soon you have two, three, five networks, all expanding simultaneously. In the meantime, the original group continues to attract users. Ning swells like a river fed by an ever-growing number of tributaries.

[TO THE PROMISE LOOP]

Once a viral loop takes hold you can accurately predict how fast your user base will grow. That's because a viral loop expands according to something known as a power law curve, characterized by a soft-edged L shape (see Figs. 4–7). It has other names, too: the 80-20 rule, Pareto's law, the law of the vital few, the principle of factor sparsity, the long tail. The concept originated in 1906, the inspiration of Italian economist Vilfredo Pareto, who realized that 20 percent of the population owned 80 percent of the property in Italy. He fashioned power law curves to posit that wealth follows a "predictable imbalance," leading to a winner-take-all society.

Although no one knows exactly why, power laws describe a dizzying array of natural and unnatural phenomena—everything from ranking the size of planets, galaxies, and lakes by volume to Newtonian physics. If you charted Earth's cities by population, listed everyone in the world in descending order of wealth, analyzed sales of music or the concentration of endowments for public and private colleges, with 20 percent of the schools possessing 80 percent of the endowments, you would end up with a curve similar to Pareto's curve for Italian land distribution. Pareto's law has been called on to characterize blog traffic, with, roughly speaking, the top 20 percent of bloggers attracting 80 percent of the readers and determining the relative popularity of websites. While the general shape of the curve remains the same, Pareto's law is not a hard and fast rule; the 80–20 rule is just an approximation. Exact percentages vary depending on the exact phenomenon under the microscope.

Chris Anderson, in *The Long Tail: Why the Future of Business Is Selling Less of More*, relies on Pareto's thesis to explore online commerce and illustrate a heavy tail argument, that 98 percent of all the possible choices get chosen by someone, and the 90 percent available online often account for half the revenue and two-thirds of the profits. The point of the "long tail" argument is that in certain Internet, digital, and frictionless domains, the dominance of the "head" of the curve (a minority of things generating a majority of activity or revenue) should be somewhat less than what you would normally see in the real world.

Applied to music it is easy to see. In the real world, retail stores stock only a small percentage of the CDs that are available. Walmart, for example, may only have three hundred CDs on its shelves, so consumers don't have the option of buying music further down the tail, which means sales are highly concentrated toward the top three hundred CDs. Then it's possible it becomes a 1:100 rule: 1 percent of the CDs generate almost 100 percent of the revenue. On iTunes, on the other hand, every track and CD is available, digitally, frictionless, easily findable and searchable. In the digital domain, because the long tail is more accessible, the head is less dominant than in the real world. Instead of 1:100, maybe it's 5:80—5 percent of the CDs account for 80 percent of the revenue, with the remaining 95 percent of releases accounting for 20 percent of the revenue—and 20 percent is a lot more than zero percent, especially in a large market. Google has been a huge enabler of this longer tail because a product near the tip is both findable and accessible.

If Ning were represented by a traditional offline power law curve, 20 percent of its largest social networks would generate 80 percent of its page views, and a few huge networks would dominate usage and traffic. Instead, while Ning's top two hundred networks are responsible for the lion's share of traffic, they're not responsible for all of it, and, in fact, not much more than half. Many networks down the long tail are also thriving. Ning is seeing a power law curve distribution, but the head is squeezed, while the tail extends outward. And it expects this heavy tail to hold sway in the future, with loads of midsize to small networks with niche audiences exhibiting the most growth despite being microtargeted and relevant to relatively small numbers of people. Users discover these networks via email invitations (users inviting other users), embedded widgets (users embedding widgets in blogs and other places, leading people back to the networks), and that old mainstay: Google searches, in addition to simple word of mouth or users browsing or searching on Ning itself.

If Ning keeps growing at this rate, it will reach the promised loop as it tips to a point of nondisplacement, adding users even if it does nothing and becoming virtually impregnable. After PayPal blossomed as an on-line transaction power, eBay launched a competing service and failed miserably (eventually buying PayPal instead). To combat YouTube, Google and Yahoo launched rival online video sites, neither of which went any-where. There's the likelihood that LinkedIn has become unassailable by aggregating huge pools of users. Ning also seems destined to achieve this point of nondisplacement. In only one instance, Friendster, has a company fallen apart after achieving this kind of reach, and it was largely done in by technical failures—network meltdowns and outages—that drove users

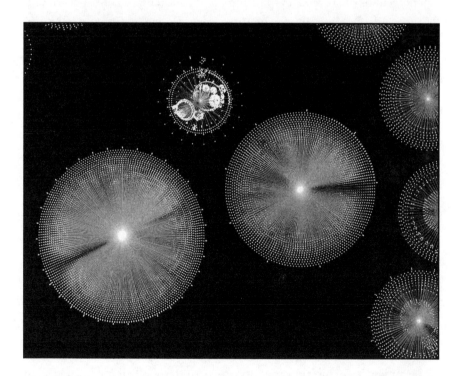

FIG. 4. Each white sphere represents a new Ning user, each line an invitation to join. The starbursts define the extent and growth pattern of a single network, centered on its creator. (*Ning.*)

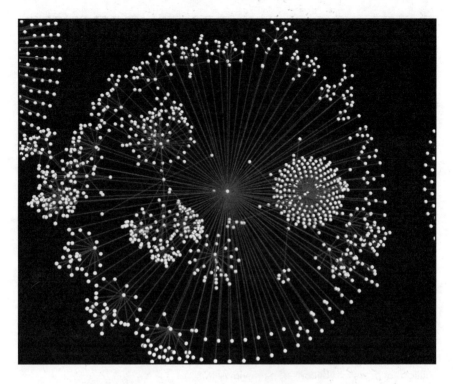

FIG. 5. In some nings, the creator invites most members. When subsequent users bring in new members, clusters form to reflect the viral chain. (*Ning.*)

FIG. 6. Ning benefits from a double viral loop, since a member of one social network will often set up another social network on a different topic. (*Ning.*)

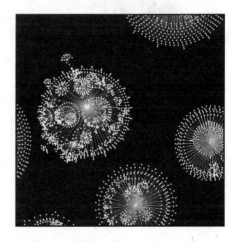

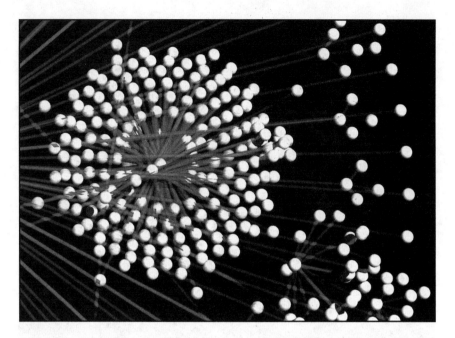

FIG. 7. This viral effect means each Ning member is equal to two users, compounded daily. That's how Ning grows and expects to amass millions of networks with tens of millions of users and billions of page views. (*Ning*.)

into the embrace of MySpace and Facebook. Twitter, too, has had trouble scaling; its network is buggy and unreliable. While it is possible it could follow Friendster to ignominy, it has an enviable connection with a deep, loyal pool of users who have weathered severe outages as its network grows.

Mass audiences on this scale carry serious potential, hence the fantastical valuations viral loop companies have achieved. That's because if you can get that many people to use your product, someone somewhere will pay you to reach them. Even if your strategy is limited to getting big and bought, you have the opportunity to auction off yourself (and your millions of users) to the highest bidder and let the next guy worry about wringing revenue from your audience. MySpace, which News Corp. bought for $580 million and Murdoch estimates is worth close to $6 billion today, chose this route. So did YouTube (Google, $1.65 billion), PayPal, and Skype (eBay, $1.5 billion and $2.6 billion, respectively). Flickr cashed out early for a modest $40 million (to Yahoo). Or you can try to monetize those bodies yourself. If Facebook skimmed a buck a month off hundreds of millions of members, that would mean yearly revenues in the billions.

That's not exactly a radical idea. Google achieved a $100 billion market cap by vacuuming up nickels, dimes, and quarters from search ads and counting clicks on advertisements. Craigslist monetizes a scant 2 percent of its site, giving away the rest in the form of free classified ads. The belief is that massive audiences like these can generate huge returns in the same way a 0.25 percent increase in sales tax for a municipality can yield millions in revenue.

SHARED CHARACTERISTICS OF VIRAL LOOP COMPANIES

This doesn't mean launching a successful viral loop company is easy. Far from it. Creating a deliciously spreadable product is merely the first step. Then comes the hard work of ramping up a business, and that's where some real challenges await, as Hong and Young learned with Hot or Not. Viral loop companies succeed for many of the same reasons, while unsuccessful ones seem to fail in different ways. For every eBay and Facebook there are heaps of social start-up failures you've never heard of. In addition to Friendster, which simply couldn't scale, there is Tribe, for example, an online community that never caught on; Plaxo, creator of a "smart address book" that didn't serve an important enough need; and Flixter, which lets users share movie reviews but has had trouble attracting repeat traffic.

Successful viral expansion loop businesses share the following characteristics:

• **Web-based:** They are far better suited to the frictionless world of the Internet.

• **Free:** Users consume the product at no charge; after aggregating a mass audience, it may be possible to overlay various revenue streams (offer premium services, for example).

- **Organizational technology:** They don't create content—their users do. They simply organize it. But facilitating can lead to a mass audience. Just ask Google.

- **Simple concept:** Easy and intuitive to use.

- **Built-in virality:** Users spread the product purely out of their own self-interest and, in the process, offer a powerful word-of-mouth endorsement to each subsequent user. (And word of mouth is widely viewed as the best form of advertising.) This means that viral loop products have within themselves the seeds to grow on their own.

- **Extremely fast adoption:** Within a month of Facebook's launch, half of Harvard's student body had joined. Within thirteen months, 12 million people had downloaded Skype. Hotmail had 30 million users within thirty months. Yet none of them required a dime for marketing or a sales force.

- **Exponential growth:** Because each user attracts more users, there is a tandem growth model. This is in sharp contrast to a "normal" business, which more typically grows linearly (and far more slowly), at a rate usually corresponding to its marketing spend.

- **Virality index:** For the user base to grow exponentially, virality must equal or exceed 1.0. In the aggregate, one user becomes two, turns into four, eight, and so on. Anything less than 1 and virality cannot be self-sustaining.

- **Predictable growth rates:** If a product is properly designed with viral hooks, it spreads at a constant rate—assuming there are sufficient numbers of people—and can be accurately forecast, in the same way epidemiologists can predict with some certainty how quickly a virus will spread through a city.

- **Network effects:** The more who join, the more who have an incentive to join. A telephone, for example, becomes continually more useful to those who already have one as more people are added to the network.

- **Stackability:** A viral network can be laid over the top of another, each fostering the other's growth (PayPal and eBay; YouTube and MySpace).

- **Point of nondisplacement:** A tipping point, when a company attracts so many users it continues to grow; it becomes nearly impossible for a competitor to take it down.

- **Ultimate saturation:** After a network has spread far and wide, it can reach a point of maturity when growth slows. This happened to both MySpace and Facebook, both of which saw their growth rates slow from 3 percent a month to about 1 percent—and in MySpace's case even decline slightly. Nevertheless, they had already amassed substantial user bases, with a full 20 percent of users considered "addicts" who made up almost 75 percent of visits.

The result is a business that spreads rapidly, scales quickly, and has the potential to create staggering wealth in a relatively short amount of time. "When your currency is ideas, people become emotionally attached," Bianchini says. "Then you become a public utility like Blogger, YouTube, or Facebook." Except that Ning doesn't want to create one gargantuan audience. (Indeed, nearly a third of its networks don't take off, but this mortality doesn't cost the company a cent, unlike unsold blenders at a Walmart.) It wants to foster millions of viral networks with narrow channels, each delivering the kind of targeted advertising that Google rode to vast riches.

[VIRAL PLAIN]

As with the microwave oven, Post-It notes, cellophane, Wheaties, the Frisbee, and aspartame, the Internet was originally conceived to fill one need, only to end up addressing another. Rand Corporation researcher Paul Baran first pitched the idea in 1959 so military commanders could communicate in the event of a nuclear strike on American soil, not so it would become the backbone of communication, commerce, information, and entertainment. What Andreessen learned from Mosaic was that built into the Internet is the cyberlogical ability to spawn almost infinitely replicable applications, which makes it a vast viral plain, pouring the foundation for another massive viral platform—the World Wide Web. Thriving in this virtual hothouse would later come other self-replicating landscapes: email, webmail, instant messaging, peer-to-peer networks, photo and video share sites, tagging and Digg-like ratings services, social networks, and VoIP (Internet telephony).

All have inherent growth traits and, when combined, unleash spectacular multiplier effects. Each not only spreads; it helps the others to spread. Email points users to photo share sites, which end up on social network pages to accompany videos, their existence shared via instant messages and disseminated via peer-to-peer networks, and so on. Virality is as much a digital imperative as propagating the species is a biological imperative in nature. It also takes advantage of our very human need to connect with one another.

Online or offline, everything begins with our concept of identity. As sociologist Craig Calhoun wrote: "We know of no people without names, no languages or cultures in which some manner of distinctions between self and other, we and they, are not made." He cites Hannah Arendt to emphasize, "We are distinct from each other and often strive to distinguish ourselves further. Yet each dimension of distinction is apt at least to establish commonality with a set of others similarly distinguished. There is no simple sameness unmarked by difference, but likewise no distinction not dependent on some background of common recognition."

Where does this basis of commonality originate? From one's culture. We are all a product of influences far too complex to decode, a tapestry of experiences from infancy to adulthood arising from our interactions with family, friends, community, and consumption of media and entertainment. It shapes who we are, how we act, what we fear and desire—and not always for the betterment of mankind. "Culture jammers," a loose coalition of media activists led by Marshall McLuhan disciple Kalle Lasn, believe that the United States has essentially become "a multitrillion-dollar brand" that is "no different than McDonald's, Marlboro or General Motors." People no longer create culture. Instead, corporations with a message to spread and something to sell have co-opted it. "Brands, products, fashions, celebrities, entertainments—the spectacles that surround the production of culture—are our culture now."

Brainwashed or not, "as human beings we are social creatures and we want to interact with other humans," says John Manzo, a professor at the University of Calgary in Alberta. Language, he points out, would be useless without someone to talk to. This need to communicate has been transferred to the Web. Today's almost ubiquitous interconnectivity doesn't replace real relationships with real people, the so-called meatspace (the yang of cyberspace), as defined by the cyberpunk movement of the 1990s. Instead, email, instant messaging, Twitter, and social networks like Facebook, MySpace, and Ning "allow us to have a richer life in totality than what we'd have before that."

Andy Warhol famously remarked, "In the future, everyone will be world-famous for 15 minutes." Really, though, in the future everyone will have his own TV show. For what is a profile on Facebook, MySpace, Bebo, or Tagged but a kind of reality show starring . . . you. Instead of fifteen minutes of fame, however, you get fifteen seconds over and over again (until the next update). As video and other multimedia transform our Web experience, these shows take on more complex modes of self-expression. Within the skein of networks unfurling through digital time and space, the sum parts of these disparate ego blasts—a tweet or blog post here, a Facebook Wall comment there, a video or photo, the results of a pop quiz that claim to tell you what kind of children's book you are or what your inner nationality is, become a documentary of your soul. "Image is everything," Andre Agassi chirped in a Canon camera commercial nearly twenty years ago. Today your reputation precedes you.

Increasingly there is your public self—the person you present to the physical world—your personal self (who you are when you are alone) and your digital self, which reaches far beyond the other two. If you spend time online, many more people know you—or think they know you—through your digital self, which can be as (or more) real to them than your real self. Indeed, people's perceptions of you can be quite vivid. Two Washington University in St. Louis researchers scanned the brains of fiction readers and concluded that they create intense, graphic mental simulations of sights, sounds, movements, and tastes they encounter in the narrative by activating the same brain regions used in processing similar real-life experiences.

These Web lurkers, people who know you exclusively through your digital deeds, base their judgments on the ideas and observations you share with the world, the photos and videos you post, the widgets you employ on your personal Web spaces, and the words others use to describe you. The memes you create spread virally, far beyond your network of friends, relatives, acquaintances, and colleagues. Once they leave your brain and hit the viral plain, they are out of your control and can take on a life of their own. Then you become more than just a guy trying to hold on to a job and pay down your mortgage. You are a brand that must be managed. With apologies to Marshall McLuhan, the medium is not the message. You are.

Why do we do it? What explains our BlackBerry-bearing, Twitter-tweeting, Facebook friend with the need for constant connectivity? As facile as it sounds, we do it because we are hard-wired to socialize. It's in our best interests. One reason we gravitate toward communities is because they multiply the impact of each individual to bring greater prosperity, security, and fulfillment to all. Aristotle believed that "man is a political animal" and we achieve noble actions by living as citizens together. What is politics, however, but the expression of personal interest manifested in the body politic? Two thousand years later Benedictus de Spinoza, a seventeenth-century Dutch philosopher of Portuguese-Jewish descent, expressed the view that men "are scarcely able to lead a solitary life so that the definition of man as a social animal has met with general assent; in fact, men do derive from social life much more convenience than injury."

Perhaps the answer is even more fundamental than Aristotle, Spinoza, or other philosophers ever imagined. Social networking makes us happy and, online or off, all of this congregating is merely a product of biological necessity. Research indicates that engaging with friends helps us live longer and better lives, with those with strong friendship bonds having lower incidents of heart disease. They even get fewer colds and flu. A decade-long Australian study found that for the duration of the study subjects with a sizable network of friends were 22 percent less likely to pass away than those with a small circle of friends—and the distance separating two friends and the amount of contact made no difference. It didn't matter if the friends stayed in contact via phone, letter, or email. Just the fact that they had a social network of friends acted as a protective barrier.

A research project by Paul J. Zak, a professor of economics and the founding director of the Center for Neuroeconomics Studies at Claremont Graduate University, found that when a test subject learns that another person trusts him, the level of oxytocin, a hormone that circulates in his brain, rises. "The stronger the signal of trust, the more oxytocin increases," wrote Zak, whose primary interest is neuroeconomics, a discipline that attempts to gauge how the brain's neurologic functions process decisions involving money. And trust, Zak learned, begets trust: the more oxytocin swimming around your brain, the more *other* people trust you. Notably, his test subjects had no direct contact with one another. All of their interactions took place by computer and with people whose identity they didn't know. "Trust works as an 'economic lubricant' that affects everything from personal relationships to global economic development," Zak says. Although he didn't explicitly state it, trust is also an integral part of social networking.

Another trust study discovered that when an investor in an experimental game was given a dose of oxytocin, he was more likely to allow someone else to control his money, no questions asked. The substance, which is sometimes referred to as the "cuddle hormone," has also been found to increase generosity and decrease fear and been associated with maintaining healthy interpersonal relationships and is a key to bonding. When virgin female rats are injected with oxytocin, they are transformed into protective mothers, taking over other females' offspring and nuzzling them as if they were their own.

Taken together, all this research strongly indicates that we are biologically driven to commingle online and off. Fortunately, as big as the world is, we are never far from one another. We are not, as the saying goes, six degrees of separation from anyone. It's actually closer to 6.6—at least that's what a Microsoft researcher estimated after combing through 30 billion electronic conversations over the company's instant-messaging network in June 2006.

[MAD ABOUT ME]

Since we live our lives through the prism of our minds, these online relationships, such as the ones that users on Ning share with one another, have the potential to become more real to us than real relationships. This isn't just true online. Have you ever attended a concert only to be disappointed it wasn't as good as the recording—the band not as sharp, the singer's voice croaky on high notes, the arrangements not as full? But that's the real music; it's the recorded music that wasn't. Yet your expectations have been shaped by the "perfection" of the sound studio, and this representation of music has become more real than the actual performance. It's true with media, too. Coverage of events is often more real to people than the actual events. Unless you have experienced Iraq firsthand, your perception is largely filtered through the interpretations of reporters, which, melded together with the braying of the American punditry, influence your own views. With children, artificial "grape"- or "strawberry"-flavored candy can seem more real than actual grapes and strawberries. In all these examples, perception trumps reality.

This is particularly true of online relationships, with many of us leading dual lives that calibrate between the physical space in front of us and the virtual space that occupies our minds. Mary Hodder is a forty-year-old Web consultant and entrepreneur whose life is spent on-screen. Survivalists live off the grid, but Hodder hates not being on it—even for a few minutes. She's more of an interface grrl. "I will go far out of my way to get my next connection to the Internet, via phone or my laptop," she says. "It's everything." Toting a laptop almost everywhere she goes, she traipses from café to café looking for Wi-Fi to hook into, and hacks her phone to connect to her computer. She downloads pirated movies and even television shows off the Net, shops there and pays all her bills, too. Her blog, Napsterization.org, explores how technology alters the media landscape. She spends much of her time on Twitter, microblogging the banal and not-so-banal nuances of her existence. Almost everything she reads, every video she watches and website link she clicks to, comes via the posse of people who follow her—and whom she follows—on Twitter. They have become her filter for the world.

Although technically based in the San Francisco Bay area, she lives, works, and plays on the Web. Even in a car, on a train, or sidewalk, she carries on simultaneous conversations with friends, associates, clients, and business contacts via email, instant messaging, and talking on her cell phone. She checks friends' blogs, scans their comments, follows the same links, mulls the same information, shares her thoughts via discussion threads or by posting comments on napsterization.org—and it's all hyper-linked, searchable, and browsable, depending on the tools available. Although Hodder may be physically disconnected from her friends, they are never far away, represented by the digital word sculptures they mold together. "They create content, I read or point to it in my blog or modify it, and they do the same," Hodder says. She refers to the material world as old-style "analog," while the Internet is strictly "digital."

Every day, Hodder becomes less of an aberration. Most of her friends and colleagues live this way, too, with the Web at the center of their relationships. The online Mary Hodder is much more widely known and admired than the real-life Mary Hodder. This is also the case for computer hackers, who identify more closely with their online "nicks" (nicknames) than their real names. Online they are powerful nemeses of corporations and governments. In real life, perhaps they are antisocial teenagers battling authority. It may also hold true for the haters, who under assumed names spray vitriolic commentary through the comments sections of blogs like graffiti. Like Hodder, they are part of a large and growing number of technophiles whose lives are one big Wikipedia. And the life Hodder et al. lead foreshadows ours. Indeed, it may mirror yours, since you are reading this book (and ostensibly have similar interests).

[HOOKED ON SPEED]

Like Hodder, we exist in multiple worlds of our own creation: the physical realm and the intellectual sphere joined. We are not only driven to connect to others, we are also hooked on speed. That's because as a society we suffer from attention deficit disorder. Work, play, family, friends, media, and marketers clamor for our attention. The more there is to do, the less time we have to do it. To adapt we have perfected the art of multitasking. At work, we surf the Web on company time and instant-message friends during staff meetings; at home we order books from Amazon while we watch CNN, prepare dinner, and help our kids with their homework. We pay bills online in darkened movie theaters and post blog entries at the beach. We text friends as we chase taxis and cruise social networks while waiting to board airplanes. Whoever said "Time is nature's way of keeping everything from happening at once" never owned a BlackBerry.

Of course, it's not just our lives that are set on fast forward. Entertainment on demand means never having to wait for summer reruns. Portable MP3 players enable consumers to hear their favorite songs wherever and whenever they want; at least one record label—Atlantic—sells more music through digital downloads than as compact disks, a trend that will eventually overtake the entire industry. You're more likely to store photos on Flickr than tote spent rolls of film in to be developed. Snail mail has become a quaint anachronism. Even Earth is spinning faster, by a second a year, according to scientists.

Our online habits are prolific, diverse, and virtually instantaneous. Many of us are media consumers, creators, distributors, and critics, often simultaneously. But skimming blogs and news sites, downloading music and videos, cruising MySpace, creating and maintaining blogs, and participating in video-game virtual worlds take time. Posting videos to YouTube requires drive and determination. Getting to the next level of a favorite video game requires persistence. All the time we make choices. We sift, filter, and ignore. Even turning it all off is an option. Today marketers use words like "fractured" or "fragmented" to describe this new media landscape, where there are hundreds of channels, thousands of publications, websites, and blogs, and a million places to put ads. It is, in short, the niche-ification of our lives. Because we are almost constantly communicating with friends, family, and colleagues over a vast viral plain, our written self-expressions, whether they be forwarded emails, ideas, jokes, links, or memes, spread virally. Not just person to person, but social cluster to social cluster. As the Internet continues to go more mobile, becoming gradually untethered from the desktop, this viral plain is both breaking up and expanding. It will offer a far greater, more diffuse surface area for ideas to spread virally. About 30 million smartphones, which enable users to email, text, surf the Web, and perform other Webby functions on the run, were sold in 2005. By 2010, an estimated 260 million will be in circulation and they will outsell land-bound PCs.

There are three primary technological innovations driving this surge in mobility: screens, microprocessors, and ubiquitous connectivity.

[SCREENS]

Display screens have been improving at breakneck speed, which is profound because they are a type of organizational innovation that can have a disruptive impact on existing industries. On a macro level, the Web is an organizational innovation because it stores and organizes information. So is the qwerty keyboard. It allows for the efficient production and organization of words. Google didn't create the Internet. It simply enables you to search it. But it is the screen that allows people to interact with virality.

As the cost of interactive displays plummets and the technology evolves, screens are becoming ubiquitous. A wide-screen flat-panel high-definition television set that cost $10,000 half a decade ago can be had for a twentieth of that price today. Multitouch screens as big as a wall and as small as the Apple iPhone are changing the entertainment landscape. Some will be as thin as a slice of wallpaper, yet durable enough to handle the most rambunctious user. They are built into walls and hung on buildings, in stores, in schools, on trains, in taxicabs, on handheld devices. One day soon you'll walk down a street and be awash in a sea of moving images. This is already happening. In New York City's Times Square there may be more moving billboards than still ones. Some subway entrances sport screens advertising television shows, and taxis have monitors in the backseat, transmitting TV news, traffic, and weather updates. You see them in department store windows, installed on airport walls, and towering over cities as mammoth moving billboards.

These flickering images may fulfill a primordial urge. Along with the need for social interaction and spreading information, humans have an innate fixation with moving pictures. Former vice president Al Gore, in a speech he gave at the October 2005 We Media conference in New York, claimed the human brain is "hard-wired" to capture the slightest movement in our field of vision. We not only notice it, we are biologically compelled to look. "When our evolutionary predecessors gathered on the African savanna a million years ago and the leaves next to them moved, the ones who didn't look are not our ancestors," he said. Indeed, they ended up as lunch. Those that noticed sudden changes in their environment, no matter how subtle, passed on the genetic trait neuroscientists refer to as "the establishing reflex." This, Gore said, is the brain syndrome activated by television and online video, "and why the industry phrase 'glue eyeballs to the screen' is actually more than a glib and idle boast."

[CHIPS]

Designing a microprocessor like the Intel Atom—the company's smallest chip ever—is like planning a city so tiny it could fit into a single bacterium. First, architects map out which routes go where so that millions of switches (the transistors) can direct traffic in the form of 1's and 0's that shoot from transmitters to transceivers across silicon expressways (called "buses"). Once schematics are plotted, designers create microscopic mock-ups of each layer, or "mask," and test them on powerful workstations, mimicking the chip's functions. Once built, the microprocessor's 47 million transistors, which are so minute that 2 million of them could sit on the period at the end of this sentence, switch on and off up to 300 billion times per second. If just one of them malfunctions, the entire processor spits up a hairball.

Then things get really complicated. The chip's fabrication phase is a logistical nightmare, with some three hundred steps involving chemicals, gas, and light. It begins with a land grab in the form of purified beach sand: silicon. This is melted and grown into cylinders and forged into thin wafers the size of LP records, which are shined until their surfaces are "perfect mirrors." With photolithographic "printing," the transistors and electrical passages are layered onto the wafers. To ready the chip for mass production, the wafer is blasted with heat and coated with silicon dioxide and light-sensitive photographic film. The masks are overlaid, with more layers ladled on top, and the whole thing etched, bombarded with chemicals, and covered with layers of metal. Each and every gate on each and every transistor is fed a positive- or negative-charged ion that will determine whether its job is to open or close. The wafers are then cut into chip-size bits using a precision saw.

Building transistors only slightly larger than the silicon atom itself is a dazzling display of design and engineering, made more so by the sheer

pace of technological innovation over the past six decades. An early transistor, created by Bell Labs, was about an eighth of an inch in diameter;
today, two thousand transistors placed side by side equal the width of a
human hair, and the cost has fallen to about one-millionth of what it was
in 1968. If Ford had innovated at the same rate as Intel, a car could go half
the speed of light, and if you were driving to New York for a week, it
would be more cost-effective to throw it out and buy a new one than feed
quarters into the parking meter.

Over the years, Intel and its rabid rivals engaged in a game of one-
upmanship over who could produce faster, more powerful chips, but they
didn't pay much heed to battery drain or heat—both natural side effects
of increased processing power. But most BlackBerry users don't need a
chip powerful enough to edit video, create Pixar-like effects, or decon-
struct the human genome. They just want a smartphone that lets them
send and receive email, open attachments, surf the Web, take and store
photos, and perform other basics without burning through the battery.

To fill this need, Intel and others have been churning out chips like
the Atom, which was specially designed for the mobile market. These
microprocessors represent a tectonic shift in thinking, because they are not
faster than previous processors nor do they do more. In fact, they do less.
But they drain a fraction of the battery power, yet offer mobile users the
entire Internet experience, unlike pre-2008 smartphones, which can't digest Flash, an Internet staple. Along the way Intel stumbled onto a whole
new category of hardware called "netbooks"—mini PCs that are lightweight, cheap, and capable of running basic PC functions such as word
processing, email, and Web surfing. Intel views the netbook as a disruptive technology that could create whole new markets. China and India
offer tremendous opportunity as the Internet becomes a staple of life there.
What's more, this new generation of chips will be driving everything
from handheld gaming machines to GPS gizmos, e-book readers, Internet tablets, and pocket video and music devices, all juiced with mobile
Internet capability. It makes possible social networking at your desk or on
the run.

[THE DARK SIDE OF VIRALITY]

All of this interconnectedness carries risks. The stronger our connections, the more vulnerable we become because the viral dissemination of information can be used as a weapon. Virus makers concoct mischievous applications that can auto-replicate and damage thousands of computers at a time, with each penetrated host a potential virus transmitter. Zombie bots unleash billions of spam, breaching Internet gateways and clogging inboxes. Hackers spark denial-of-service attacks to block websites and slow down corporate networks, while another favorite strategy involves a buffer overflow attack, which floods a software program with too much data. The perpetrator can then track and manipulate the overflow and trick the system into following his instructions as if he were the system administrator. There's even a Swiss-based eBay-like auction site, WabiSabiLabi, for black-market hacker code that can penetrate the software run by governments, corporations, and private citizens. The biggest buyer? The United States, which one government source claims is less interested in using black-market code for espionage than in stockpiling munitions in the event of cyberwar. "These things are powerful," seconds Charlie Miller, a security researcher and former National Security Agency employee who once hacked a MacBook Air in less than two minutes at a competition. "And compared with the price of a jet fighter, they're very cheap." More to the point for a viral loop business, infinitely replicable information can even be used to hijack a company.

In the summer of 2000, a few months before Hot or Not entered the dot-com lexicon, two Harvard physics students, Greg Tseng and Johann Schlier-Smith, decided to create an online dating business. From the day he had arrived on campus three years earlier, Tseng, in particular, had found the social scene at Harvard difficult to navigate. He had grown up in a middle-class northern Virginia suburb, but in Cambridge there were scads of rich blue bloods, people with vastly different approaches to life and money. The ritual of courtship was fraught with potential embarrassment—something he would just as soon avoid.

Wouldn't it be great, he thought, if you could short-circuit the dating process? The only way to do that, he figured, would be if you knew for sure that someone secretly liked you. But to accomplish that he would need to get everyone on campus into a database that listed every single person each person had a crush on. Then he came across an article by venture capitalist Steve Jurvetson about the rise of Hotmail and how its viral growth had killed Juno, which dropped millions of dollars on marketing while Hotmail spent virtually nothing. Tseng realized therein lay the answer.

When the fall semester started, they launched CrushLink, a combination Web and email scheme. "It was," Tseng says, "a very tight viral loop." A user would register on the site and list his crushes and their email addresses. The site would alert each recipient via email that someone had a crush on her. She would register, list her crushes, and the loop continued. Tseng seeded it by anonymously posting on message boards: *Wow! I just found this new site and met the love of my life. It's called CrushLink.* It got them fifty users a day. After about a week, they calculated their viral coefficient at about .3. There was a multiplier effect to be sure, but it was far from viral. So they experimented.

Tseng quickly learned that fewer registration steps meant higher conversion rates, and that had an impact on the coefficient. That's because multiplying all the conversion rates in a viral loop gives you overall virality. If you increase conversion rates, even by a fraction, you increase virality, which in turn encourages the overall spread. He also found that bland colors worked better than garish backgrounds, and speeding up the service so that pages downloaded faster also helped. That's because humans can perceive anything over 150 milliseconds—half the time it takes for the human eye to blink. Adding a smiley emoticon in email subject boxes raised their viral coefficient a full 10 percent. "No kidding," he says.

But the big adjustment came when they began emailing hints to prospective crushees, things like, "Your secret admirer's last name has six letters in it," "Your secret admirer's first name starts between *A* and *F*," or "Your secret admirer's email address is different from your domain." This attracted more people to the site, and for every ten of them, at least a few added more crushes to the database. In three months, they registered tens of thousands of users and broke one hundred thousand users on October 27. By February, CrushLink had gone viral, and a month later it registered its millionth user. It crossed 1.5 million on March 2 and 2 million on March 22.

The two college seniors made money by having users fill out advertising offers, which were basic sign-ups for other sites. They simply treated hints as a form of currency, giving away the first few, then requiring users to fill out questionnaires to get more. Enough did that Tseng and Schleir-Smith generated $2 million in revenue. Not that they actually saw that much. First, some advertisers claimed they had tricked users into filling out forms, so the traffic wasn't authentic. Tseng sued, and in the end the two were able to recover about half the money they believed they were due.

After graduating, the two enrolled at Stanford to study physics. They tried to sell CrushLink, but the dot-com bust prevented them from getting their price. They created a tech incubator called JumpStart Technologies with the money they were earning from CrushLink to fund other businesses and hired a barebones staff to keep the site going. But their viral schemes began to unravel when spammers began mimicking Crush-Link emails, blasting out millions of them all over the Internet. CrushLink went from being a cute concept to, as a writer from Salon described it, "the latest excrescence of an Internet marketing machine grown unfathomably sleazy."

Then the Federal Trade Commission fined the viral duo $900,000 for violating the CAN-SPAM Act. In the complaint, the FTC alleged that JumpStart offered consumers free movie tickets if they provided the names and email addresses of five friends. JumpStart then spoofed the person's email address so that the message looked as if it had come from the friend when in fact it hadn't. The subject box added to the illusion, containing a personalized message like "Hey," "Happy Valentine's Day," or "Movie time. Let's go." "In this way," the complaint claimed, "JumpStart's commercial emails circumvented certain spam filters and were opened by consumers who thought they contained personal correspondence."

Of the fine, Tseng says, "We were definitely unlucky to get targeted (many others were doing similar or worse things) and should've had better legal representation but we were twenty-four and didn't know better. And suffice it to say, since then we have never sent any emails that could possibly be construed as misleading." He also claims that CrushLink never spammed or sold email addresses to spammers. Neither has Jump-Start.

If true, CrushLink is the story of a viral loop company that was sabotaged by an even greater informational force: spam. If false, CrushLink simply went amok, using its architected virality for malevolent gain. Either way it is a cautionary tale, the kind of event we will be seeing more of in the future. In fact, we already have—and with the same players. In July 2009, New York State attorney general, Andrew Cuomo, accused Tagged, a social network that Tseng and Schleir-Smith founded in 2004, of stealing "the address books and identities" of more than sixty million users, alerting recipients to view a photo that in reality did not exist. Instead, the recipient "was forced to become a new member of Tagged," Cuomo said. Tseng blamed a "confusing new registration process," which Tagged immediately discontinued, for the problem.

As technology marches on, it's important to consider that the ability to stop is as important as accelerating. It wasn't until George Westinghouse invented the air brake in 1868 that trains could run faster and pull hundreds of cars. Before then, train wrecks were common even as trains moved slowly across the land. We require an equivalent innovation to protect us from being crushed in the viral melee.

If history is any guide, we'll get it. Whenever companies have resorted to coercive viral hooks—by, say, hijacking your email address book when you try to sign up—any short-term viral growth has been offset by customer alienation, which is itself broadcast virally, user to user, across social networks and the blogosphere.

Nowadays virality works both ways. It's the world we live in.

[UBIQUITOUS INTERNET]

Whether Wi-Fi, cellular networks with broadband capability, satellite connections or other measures, smartphone users have many ways of getting online. But the wireless Internet means more than being able to check email at Starbucks. Imagine if your town was transformed into one gigantic wireless hot spot overnight. You could feed parking meters with your MasterCard instead of hunting for quarters. Utility companies might read meters in real time and pass the savings on to customers. The next time you saw a pothole, you could instantly email a camera phone photo to city hall. Municipal wireless wouldn't just make life easier for citizens. It would have the potential to save lives. Firefighters would be able to turn traffic lights green as they raced to put out a blaze. Police could tap into a bank's surveillance cameras to get a head start on cracking a heist. Emergency responders would be able to communicate during a natural disaster or terrorist attack.

The ubiquitous Internet means that anyone, anywhere, can tap into this mobile informational grid, with millions of memes spreading from screen to screen to screen. Entertainment, news, email, texting, and phone conversations will be held at 60 miles per hour. What you do at home—watching TV, viewing movies, listening to the radio or your iPod, downloading music, accessing MapQuest or global positioning systems, surfing blogs and posting updates to your Facebook profile—you'll be able to do on a bus, in your car, or walking down the street. Odds are, you'll do it on a smartphone or other small mobile device, and this yields almost limitless levels of virality. It took only a few years for social networking to comprise more than 25 percent of all Internet traffic, and these connections are sprouting ever more connections. It creates a three-headed viral hydra: the user base is viral, the content is viral, and it all sits atop a vast viral plain.

Taken together, better screens, chips designed to offer the full-color Web on handhelds, and universal connectivity mean that people will be spending more time online, more time plugged into the viral plain, transmitting memes and messages, links and ideas, touching one another digitally over social networks. It's a gargantuan business opportunity for the ones who seem to have figured it out—like Ning.

Because in this new phase of webonomics, it's not just the eyeballs, as it was before the dot-com crash, it's the kind of eyeballs you collect and how you slice, dice, and direct them. When a user signs into Ning, she is already expressing an interest just by virtue of joining a specific social network. Then Ning displays the kinds of ads Web surfers are accustomed to seeing on blogs, news sites, all over the Internet, especially tailored to their particular social-net niche. Extreme skiers see ads targeted to extreme skiing, and so on, and the click-through rates on these, Bianchini reports, are far higher than with traditional social networking banners. Right now, Google places threads; eventually, however, Ning will serve its own. And even today, if you want to control the ads on your Ning network, you can pay as you go for the infrastructure for a monthly fee of $20. About twelve thousand group leaders pay the maximum $55 a month for premium services that enable them to choose their own URLs and buy extra storage for photos and videos, generating $600,000 in revenue. Either way, Ning makes out.

"It would be very difficult for MySpace or Facebook to shift gears and directly offer a competing service to us," says Bianchini. "They have a huge set of technical challenges just scaling what they're already doing, and we have spent three years building a serious architecture and technology lead for what we do." One of her engineers compared that kind of course correction with "swapping out the engine of a 747 during midflight." By the time Facebook—or anyone else—could do that, Ning might well have ridden its double viral loop to impregnability.

Because once it hits critical mass, the road is paved. Then no one can stop it.

II

VIRAL
MARKETING

4

The Perpetual Viral Advertisement

Viral Tag: P.S. I Love You.
Get Your Free Email at Hotmail

In the early to mid-1990s, after Mosaic and Netscape laid the foundation for the Internet's viral plain, populating the Web with sites and content channels, virality was a simple value proposition. If someone liked something, she passed it on to her friends via "word of mouse." Until Sabeer Bhatia and his partner Jack Smith created the first webmail service, no one had ever thought of incorporating viral marketing into the actual product. At first, though, things didn't look very promising. In February 1996 Bhatia was pitching his twentieth venture capital firm, Draper Fisher Jurvetson (DFJ), on Silicon Valley's famed Sand Hill Road, and it appeared the meeting would end like the previous nineteen: no money, no prospects, a bad TV drama played over and over with a slightly different cast.

Bhatia was explaining the concept behind JavaSoft, a set of developer tools his partner had created to stow personal information from users—sign-up information, addresses and phone numbers, surveys—then display it on a website. DFJ cofounder Steve Jurvetson doubted there would be much pent-up demand for it. At best, it might appeal to a hard-core geek audience, but with the vast majority of Web users on dial-up modems over pre–fiber optic cable phone lines, this was a small sample. He doubted there was enough to create a sustainable, stand-alone business. Over the past two years he had received pitches from twenty or thirty different Web tools companies pushing JavaSoft-like applications and had the same qualms with them all: How do you get discovered, grow, become huge? How would users learn you exist? Just having a webpage with a great product didn't automatically translate into success. You needed a marketing strategy.

Unlike other VCs Bhatia had met, however, Jurvetson had no problem with a couple of twenty-seven-year-old engineers with no managerial experience, no history with consumer products, no expertise in software running a company. He was, after all, barely a year older than Bhatia. A former engineer with a background in mathematics, Jurvetson worked in research and development at Hewlett Packard where several of his chip designs were manufactured and at Apple and NeXT in marketing. As a venture capitalist, he didn't pigeonhole people. He was solely interested in the big idea. As Jurvetson finished his critique, ready to show his visitor the door, Bhatia claimed they did have a marketing plan. A programmer who used JavaSoft would marvel at how well designed it was and say, "Wow, you really built this cool web-app in three months? I want to buy those tools." Before Jurvetson could point out that this wasn't much of a strategy, Bhatia mentioned an additional application: webmail, which users of JavaSoft could use to communicate with one another.

Jurvetson perked up. People were largely tethered to their own computers because of email. At work they had a work account, at home a personal one, and on the road they couldn't dig into email at all unless they were dialing in from their own laptop. Jurvetson had spent much of his twenties as a student and then as a consultant who put in a lot of miles. Webmail would have made life a lot easier. The utility was crystal clear. As Bhatia sketched out the idea behind it on a whiteboard, Jurvetson was amazed no one had thought of it before. He advised Bhatia to forget about JavaSoft—webmail was the killer app. "We're going to get one of our partners to come in and take a look at this because it could be big," Jurvetson said.

[HAGGLING WITH A VENTURE CAPITALIST]

The following week Bhatia and his webmail co-creator, Jack Smith, met with Jurvetson and his partner, Timothy C. Draper, a rare third-generation venture capitalist—his grandfather, William Henry Draper Jr., was Silicon Valley's first venture capitalist and President Ronald Reagan had appointed his father, William Henry Draper III, to be chairman of the Export-Import Bank of the United States in 1981. With unquenchable optimism Bhatia listed projections for webmail's subscriber base that, if true, would mean it would expand faster than any company in history. The VCs dismissed these brash figures out of hand, but they believed that if the two engineers achieved a fraction of this success, webmail would prove to be a stunning investment. After a third meeting, Draper said, "OK, we're ready to fund you. We like this very much. How much do you want?"

Bhatia asked for $3 million, which he calculated would be enough to hire a few engineers and get the company rolling.

Too much, the VCs said. First they wanted to see if it was even possible to make email work on the Web.

Bhatia requested half a million and they countered with $300,000.

"Alright," Bhatia said. "I'll take it."

Naturally there were strings attached. Draper and Jurvetson, offering their standard term sheet, wanted 30 percent of the company, which would value the fledgling enterprise at $1 million. Bhatia contended the company was worth much more, on the order of $10 million. At one point Jurvetson offered $600,000 in exchange for 30 percent of the company, but Bhatia didn't want to give away so much this early on, and insisted DFJ's share entitled it to 15 percent. They couldn't bridge the gap and Bhatia threatened to seek funding elsewhere. He didn't act like someone who had riffled through almost two dozen VCs without a nibble, and, the two sides still far apart, Bhatia and Smith left without a deal.

The following evening, Jurvetson, intent on hammering out an agreement, phoned Bhatia, who pushed back. He claimed other seed investors were waiting in the wings, although he didn't mention it was actually Smith's father willing to write a small check or a nebulous band of investors from China who had never before financed a company. Jurvetson assumed these were paper tigers and didn't pay much heed, until Bhatia told Jurvetson he had lined up a meeting with venture capitalist Michael Moritz of Sequoia.

Oh my God, Jurvetson thought. Moritz had beaten him out of seeding Yahoo, on its way to a billion-dollar valuation, the most watched IPO since Netscape. The negotiations seemed to be proceeding smoothly with Jurvetson presenting the first terms sheet to Yahoo until Sequoia swooped in and he never saw them again. Jurvetson lost out on one of the biggest scores in Silicon Valley history. Earlier, in trying to express how well he understood the Internet, Jurvetson had confided the Yahoo story to Bhatia, who was now using it against him. He had made a terrible negotiating mistake. Not long after, Jurvetson and Bhatia agreed that DFJ's $300,000 in seed money would entitle the firm to 15 percent of the company, valuing it at $2 million post money. In exchange, Jurvetson was able to insert a clause that gave his firm the right of first refusal, which meant it couldn't be passed by in the event that Bhatia sought additional financing down the road.

Jesus, Jurvetson thought. *This guy is a masterful negotiator.*

[THE IDEA FOR WEBMAIL]

Sabeer Bhatia had absorbed the art of negotiation in the bazaars and markets of India. His family was part of the professional class in Bangalore; his father had spent a decade in the army, then bounced around public-sector bureaucracies, while his mother worked at the Central Bank. Haggling was part of everyday life—he often watched the family servants whittle down the prices of food, clothes, and other staples. A man, no matter how rich, was judged in part by how well he bargained. It required great persistence. First, approach the vendor but act like you aren't interested. Don't believe a word he says. You're almost assuredly not the first customer of the day, he's not giving you a special price, and he's not your friend, no matter how many times he calls you that. Walk away but don't wander far. He'll shout a lower price and it would be rude not to return to the negotiation. He comes down a little, you go up a smidgen, then he might feign concern over your economic plight. You must be very poor, he might say, and for dramatic effect offer you a few rupees out of his own pocket. But it was all part of the game until you finally arrived at a mutually acceptable price.

During Bhatia's first year at Birla Institute of Technology (BITS) at Pilani, the nineteen-year-old engineering student became the only person in the world in 1988 to receive a passing grade on the notoriously difficult California Institute of Technology's transfer student examination, scoring twenty points higher than anyone else. After three years at Caltech, he enrolled at Stanford for a master's degree in electrical engineering, where he became smitten with the idea of becoming an entrepreneur. In India young men did not become entrepreneurs—too much corruption, too many risks, too hard to succeed. Those from the middle class took the safe route, which was what Bhatia had expected to do. His original plan was to earn his doctorate and return to India to work as an engineer at a large Indian company.

At Stanford, his worldview changed. He attended informal discussions with entrepreneurs like Marc Andreessen and Apple cofounder Steve Wozniak, in his mind, regular guys with big ideas, who offered the same fundamental advice: if they could do it, so could he. Instead of returning to India after graduation, Bhatia took a job at Apple, where he met Jack Smith. Although the tall, stocky technophiles were worlds apart in temperament, they became fast friends. Smith was a dropout from Oregon State University. His most cherished Christmas toy growing up had been an oscilloscope he used to chart radio waves. He began his career at Apple as an intern and chose to stay rather than earn his diploma. While Bhatia was charismatic and a mainstay of the party scene, Smith was quiet, a homebody, married with a child. Bhatia became a fixture at cocktail parties organized by a community of Indian expat entrepreneurs who had scored in the United States. He made it a habit to come in the next morning to regale Smith with stories of people who, starting from scratch, had sold companies and ideas for millions of dollars. It became part of his sermon. "Jack! There is opportunity everywhere," Bhatia would say. "It's just ours to lose." Or "Jack, we're wasting our lives here." He would reel off entrepreneurs who, with little training or track record, had reaped fortunes. "There's no reason why we can't, too." In fact, if they couldn't, they would be "failures" because in this country there was simply no excuse for not being wildly successful.

Before venturing forth on their own, they quit Apple to follow their boss to a start-up called FirePower, which created hardware that could run multiple operating systems on Apple hardware. While there, Smith came up with the idea for JavaSoft. Bhatia pounded out a business plan in one night and walked into work looking particularly bedraggled, so much so his boss assumed he had been out all night partying and gave him the rest of the morning off. Bhatia set up meetings with venture capitalists and they fell into comfortable roles: Smith handled the technology while the garrulous Bhatia was their big-picture front man.

Since they didn't want their FirePower colleagues to know what they were up to, they didn't converse through work email. Instead they sent each other handwritten notes or exchanged floppy disks, spoke in person in the parking lot or while walking around the block, and chatted over the primitive mobile phones of the time. This struck them as ludicrous. Here they were on the cusp of a technological revolution, yet they couldn't access their personal email accounts privately and securely through the corporate firewall. It was a major inconvenience. Meanwhile Bhatia wasn't having luck attracting backers for JavaSoft, with fifteen, sixteen, seventeen potential firms passing on it. They told Bhatia he and his partner were too young and inexperienced, the company at too early a stage of development. It would be virtually impossible for JavaSoft to attract enough users, and even if it could, Microsoft would eat them for lunch.

One day, as Smith drove to his home in Livermore, he called Bhatia on the 3-watt car phone that sat in a bulky case on the passenger seat next to him. After another frustrating day of not being able to communicate with his partner over email, he had thought of a way to combine a solution to their extracurricular communication woes with a plan to market JavaSoft. Smith figured he could create a method for people to email over the Web, which would, he told Bhatia, meld two of the greatest uses of the Internet: email and the Web. "We could make it free, have an advertising banner to fund it, and go from there," Smith told him.

"Interesting," Bhatia replied. "I'll think about it."

Smith didn't take Bhatia's lukewarm response personally. That was the way his friend was. He would absorb information and only after running through countless scenarios arrive at a conclusion. Sure enough, the next day Bhatia crowed, "Jack, that is a brilliant idea!" They agreed to use Smith's webmail idea to get JavaSoft funded.

But their fear was that, unlike JavaSoft, a somewhat nebulous concept that required deep programming skills, webmail would be easy to steal. All they had was an idea. The venture capital community was deeply connected and a mere slip of the tongue could lead to the wrong person getting hold of it. What if one of the would-be financiers mentioned the idea to Netscape or Microsoft? Whoever built it first might gain an insurmountable lead, so they had to be careful whom they told. Bhatia decided he would size up a potential investor, and if the VC dismissed JavaSoft because of their age or inexperience, he wouldn't mention webmail. If the VC had a clue, he would suggest the free Web-based email as a traffic-building strategy. While webmail was the killer arrow in their quiver, they figured they would make money on JavaSoft until they could develop it.

Following months of fruitless meetings, Bhatia entered the offices of Draper Fisher Jurvetson in February 1996.

[P.S.: I LOVE YOU. GET YOUR FREE EMAIL AT HOTMAIL]

After the two sides worked out terms governing the initial $300,000 seed investment, Bhatia and Smith walked out with a $50,000 bridge check in their hands and quit their jobs at FirePower. Working out of his house, Smith, after bringing onboard another engineer, got down to building a prototype. They also needed to come up with a name, which fell to Smith, who stayed up late with his wife to brainstorm. Sitting with a blank sheet of paper they listed possibilities that contained "mail" in some form. Out of two dozen there was Cool Mail, Run Mail, this mail, that mail, but no "Aha!" moment. Finally his wife suggested, "Hotmail." Smith wrote it down. He wasn't sure about the "hot" part, but given everything else this seemed the best candidate. Then he noticed it contained the letters h, t, m, and l, which together formed the acronym for hypertext markup language, the lingua franca of webpages. Smith canvassed Bhatia the next day while riding in an elevator to their attorney's office. As usual, his friend initially gave it a cool reception, but they were running out of time so he went along with it. On March 27, 1996, Smith registered the Hotmail domain.

At the same time he finished a prototype within two weeks, sharing it with a small circle of friends who provided valuable feedback, mostly relating to layout, how email should be viewed and the index page arranged, the look and feel of the interface, how the columns should appear on the screen. Smith demonstrated it at the next meeting with Draper and Jurvetson, who were duly impressed.

Draper asked, "How are you going to get the word out there?"

"We'll put it up on billboards," Bhatia said. He also mentioned radio advertising.

"God," Draper replied, "that's expensive marketing and we're giving this away?" He thought for a moment. "Can't you just give it out to all those guys on the Web?"

That would be spamming, Smith replied.

I guess spamming is bad, Draper thought. He hadn't heard the term before. Then he flashed back to Harvard Business School, where he had received his MBA, a case study his professor covered in class: women holding parties for their friends, then selling to each other. A certain percentage of the women at each party became salespeople by referring more business. Tupperware, that was it. He also recalled MCI's friends and family plan, which harnessed the power of social interactions to spread the product. He wondered if they could do something like that with webmail.

"Jack," Draper asked, "could you put a message at the bottom of everybody's screen?"

"Oh, come on, we don't want to do that!" Bhatia blurted out.

"But can you technically do it?" Draper asked.

"Of course we can technically do it," Smith said.

"Oh, great," Draper said. "And it can persist, right? You can put it on one message, and if he sends an email to somebody else, you can put it on that one, too, right?"

"Yeah, yeah," Smith said, not convinced.

"So put 'P.S.: I love you. Get your free email at Hotmail' at the bottom."

Bhatia and Smith communicated through pained expressions. "Oh, no," they seemed to be saying. Draper had seen that look before. Of all the investors in the world, why did we end up with this idiot? Frankly, he didn't care what they thought. This just felt right.

"Wait a second, guys, don't you get it?" Draper asked. A tagline at the bottom of each message would act as free advertising. "I can send you an email and you can send it to all your friends and they get it and they can sign up and send it to their friends and pretty soon it takes off."

Smith said, "I don't think . . ."

Bhatia interrupted, "Let's move on to other business."

Draper agreed to table the discussion for now, but he had no intention of letting it go. He vowed he would keep pounding until they listened.

They launched HoTMaiL on Independence Day 1996. Not only did they like the symbolism—they viewed webmail as a populist tool because any user could log in from anywhere in the world—Smith had long promised the service would be ready by then. After turning on the registration function and hitting the switch in the early afternoon, Smith accompanied his tiny technical staff to Chili's Grill & Bar in San Jose to celebrate. To keep track of sign-ups he brought along a laptop with an attached radio modem receiver on the back, the antenna sticking up like a divining rod. Over quesadillas Smith counted one hundred registrations in the first hour. After lunch they went to the movies, and by the time the summer blockbuster *Independence Day* began to roll, he tallied a total of two hundred sign-ups. Upon exiting the cinema, Smith logged in again to find that fifty more had joined HoTMaiL. They were finding the site via word of mouth *and* word of mouse. People were talking about it, and letting their friends and family in on the deal via email, using the Hotmail message as a proof of concept: 80 percent of those who signed up said that they learned about it from a friend.

Growth was robust but not staggering for the week. At the next meeting at DFJ Tim Draper once again pushed the two young entrepreneurs to insert a tagline into each message. Bhatia and Smith were adamant about not adulterating email. It just wasn't done. They would feel like they were polluting emails with advertising, and what about privacy issues? If someone was adding a tagline, what else were they doing? A user would wonder what else they had access to, and they were also fairly certain it was unethical. But Draper wouldn't let it go. The benefits, he contended, far outweighed the risks. If they were predicating their entire business on the size of their user base, they should be doing everything in their power to increase it as fast as possible. "P.S. I love you. Get your free email at HoTMaiL." The more he said it, the more he liked it.

The next day Bhatia phoned Draper with the news that they agreed to do it, but without the "P.S. I love you" part. The impact was almost instantaneous. Within hours Hotmail's growth took on the shape of a classic hockey stick curve. They started averaging 3,000 users a day, compounded daily. By Labor Day they registered 750,000 users and within six months they were up to 1 million. Five weeks after that they hit the 2 million user mark, adding more than 20,000 sign-ups a day, with Smith desperately trying to keep the servers up and running. At times, the site became slug-gish and suffered major outages. But through it all, Smith, using little more than virtual spit and glue, kept Hotmail (they had dropped the awkward capitalization by this point) afloat.

The tagline with the clickable URL that Draper insisted be inserted in every outbound message served as a promotional pitch for the com-pany. Simply by using the product, every customer became an involuntary salesperson. This implied endorsement from a friend or peer made it more powerful, and more far-reaching, than traditional advertising. The receiver of a Hotmail message could see that (1) his friend was a user, (2) it worked, and (3) it was free. Successful consumer branding is often based on user affiliation. (The cool kids wear low-cut jeans, so I will, too.) This plays to our tribal instinct, and resulted in clusters of users. Bhatia sent a message to a friend in India and within three weeks Hotmail registered 100,000 users there. It also became the largest email provider in Sweden without spending a nickel on advertising there. In contrast, Juno blew through $20 million in marketing and advertising, while Hotmail gained three times as many users in half the time.

As Jurvetson related in a white paper, the Hotmail adoption pattern was similar to that of a virus "with spatial and network locality." A per-son's email address book is a type of virtual social network that is not en-cumbered by geography. A certain percentage of contacts will be friends, family, and colleagues who reside relatively nearby; others may be scat-tered throughout the world. A Hotmail message sent across the country might result in a new cluster of users. "We would notice the first user from a university town or from India, and then the number of subscribers from that region would rapidly proliferate," he wrote. "From an epide-miological perspective, it was as if Zeus sneezed over the planet."

Jurvetson noted a "mathematical elegance" to Hotmail's "smooth ex-ponential growth curves" in the company's early days:

$$\text{Cumulative users} = (1 + \text{fanout}) \text{ cycles}$$

Where "cumulative users" related to the number of Hotmail registered subscribers, "fanout" was the rate by which the product spread and "cycles" was the number of times the product was used in the time period since launch (or frequency multiplied by time). At the beginning, each Hotmail user, on average, brought in two new users each month. (In other words, the fanout equaled 2.) These two new Hotmail subscribers attracted two new users, and so on. That meant that one seed user equaled three users at the end of the first cycle, nine by the second, twenty-seven by the third, each cluster growing exponentially. Of course, this was a simplified model. There were other variables at play, like retention rates and "churn"; ultimate saturation, when Hotmail reached so many users that its growth inevitably slowed, et al.

[AN INSURMOUNTABLE LEAD]

While companies like Hot or Not could toss more servers into the mix to keep up with increased bandwidth demand, Hotmail, which was suffering brownouts, system failures, and painfully slow download times, had to completely restructure its systems on the fly. This fell to cofounder Jack Smith, who had originally launched Hotmail on a nonscalable architecture because the company simply couldn't afford anything else. He could only "silo" a limited number of webmail accounts on a given machine. "To add accounts we had to add machines," Smith says, "but the registration system was a global concept. We had a hard time spanning the machines and we didn't have a universal database." He and his engineers were forced to manually customize machines to handle additional traffic, an inefficient, time-consuming process. "We were still growing like crazy, but some days we had such a hard day we had to shut off registration because we couldn't accept more new users at that moment."

As Hotmail was poised to register its millionth user, Smith designed a multitiered architecture to scale without limit. Instead of his original single-tier system, which stowed emails on one set of machines, the registration database on another, and the site on a third, he set it up so the load could be balanced across the entire network. "You had your database on one tier, the front end on another, and your mail spread over numerous machines instead of one per account," he says. At the time there was no out-of-the-box server software with this capability, so Smith had to create new technology.

It took a month to design three major components—an email transporter, a back-end database, and a customer authentication database. Once it was in place, any technician could blindly add machines without reconfiguring anything if the site started getting slow. But when Smith cut over to the new architecture it immediately melted down, and he quickly switched back to the old system. It didn't take long to diagnose the problem. Because of budgetary constraints, Smith had skimped on hardware. He went out and bought two dozen far more powerful motherboards, grabbed whomever he could find in the office, and brought them into their data center, where they swapped out the old ones. "The next night we cut over to the new architecture and it worked beautifully," he says.

With a robust infrastructure Hotmail continued its frenetic growth, reaching 3 million users in two hundred countries by April, becoming the third largest email provider after AOL and CompuServe. Bhatia returned to the financing table for more money, this time securing $3 million from DFJ and Menlo Ventures at a more agreeable valuation. Hotmail had topped 5 million by its one-year anniversary, registering 60,000 new users a day, and on the way it had earned a reputation for speed and reliability. While messages could take a minute to transmit between two AOL accounts, and between fifteen minutes to several hours to travel between AOL and non-AOL accounts, Hotmail was significantly faster. And after a shaky start, it didn't suffer the kinds of outages plaguing AOL, which at times simply couldn't handle the flood of email.

In addition to its growth, the company was generating advertising revenue. For the first few months of Hotmail's existence, Bhatia posted ad banners for free, just to give the site the patina of e-commerce professionalism; then he began layering in paid advertising. Revenue for the fourth quarter of 1996 was $350,000. Bhatia quickly found that he had neither the time nor the inclination to sell ads, so he outsourced this function to another company in exchange for a percentage of the revenue. According to Bhatia, the deal involved a million-dollar-a-month minimum. While Hotmail was still hemorrhaging money, it showed signs of profitability, and one month it actually flirted with breaking even.

By September 1997, with Hotmail edging toward 7 million subscribers and adding more features—instant messaging, a spell-checker, email search, and the ability to attach multiple files to a message—potential suitors appeared. General Electric pledged to head another funding round and offered to hook up Hotmail with its back-end credit card service to distribute monthly bills to consumers. John Doerr of venture capital firm Kleiner Perkins also wanted to lead a financing round and take a seat on the board; this would put Hotmail into a position for an initial public offering. An investor in Excite, valued at some $400 million, was interested in negotiating a merger, which would give Hotmail 33 percent of Excite's stock and the opportunity to handle the Web portal's email. Yahoo also floated the idea of joining forces with Hotmail, and Microsoft, after broaching a partnership, made an offer to buy Hotmail outright.

Each came with pluses and minuses. GE had enviable connections with NBC and MSNBC, which could transform Hotmail from a simple emailer to a destination site providing news and entertainment, but it valued Hotmail at $105 million, $20 million less than Bhatia wanted. Kleiner Perkins was the gold standard in tech IPOs, but arrived at an even lower valuation for Hotmail than GE had. Both Bhatia and Smith believed the offers from Excite and Yahoo, which was willing to bid $200 million, were far too low, and their mantra became: if you come in with anything less than half a billion dollars, get lost! That left Microsoft or the option of going it alone, building the business, then looking to cash in on an IPO.

Jurvetson advised Bhatia to spurn Microsoft and march toward going public. Unlike Netscape, which despite its staggering IPO was vulnerable because Microsoft could require PC makers to install Internet Explorer as the default Web surfing software and separate it from its user base, Jurvetson believed Hotmail could weather anything Bill Gates threw at it. He had been following discussion among analysts who believed the Web challenged Microsoft's chokehold on the industry, a view he shared. The Windows environment didn't matter much if you could jump the on ramp to the Web from any computer at any time. Microsoft had created its own webmail service on the Microsoft network (MSN) but had been having tremendous scaling problems. And while Hotmail was coasting past 10 million sign-ups (Fig. 8), MSN barely broke 2 million.

VIRAL MARKETING

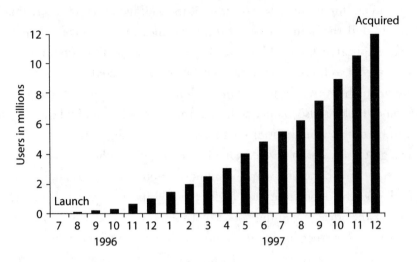

FIG. 8. Hotmail subscriber growth, 1996–1997. *(Draper Fisher Jurvetson)*

It was, Jurvetson thought, an almost insurmountable lead, and the key was Hotmail's viral marketing. Even if Microsoft could somehow buy its way out of MSN webmail's lagging growth, its viral coefficient still would never match Hotmail's. Assuming it doubled at the same rate as Hotmail, only time shifted, and this meant the delta between the two got even bigger. When Hotmail hit 20 million users, Microsoft would only be at 4 million; Hotmail at 40 million subscribers, Microsoft at 8 million; Hotmail at 80 million, Microsoft at 16 million. Then came ultimate saturation. The way Jurvetson saw it, Microsoft's only chance was to sabotage Hotmail's servers.

[HAGGLING OVER PRICE]

Bhatia, however, was pondering two potential endgames that had recently played out with other tech companies: The first involved AOL, which rejected an offer from Microsoft and went on to multibillion-dollar revenues. On the other end of the spectrum was another toast of the Valley, Point-Cast, which had rebuffed Rupert Murdoch and News Corp's $400 million bid and then faded into oblivion. Bhatia decided to re-enter the bazaar and try his hand at haggling with a team of Microsoft negotiators, who in the fall of 1997 jumped a plane from Redmond in a group of six to sit at a table in Hotmail's conference room. At first they talked of a partnership, with Hotmail providing webmail to MSN, but after learning that Hotmail planned to move into news and entertainment to become a portal like MSN they said they couldn't partner with a potential competitor. Instead, had Bhatia considered acquisition? At the right price, Bhatia replied, he could think of anything.

In October 1997, Bhatia, Smith, and Hotmail's vice president of marketing traveled to Redmond and, after a tour of the campus, met with Bill Gates and two senior executives in his office. No small talk, right down to business. Initially intimidated by Gates, who was renowned for tearing apart weak arguments and weaker minds, Bhatia quickly recovered his bearings and the meeting lasted an hour and a half. Afterward Bhatia and Smith sat at an enormous table, facing a team of fifteen Microsoft negotiators—the chief financial officer, lawyers, business development staff, and accountants—who told them they wanted to buy the company for $160 million.

Bhatia thanked them for the offer and said he had to discuss it with his board.

"C'mon," Gregory Maffei, the CFO, said, "is that in the ballpark?"

Bhatia refused to negotiate with so many people, knowing it put him at a distinct disadvantage. Back home, he polled his investors, half-joking he could get a billion for the start-up. The lowest figure came from Doug Carlisle at Menlo Ventures, who promised Bhatia that if he could get $200 million, he would commission a bronze sculpture in his likeness and install it in his lobby.

Returning to the bargaining table, Bhatia informed Microsoft's swarm of negotiators that he wanted $700 million. This prompted the predictable storm of invective: "You're crazy," "Out of your mind," "You've blown it," amidst a stream of obscenities. Bhatia recognized the bluster for what it was: the American version of the Indian bazaar. Perhaps he should turn out his pockets and offer them a few dollars. *You must be poor.* He consulted his beeper and recited Hotmail's latest subscription numbers, which were growing by the second. At that rate, by the end of the year they would have more than 12 million users and be, by far, the number-one email provider in the world. Microsoft upped its bid to $200 million and Carlisle crowed, "It's statue time," but Bhatia stayed the course.

The weeks dragged on and the pressure mounted. Several times Microsoft team members stormed out, but they always returned. Microsoft raised its offer to $300 million and negotiators hinted it could always buy RocketMail, a much smaller competitor. Bhatia didn't waver. Jurvetson backed him. "You don't have to sell now," he said. "Why don't you wait until you're big enough to buy Microsoft, rather than them buying you?" But his own executives, with dreams of a quick cash-out on their minds, urged him to take the money. Even his parents got into the act. He told his father that he had turned down $325 million. His father mumbled, "Um, okay," and they hung up. A minute later the phone rang. It was his mother. "Sabeer, listen to me. You call that Mr. Gates back right now and you take his offer! Do you know how much that is in rupees?"

After Microsoft placed $350 million on the table, Hotmail management took a straw poll and voted to accept it. Bhatia overruled them, although he would later admit it was the scariest thing he had ever done. He heard more than once that it would be on his head if he screwed things up. Finally, on December 31, 1997, a few days after his twenty-ninth birthday, Bhatia closed the deal and Microsoft transferred ownership of 2,769,148 shares of stock, worth almost $400 million.

Less than two years earlier, Bhatia had entered the offices of Draper Fisher Jurvetson with little more than an idea—no prototype, not even a mock-up—which he sketched on Jurvetson's whiteboard. Now he and Smith had created a viral loop business that had grown faster than any company in history and in the process had made each of them $75 million richer. But Carlisle never commissioned that statue. Bhatia's mother told her son it was bad luck to have one modeled on a living person. Instead, Hotmail set the stage for other viral companies to follow suit: The first was ICQ (short for "I seek you"), an instant-messaging program launched by five Israelis four months after Hotmail. Within six months it amassed 850,000 users, doubly impressive since users had to install software.

After the company was rebranded MSN Hotmail, it grew to 30 million registered users within eighteen months of launch. Over the course of the decade, Hotmail continued to increase its ranks of users, counting more than 260 million registrants; at one point, one in four people on the Internet maintained a Hotmail address. Microsoft removed the viral tag and replaced it with simple advertising, which irritated many users but didn't lead them to quit en masse. In 2005 Hotmail was folded into Windows Live and continues to be one of the three most popular webmail programs in the world, along with Yahoo and Gmail.

5

When the Audience Decides What's Good

Collective Curation; Boom, Bust, and Beyond, and the Viral Reality Show of Your Life

The great digital push is under way. We live in an age when the tools of self-expression have never been more accessible. Stripped-down technology with ever-greater capabilities—lighter, simpler cameras, for instance—let just about anyone shoot, edit, and post videos and photos on the Web. Broadband allows webizens to consume it instantly, and when users decide something is good, they share it with their network of friends via email, by embedding a link in their blog, or by posting on a discussion thread. Without gatekeepers to filter content, the audience attains a power never before seen, exemplified in the experiences of one Arin Crumley, a tall, Twizzler-thin videographer living in Brooklyn, New York.

His story begins like many of his peers, with the twenty-one-year-old Crumley trawling for a girlfriend on the Internet, blasting notes to more than one hundred likely prospects who posted personals on *Time Out New York*'s website. Shortly afterward, Susan Buice, a young, self-styled "artist in theory, waitress in practice," clicked open his email: "What made you move to NY? Do you have any more pix? I think I might find you hot."

Unlike the others on Crumley's hit list, Buice decided to give him a chance. She told him to drop by the restaurant where she worked the late-night shift. Crumley showed up, ready to shock, disguised in sunglasses and baseball cap, packing a video camera, and snapping surreptitious candids, then trailing her as she left the restaurant for the subway. "Dear Stalker," Buice replied, after the photos arrived in her in-box. "So this is what the world sees. Just an innocent bystander. So pedestrian. Nothing like the tragic hero I feel as I trudge through each day." She told him the typical date wouldn't do justice to the stalking experience. "We need to think of another unique scenario—something challenging." Channeling his inner mime, he suggested they avoid small talk by communicating without speaking. For their first date, they silently wandered the Brooklyn waterfront, passing notes, drawing pictures, listening to music on each other's iPods. Later, when Buice attended an artist colony in Vermont, they mailed videos back and forth; six months after they first met, they moved in together (they lifted the no-talking edict). Along the way, they amassed a collection of artifacts most couples would call "keepsakes." Buice and Crumley considered them artistic "by-products."

Eventually, in the way of youth the world over, they concluded that their courtship had to be immortalized and only a full-length feature film would suffice. They quit their jobs, pooled $10,000 in savings, lined up a stack of credit cards, and flew in a friend from the Left Coast to operate their prized possession: a Panasonic DVX100 digital video camera. The saga of *Four Eyed Monsters*, their self-directed, self-obsessed movie, had begun.

It was an unlikely way to make a movie, and if it sounds self-indulgent and a tad meta, well, it was. But there was method to their madness. Until recently, making a movie meant using a shaky Super 8 or low-resolution camcorder, or taking a flier that required tens of millions of dollars, hundreds of personnel, and superior technical expertise. It also meant dueling with the studio executives and distributors who decided which movies made it into theaters and which didn't, and who exerted ham-fisted control over the industry, making it all but impossible for neophytes like Buice and Crumley to break through. (And even if they did, they were often roundly fleeced: bought off with a nominal take-it-or-leave-it offer, stripped of control of their work, and sent packing back to Mom.) Now the same pair of lovelorn kids who would have vanished completely in another age can pick up a camera, teach themselves the art of filmmaking for next to nothing, and make a commercial-quality movie. They might even hit it big.

Of course, digital movies are not new. More than a decade ago, *Love God,* long since forgotten, was one of the first—if not *the* first—independent film entirely shot and edited in digital video. Back then, the format was merely a curiosity; now, with the price of a decent camera dipping below $3,000 and quality steadily improving, digital is reshaping entertainment the way the talkies did eighty years ago, with similarly revolutionary effects. Even the notion of a "film" has begun to seem a little quaint: sure, there are still your standard ninety-odd-minute narratives, and they might be around forever, but because moving images are increasingly being viewed in and over a variety of venues and devices—from 3-D high-definition digital theaters to TVs to laptops to PDAs, cell phones, iPods, and everything in between—even that form is morphing and the ninety-minute canvas that has characterized movies for the past eighty years might change. A film today might be a series of three- to five-minute episodes or a twenty-minute short. The Beastie Boys handed out fifty hi8 videocams so that fans could capture them in concert (the band later returned them for a refund). For $164,000, South African director Aryan Kaganof created *SMS Sugar Man*, the first feature-length movie shot entirely on cell phone cameras. Independent filmmaking is thriving in places as far-flung as Iran, Jordan, and Malaysia, and here in the States, partly because the tools of the trade are increasingly affordable. And it's not just indies. Mel Gibson shot *Apocalypto* in digital, Michael Mann used it for scenes in *Miami Vice*, and television has been dominated by digital video for years.

As a practical matter, it opens up other opportunities as well. Not only is it cheap (35-millimeter film costs about two hundred times more than digital tape), it's lightweight, simple, and subtle. For documentary filmmakers the format lets them make movies they couldn't do otherwise. James Longley, director of the Oscar-nominated *Iraq in Fragments*, used the same relatively compact Panasonic camera as Crumley and Buice. "Just imagine trying to shoot on 16-millimeter film stock during a three-hour Friday sermon, stuck in the middle of the Kufa Mosque in southern Iraq, sandwiched between seven thousand followers of Moqtada Sadr in 110-degree heat," he says. "At a minimum, you would need a camera assistant to load and unload the eighteen film magazines and a soundman to record the audio. You would probably need lights as well, as the sun goes down." With digital, however, he was able to capture the scene on three DV tapes, without the obtrusive camera crew, using a camera light enough that he could hold it for hours and not grow tired. Later he rode in the back of a pickup truck filled with Mahdi Army militia, recording everything as they arrested alcohol sellers in a local market, took them back to the Sadr office, and interrogated them. "A large part of being able to record that kind of material is the ability to be unobtrusive," he says, "to let the mechanism of the camera nearly vanish, unencumbered by lights, sound recordists, and film-changing bags."

That doesn't mean that everyone with a digital camera has talent. Ronald Steinman, executive editor of *The Digital Filmmaker,* says, "The typewriter didn't make better writers. You can buy a digital camera, do digital editing on your laptop, but it doesn't mean everyone who learns it will know how long a dissolve should last or where to cut. It's one thing to have the equipment. It's another to be able to use it."

[OPEN WATER]

With billions of videos streamed online, it's not surprising new businesses are sprouting up around this digital efflorescence. Each day on YouTube, millions of video views are delivered and thousands of clips are uploaded. Apple's iTunes Music Store sold 12 million video clips for $1.99 in its first few months. These aggregators are fast becoming the central nodes of an entirely new video marketing and distribution system, one far from Hollywood's control, except for Hulu.com, the industry's answer, which sells downloads of movies. Nevertheless, the big studios may increasingly find themselves competing with films made by the masses. Part of the issue is lowering the transaction cost for making and distributing programs and films, and part of it is the low cost of user-generated content (usually free). It's completely disintermediating. That process of cutting out the middleman, while still in its infancy, has the potential to upend the balance of power that has governed the film industry for decades.

One early indication that homespun digital could deliver Hollywoodworthy numbers was the 2003 release of *Open Water,* a psychothriller with a cast of two, a crew of three, and a pack of sharks. Chris Kentis, who had been cutting film trailers for a production company, pounded out a script, auditioned actors, bought two digital video cameras, and shot the movie over the course of two years, mostly on the open ocean. "We were chasing weather, and weather was chasing us," Kentis says. "We could see a storm approaching with lightning, and the captain would tell us we had fifteen minutes to shoot the scene. We could react immediately. It was guerrilla filmmaking on the water." With low expectations he submitted it to Sundance, figuring that festival organizers would take a dim view of a movie with so few credits (written by Chris Kentis, directed by Chris Kentis, cinematography by Chris Kentis . . .). Not only was *Open Water* accepted, it attracted a distribution deal from Lion's Gate and, later that year, opened at 2,700 theaters across the country. Made for $130,000, it grossed $30 million at the domestic box office and close to $100 million worldwide (counting DVD sales).

In the time since *Open Water* debuted, the technology has improved at a fierce rate, and this is helping to mitigate the risks often associated with filmmaking—namely, big budgets coupled with unpredictable returns on investment. This was the thinking behind *Samaritan*, a short movie produced by Star Circle Pictures, about a mysterious stranger who thwarts an armed robbery, and a police detective who is left with more questions than answers. Every time you say the word "film" on the set of a Star Circle Pictures project, you have to fine yourself 25 cents. That's because the company doesn't "film" movies. It doesn't even use digital video, which it views as so last year. It made the world's first micro movie with the Panasonic AG-HVX200 high-definition camera, using memory cards. Producer Ethan Marten says they wanted to show investors how much cheaper and efficient it was to create movies in the newer formats. A typical director shoots five or six setups a day. *Samaritan*'s director Kimball Carr was able to do eighty-one over the course of two nights with a crew of ten in what he called "controlled insanity."

Part of the efficiency stemmed from preplanning. Carr storyboarded the entire movie in advance with animated characters with Innovative Software's FrameForge 3D Studio software. This enabled him to display each scene—every camera angle and character nuance—to the cast and crew before shooting. (In the future, a director could animate an entire production instead of tucking a spec script under his arm to show potential investors.) They switched between handheld shots, shoulder shots, and tripod mounts with the same camera, which made it easy for the crew to anticipate what the director needed, and deployed three computers on the set. One had the script, the other the animated storyboards, and a third collected the data from two 4-gigabyte memory cards, which meant they could shoot sixteen straight minutes, download the data to the laptop, and reuse the cards.

"We didn't just have dailies," Marten says. "We had instantaneousnesses. Yet we also have our old film look. You'd have to be the equivalent of a wine connoisseur to tell the difference. Some actors and actresses are worried because you can pick up every imperfection, every crater in their faces." He muses that in the future, a star's agents might have to write degradation clauses into contracts, requiring directors to degrade closeups because they are so crystal clear.

At the outset, Buice and Crumley had little of Kentis's skill or Star Circle's technology. For starters, they had no idea how to frame a shot or do basic cinematography. Their cameraman wasn't familiar with the camera. They had never acted before. After each shoot, they beamed the dailies on a wall of their cramped loft and edited footage on a Mac G5 computer with Final Cut Pro software. "Sometimes we ended up shooting and re-shooting a scene four or five times before we got it right," Crumley says.

Then, a year into the project, with our young heroes maxed out on seven credit cards, *Four Eyed Monsters* was accepted into Slamdance, the rogue sidekick to the Sundance Film Festival in Park City, Utah. That led to invitations to other festivals—eighteen in all, including South by Southwest, the Sonoma Valley Film Festival, and Gen Art. Along the way, the pair collected several awards and glowing reviews. *Variety* called *Four Eyed Monsters* "fascinating," a film that "deliberately smudges the line between nonfiction and invention." The *Boston Phoenix* said it was "spry, brainy, endlessly inventive," an "*Annie Hall* of the 25-year-old set." Others described it as "exhilarating," "accomplished and endearing," a movie that contained "frantic vibrancy" and "delivers a powerful narrative punch." It felt like the beginning of a Nora Ephron script that would, inevitably, end with Buice and Crumley better dressed, in a fabulous apartment, and very much in love.

Alas, their whirlwind tour yielded nothing. After eighteen festivals, they were still without a distribution deal to get *Four Eyed Monsters* into theaters. Their work seemed to resonate, but they had no money and no access to the pipeline. All they had was a mounting sense that people liked the thing. "We had a film that nobody knew about and nobody wanted to distribute," Crumley says. "Companies told us that the 'target' audience for our film was 'hard to pin down.' What they meant was that they had no tried-and-true formula for how to release a film to the type of audience our film appealed to, so they didn't want to take a risk."

Which got them thinking. At the time, MySpace had about 75 million members. Children of the Web that they were, Buice and Crumley understood that social networking sites could generate interest and create buzz, a free, self-fulfilling wave of publicity with a veritable army of users, the vast majority under thirty, marketing their movie for them virally by blogging about it or posting video clips. As any ad person will tell you, that kind of lightning-fast word of mouth is the most powerful form of marketing, and the Internet's viral plain makes it possible on a scale never before seen. So Buice and Crumley embraced what Crumley calls "collective curation," the idea that a loyal, intimate, motivated fan base is better able to judge quality than any individual and a thumbs-up from the "netgeist" can be life-changing.

It was here that Buice and Crumley began butting up against the film establishment and the Web became a transformative vehicle for independent filmmakers looking to crash the gates of the old system.

[BOOM, BUST, AND BEYOND]

All of this was made possible by the advent of a fast, efficient mode to disseminate content, which arose from a deep, almost perilous crash, a cycle of failure that created the world we live in today. The pattern starts with a new technology that is greeted by equal parts ardor and ire. As the past two centuries have shown, great technological innovations—railroads, telegraph, telephone, electricity, cars, radios, the personal computer—first overcome skepticism, take root, then spin into a predictable cycle: entrepreneurs recognize a novel technology's potential; newcomers rush into the market, drawing venture capital, which in turn spawns even more companies and investment. Because stock price in this phase is pegged to possibility, not revenue and profit, almost all the players do well, even though most, if not all, of the companies, bleed red. Some succeed spectacularly at this Ponzi-like scheme. Share prices shoot skyward in a speculative frenzy.

Eventually, though, reality sets in. After burning through their cash, companies start to fold, leaving investors to wonder when and how someone will actually make money. Pessimism supplants enthusiasm. Stock prices crash and the economy tanks until, over time, the core technology is woven into the fabric of life and the market stabilizes. It's a cycle of boom, bust, and sustained growth (a golden age, if you will), followed by decay when a better mousetrap comes along.

Bubbles, however, don't recur just because people have failed to learn from experience. They are a necessary stage of technological development. After railroads supplanted canals as the hot investment of the early nineteenth century, they followed essentially the same arc. According to Alasdair Nairn, author of *Engines That Move Markets*, between 1825 and 1826 about as many railroads were founded as had been started in the previous twenty years. And when the market crashed, it crashed hard. By the mid-1870s, 40 percent of American railway bonds were in default and bankruptcies surged. But the bubble wasn't for naught. Before the crash, 45,000 miles of track had been laid; by 1900, there was a national network more than 200,000 miles long, and this made it possible for the United States to grow and prosper from the Atlantic to the Pacific. Similarly, the later rise of the automobile spurred the development of the American highway system, which ate much of the railroads' freight business but served to populate the entire country.

Capacity, or rather, overcapacity, is the key to progress. For us, broadband is the new railroad, the new highway system, the new electricity. Electricity spawned entire new industries as consumers chocked their homes full of appliances that simply did not exist before power companies flipped the switch. Telephone companies, many of them small regional operations, unfurled a skein of cable that connected people around the country—and the world. Trucks and railroads revolutionized shipping and transportation. Even the recent mortgage crisis and corresponding real estate boom and bust offer a glimmer of good news in a sea of bad.

All that cheap money made it possible for Americans of all stripes to finance the purchase of homes and college educations when in the past they largely were shut out of credit markets. The same dynamic is at work with high-speed Internet access. After all those years of laying fiber-optic cable, DSL, and other high-speed lines, we have created huge stores of capacity, and they make all sorts of innovations possible.

So begins the postcrash push, when all of this investment starts to pay off. Broadband use in the United States jumped from 6 percent in June 2000 to more than 30 percent in 2003. Today, most of us have access to it at home or work. (Significantly, we signed up for it after the dot-com crash.) Now, instead of engaging in theoretical thumb-sucking about "what broadband will mean," we're doing something with it. And unlike the 1990s, when experiments failed because entrepreneurs misunderstood the Internet's usefulness, or because it simply wasn't ready, we're working with a known quantity. It took thirty years for electricity to have a serious impact on the U.S. economy, after all, but by 1930, virtually every home had juice and it was driving refrigerators, toasters, lamps, radios, and other appliances. As Henry Blodget put it, our exuberance, irrational or otherwise, builds industries.

We have been experiencing a similar, but vastly accelerated, process, with high-speed connectivity plowing under the business landscape and remaking it in its own image. Those most adept at leveraging all of that capacity within their own markets are likely to flourish over the coming decade and beyond. The ones that don't may go the way of all extinct life-forms. Amazon founder Jeff Bezos has likened the impact of the Internet to the Cambrian era, when single-cell life-forms gave way to multicell life. It was a time when the number of life-forms exploded; it was also the period of the greatest rate of extinction. It poses an almost Darwinian challenge.

The fluidity of information is bringing about a radically democratized business world where consumers enjoy unprecedented power. At its most basic level, companies must meet our expectations or face our anger, amplified through countless channels (from blogs, to search engines of video and text, to others yet to be developed; there is such a thing as bad PR). A single bad review can grow into a consumer revolt. And as the newspaper industry exemplifies with its recent implosion, any leap into the unknown leaves some bodies broken on the rocks below. After the introduction of electricity, the U.S. population grew by 15 percent between 1910 and 1920, but the number of personal servants fell 25 percent, replaced, in large part, by appliances. In the early part of the twentieth century there was a whole industry built around delivering ice to homes, a business that melted away with the advent of the electric refrigerator and freezer. Trucks picked up dirty diapers and dropped off clean ones until Pampers hit store shelves. When was the last time you used a typewriter—or stored information on a floppy disk?

Horror flick auteur Wes Craven, director of *Scream* and the *Nightmare on Elm Street* series and an early adopter of editing software, views this growing global linkage of computers "as the beginning of neural pathways to planet consciousness," a "digital central nervous system." There is, he says, "a brain forming around the skin of the planet." And moviemaking wannabes like Buice and Crumley, with no stake in the old ways of doing business, are there to pursue the new paradigms.

MUSIC: THE PROVERBIAL CANARY IN THE COAL MINE

Naturally the winds of change swept in well before broadband hit critical mass. In the late 1990s, music pirates began to proliferate on the Web. One eighteen-year-old, who called himself "The Lair," became a star in the underground. In many respects he was your typical T-shirt-clad teen. During the school year he attended classes. In the summer he slept until noon, grabbed a bowl of Honey Nut Cheerios and padded over to his computer, where he checked on his website to make sure it hadn't crashed, answered email, and swapped music over the Net. Those who knew where to find his site were free to "leech" from his personal cache of tunes, hundreds of them, neatly organized by artist. If you wanted a taste of Will Smith's rap, "Men in Black," all you had to do was surf over to The Lair's site, click on your mouse, and let the music pulse into your hard drive. Were you feeling nostalgic? How about a trip down "Penny Lane" with the Beatles? Cared to sample the latest Sheryl Crow or Pearl Jam? The Lair, a self-professed music junkie, had you covered. Because on his site, the hits kept on coming.

It was like the 1990s version of trading baseball cards, except for one off-key difference: it was illegal. And if you listened to the strains emitted by the Recording Industry Association of America (RIAA), which represents the interests of the major labels, The Lair and the thousands of other music pirates who called the Net home were causing the record industry "incalculable harm." In the past, the authorities, with much fanfare, had raided warehouses stacked floor-to-ceiling with records, then later, cassettes and CDs. But like an irritating tune they couldn't get out of their heads, the question reverberating inside the minds of industry executives was: what would they do when all the average Joe needed to warehouse millions of bootlegs was a laptop and a fast Internet connection?

Music had entered a brave new domain: the Internet, the largest and most efficient copying machine in history. It was also the world of music pirate guerrillas, geeks armed with powerful computers and high-speed Internet access who got a thrill playing cat-and-mouse with the recording industry. Since it's hard to feel sympathy for a multibillion-dollar industry, the recording industry had (and has) trouble rallying the public around its cause. Whether offered knockoffs of Rolex watches, illegally copied videocassettes, or CD bootlegs, Americans have shown they are only too happy to shave a few bucks off the retail price, sometimes for shoddy merchandise, even if it means, technically speaking, breaking the law. As The Lair said, "My parents were kind of concerned when I told them what I'm doing is illegal, but as long as I can supply them with some songs by the Beatles and Tom Jones, it doesn't seem to bother them."

Claiming a 2.1-gigabyte hard drive crammed with two gigs of music files and a site that had been visited by more than one hundred thousand users, The Lair wasn't worried about the long arm of the law. "By coming after sites like mine with court orders, RIAA is bashing a thumbtack with a sledgehammer," he said, "but if they're not careful, that thumbtack is going to get caught underfoot and hurt. The MP3 scene has already begun to adapt by going deeper underground, and these days, all you need to adapt is to change your IP address." And no matter how many encryptions, watermarks, and other high-tech approaches to stamping out piracy software companies tested, nothing worked. Pirates displayed an ingenious talent in cracking whatever new techno-wrinkle was thrown at them, often within forty-eight hours.

The Lair was but a single voice in a vast cacophony. With greater access speeds and bandwidth, improved compression technology, and Napster—the first of the peer-to-peer networks—piracy grew a thousandfold when regular users (like students on college campuses on powerful university network connections) got wise to what was out there. By 2004 the hierarchical pirate culture had vanished and piracy became a mainstream pursuit, with 13 billion songs available through peer-to-peer networks, far more than the 800 million compact disks (about 10 billion songs) record companies were shipping each year. The record companies were powerless to stop it, especially as compact disk sales slumped while digital downloads grew. In other words, pirates like The Lair, who were at heart little more than overzealous consumers, had dictated how the music industry would change.

And if Buice and Crumley had their way, Hollywood, too.

[THE VIRAL REALITY SHOW OF THE MAKING OF THEIR MOVIE]

The pair's strategy began taking shape when they attended South by Southwest, where they posted a daily online video diary of their experiences. The diary proved popular and helped draw an audience to their screenings. For Buice and Crumley, it also drove home the point that the battle to get their film recognized (not to mention the peripheral tales of their own interpersonal combat and financial woes) was something their peers could relate to—that the story about their story might help them get over the hump.

So they sketched out a series of ten 3- to 5-minute video podcasts they planned to post once a month, a kind of reality show about the making of their movie. One episode told how they got started. Another related their experience at Slamdance, detailing fights that broke out when an acting teacher and some of his students who appeared in the movie clamored for more credit. A third looked at the impact on their relationship, which teetered on the brink of disintegration. Their first podcast was a viral hit and it didn't take long for each new installment to attract sixty-five thousand downloads via iTunes, YouTube, Google Video, and MySpace. Their audience attracted an even bigger audience. The first seven episodes were downloaded half a million times, unleashing a platoon of citizen marketers, their clips posted online, emailed to friends, or played on iPods.

The marketing was so effective that a *Four Eyed Monsters* screening at the Brooklyn Museum sold out: 470 tickets in five minutes. After Buice and Crumley posted their final podcast, they threw screening parties across the country, organized by volunteers. They tried out a service that let filmmakers distribute their work to art-house theaters; the more advance tickets sold, the more theaters signed on. Simultaneously, they released *Four Eyed Monsters* through their website, on DVD (complete with the podcasts, for around $15), or as a digital download. Eventually they earned a deal with the Independent Film Channel (IFC) to broadcast it on television and their DVD was available at Borders. Crumley viewed their strategy as a showdown between Hollywood and the New Economy: "If we are successful with releasing our film by building our own audience, getting the film directly to that audience, and using what they say about it to get to a bigger audience, that would prove that the distributors' existence is completely unnecessary. It's better than a couple of guys in an office making a multimillion-dollar decision based on their own personal taste."

Buice and Crumley are early examples of the millions who have been flowing into this filtration process. It's a process that may have some unlikely by-products of its own, possible alliances, say, between low-rent filmmakers and theater owners, who in the past have been separated by a gulf of power and influence. The rise of digital makes it easy enough to imagine a day when theater owners look to the Internet to find movies (or compilations of shorts, or animation, or any other sort of content that can be screened) to supplement the list coming out of Hollywood or the not-so-indies. Even now, they could gauge an audience's interest in advance, based on metrics such as the number of downloads or click-throughs, and deliver specialized, microtargeted content on nights when they're tired of projecting unpopular movies to an empty house. Remember, Buice and Crumley's online presence translated into a packed theater, with real tickets.

There are, of course, a number of things delaying that day. It would cost about $3 billion to convert all thirty-six thousand movie screens in this country to digital, and the process has barely begun. But as Bud

Mayo, president of AccessIT, a company that offers financing and expertise to theaters looking to convert to digital, explained, delaying that
process leaves a lot of money on the table. "You have a $9 billion domes-
tic box office, and that's using 15 percent of available seats," he says. "If
you can impose digital cinema and all its benefits, and attract 5 percent
more customers to fill some of those empty seats, that's a $3 billion to
$4 billion opportunity."

Adding to the power of the digital model is the fact that the big studios
themselves stand to benefit from digital conversion. The studios now spend
upward of $10 million to dispatch 35-millimeter prints of a single block-
buster, at $1,500 per print, to the thousands of theaters across the country
(and $5 million for a more modest release). A digital release would bring
that number down to about $200 per movie, transmitted at the push of a
button. Within ten years, your local cinema will probably have digital capacity (although it may retain film technology for a time, to appease the
purist Hollywood directors), and this will profoundly shift the economics of
the movie business. AccessIT alone plans to convert ten thousand screens
by 2010, by ponying up the initial costs. (In return, film studios pay a
$1,000 fee per screen the first time a film is shown, which Mayo says would
generate about $15,000 a year per screen.) AccessIT then transports the
film via satellite or fiber-optic cable from a central server; theater owners
could add advertisements or trailers, track concessions, and even monitor
lights remotely. They would have the technical capability to change their
lineup on the fly, substituting 3-D rock concerts, video-game competitions,
religious revivals, World Cup matches, versions of a movie dubbed in Chinese or Spanish, or indie efforts like *Four Eyed Monsters*.

"The studios are afraid of the loss of control that digital sets forth,"
says Ira Deutchman, president and CEO of Emerging Pictures, another
company that converts theaters to digital. "Once you have digital equipment, exhibitors can play whatever they want on a given day. This changes
the balance of power between exhibitors and Hollywood." Standing between the studios and the theaters, however, are the distributors, and they
still wield enormous clout. "If a theater pulls a movie before the contract
stipulates, it's going to have a problem," says David Zelon, head of production for Mandalay Filmed Entertainment. "It's worse than getting sued:
you won't get the next big picture."

Zelon claims Hollywood studios aren't losing any sleep over the ascendance of digital filmmaking or its ancillary benefits to small-scale indie directors. "Every once in a while, you'll get a *My Big Fat Greek Wedding* or *The Blair Witch Project*. But you really need a studio-marketing campaign. At the end of the day, you need stars, because the first question people ask about a film is, 'Who's in it?'" he says. "Without mass marketing, you won't capture the attention of a mass audience, and the Internet is not a viable way to attract a mass audience."

Fred Zollo, a producer of *Mississippi Burning*, didn't bother to contain his contempt for moviemakers like Crumley and Buice, perhaps reflecting the views of many of the Hollywood elite. "The idea that you go out with some girl, make a movie about it, and put it on the Internet is preposterous. How can you watch a movie on a computer screen? The only use for the Internet is misinformation and pornography. It's the Cliffs Notes of our age." The problem with digital technology, he continued, is "it lets people make movies who have no business making movies. Now any idiot can make one. They wouldn't know *Gone with the Wind* from 'Blowin' in the Wind.'"

Harsh words indeed. But even if Zelon and Zollo are right, that doesn't make movies created for, marketed, and distributed over the Web negligible. After all, NBC, Fox, and a number of other entertainment companies banded together to launch Hulu.com, which offers TV shows and movies online—free. And if 85 percent of a cinema's seats lie fallow every year, a hundred smaller movies that attracted a following would become a force, while a thousand events—from films to sports events to rock concerts—could represent a revolution. How long could theater owners turn their backs on that kind of upside? If they caved, how long could distributors afford to withhold their films, especially as more theaters joined the digital ranks? And perhaps most important, how long would studios back distributors in that battle if they could deliver their films directly to theaters in a few minutes, for a fraction of the cost?

[LEARNING FROM NEWSPAPERS]

In the way that consumers forced the music industry to adapt, and pushing newspapers to do likewise, Hollywood should pay attention because it could be next. In this broadband era of YouTube, iPhone, BlackBerrys, email, IM, and RSS feeds, most of us dash through life at a frantic pace. We are bombarded with text, images, ads, and digital come-ons. We don't read news—we consume it, often by clicking headline to headline in pursuit of whatever catches our eye. Standing in line at the pharmacy, we update our blogs; we check our BlackBerrys and Treos idling at traffic lights and our voice mails on train platforms, we Google the sales manager we're supposed to meet in fifteen minutes. What's more likely in the coming years: suddenly we will return to a slower, simpler time, or our culture will continue this acceleration as information, the lifeblood of our work, leisure, investments, friendships, and family, cascades all around us?

Contrast this glitzy postmillennial lifestyle with the premillennial, time-consuming trek your local newspaper makes each day. It owes its analog existence to trees that are chopped down, trucked to a mill where they are mashed into pulp, flattened into paper, and transported to printing presses. There the huge rolls of paper are sprayed with letters and numbers, photos, crossword puzzles, sudoku, and drawings, cut, stacked, bound, and stuffed into trucks. These bundles are dropped off at newsstands or distributed to people whose job entails flinging each copy, one at a time, house to house. Later you step onto your porch, pick up the paper, scan the headlines, and realize everything in it is a day late. You've already skimmed these articles on the Web, were fed email links on your PDA or cell phone, or accessed RSS feeds, watched them on CNN, heard them on the radio, or caught a glimpse of them on a news ticker atop a taxi cab. By the time you read the paper, the news has moved on and so have you. It's one thing to rely on such an intricate supply chain to manufacture a Stealth bomber. It's a complete waste of scarce and expensive materials and fuel for the dissemination of mere words and pictures on a page, and it takes far too long.

The decay of the printed word on paper is part of a predictable pattern of development. The incipient form of a new technology tends to mirror what came before, until innovation and consumer need drives it far beyond initial incremental improvements over its predecessors. The first battlefield tanks looked suspiciously like heavily armored tractors equipped with cannons; early automobiles were called "horseless carriages" for a reason; the first motorcycles were based on bicycles; the first satellite phones were as clunky as your household telephone. A decade ago, when newspapers began serving up stories over the Web, the content mirrored what was offered in the print edition. What the tank, car, and newspaper have in common is they blossomed into something far beyond their initial prototypes. In the way an engineer wouldn't dream of starting with the raw materials for a carriage to design a rad new sports car and Hollywood might have to branch far beyond the local multiplex, newspapers will eventually cease to use paper and ink.

Journalism might be a public trust, depending on who is doing the journaling, but most reporters and editors don't work for free. Whether or not they like to admit it, journalism is a business. When a reader plunks down two dollars for a *New York Times* or 50 cents for the local paper, he barely covers the cost of the paper and ink. Someone else is playing Sugar Daddy or Mommy: advertisers. Indeed, a typical paper generates about 80 percent of its revenue from advertising. Journalists don't sell news. They attract an audience that publishers can sell to advertisers, and make a few bucks in the process. The news is simply a lure to aggregate eyeballs so that someone with something to sell can try to reach them. The system has persisted for more than a century. Reporters write, readers pay a pittance to read their writings, and someone else gets stuck with the bill.

In recent years, however, the newspaper industry has come under assault. Circulation is falling—more than 10 percent between 2004 and 2008 alone. The decline is not a recent phenomenon. According to Newspaper Association of America statistics, this has been going on for twenty-five years. The Internet may be hastening the problem, but it didn't cause it. Still, advertisers have been migrating online, and because readers are but a click away from other news sources, there is intense competition.

In days past, when you bought a newspaper to read on the train, you were a captive audience. You either read what was in your hand or were stuck talking to the guy sitting next to you. Newspapers held a monopoly over your time, and because of geographic relevance, they acted like local information monopolies. Seventy-five years ago, nearly every community in America had at least one newspaper. They had names like the *Tyrone*

Herald in Pennsylvania, the *Milford Mail* in Iowa, or the *Moberly Monitor-Index* in Missouri. Costing pennies each, they ran a few local stories mixed with wire service copy from the Associated Press, United Press International, and the New York Times Syndicate.

Over the past century, the number of newspapers has declined steadily. Research shows that in 1910, there were 2,600 daily newspapers in the United States, the vast majority independently owned and operated. By 1990, there were 1,600 papers nationwide, largely under corporate control and overseen by fifteen chief executive officers. Consolidation killed numerous local papers, and the *New York Times* contributed. When it began publishing a national edition, the *Times* helped push many smaller papers out of business by grabbing lenders and ads. Now, the Internet is doing to the *Times* what it did to small, local newspapers. *Times* chairman Arthur Sulzberger thought he had competition with the *New York Post*, the *New York Daily News*, and the *Washington Post*. But today there is a mind-bending number of options for the curious reader online.

That means the old way of doing business—taking advantage of the monopoly you held over your audience so that advertisers were forced to go through you to reach them—is no longer a viable business strategy. The balance of power has shifted from the monopolies providing access to their audiences to the advertisers who can reach exactly the kind of people most likely to buy their products. As a result, advertisers have been moving online, where they can track their return on investment far better than they can offline. An advertiser who takes out a full-page ad in the *Times* print edition has no idea how many people actually see it, and knows even less about how many are prompted to action. All it knows is a *Times* print reader's average age is forty-two. Several generations of readers are growing up and coming of age on the Web. Meanwhile newspapers also are not just losing advertisers; they are hemorrhaging readers of the print editions, the other side of the monopoly they once held.

Newspapers have set up shop online, but not all the money has been following. For years, papers cleared 40 percent margins. It made being a newspaper owner a very profitable business. The *Times* earns hundreds of dollars for each of its approximately 1 million print subscribers, but only a fraction of that on each of its approximately 15 million online readers. Its online audience spends only a few minutes on the site each visit—when they bother to come at all—and about thirty minutes a month, on average. The culprit: as with newspapers, virtually unlimited choice and very low yields for banner advertisements. This embarrassment-of-niches syndrome is beginning to afflict the film studios and TV companies, which are also seeking revenue models online to replace far more profitable real-world sales of DVDs—up until recently, viewed as Hollywood's savior.

[NOT A HAPPY ENDING—NOT EVEN AN ENDING]

In the end, of course, Hollywood might respond to the threat posed by Buice, Crumley, and the rest by doing what it did to indie film in the 1990s: co-opting it. The Web could simply become a farm team, a place to scout talent. It seems a safe bet that someone from Hollywood must be watching social networks like Facebook and MySpace for the next break-out star, whether of film, music, or anything else. (Even this scenario should give distributors the shakes, however.)

Meanwhile, filmmakers Buice and Crumley had to defer their Nora Ephron denouement. Their 450-square-foot loft in a former factory build-ing in Bushwick, Brooklyn, was awash in digital videotapes. An archaic gas stove was set right inside the front door; their bedroom was little more than a mattress stuffed into an alcove, secreted behind a red curtain. A whiteboard was covered in notes, an almost endless to-do list. Two Apple monitors bathed the room in light. Crumley was wearing ripped blue jeans and a faded T-shirt, while the blond-haired, blue-eyed Buice had a style all her own: gray dress, light green leggings, black shawl, and brown leather boots with laces. The pair had racked up $54,000 in credit card debt and were so broke dinner often consisted of almond-butter sand-wiches. Still, asked if they would accept a $2 million offer from a distribu-tor for the rights to *Four Eyed Monsters,* Crumley said, "No."

Buice wasn't so sure.

"Only if we maintain control," Crumley insisted.

What if that wasn't part of the deal?

"No."

Buice bit her tongue. She and Crumley fought almost every day while they were making their picture. She once got so fed up, she told him she was leaving as soon as they finished the damn thing. But their arguments smacked of truth. Authenticity, even. They made the couple's story—what's the word?—cinematic.

6

Viral Video as Marketing Strategy (Psst. Pass It On . . .)

Letting Go of Your Brand, Joke Cycles, and Not Acting Like Some Guy in His Mid-40s Trying to Be a Hipster

Mint-maker Mentos was in a rut. A unit of Italian confectioner Perfetti Van Melle, Mentos spent $20 million a year on marketing, most of it on famously campy "freshmaker" TV commercials that had run for the previous fifteen years. Vice president of marketing Pete Healy believed Mentos needed to, as he put it, "reassess, redefine and reposition its brand." This prompted him to sit down in 2008 with other executives for a brainstorming session to personify what the product was all about. If Mentos were a car, they wondered, what kind would it be? A sporty convertible. If a recreational activity, rock climbing or beach volleyball. And what celebrity was most like Mentos? Adam Sandler, former *Saturday Night Live* cast member and star of such cinematic shtick as *Happy Gilmore* and *The Waterboy*. Then in April 2006 a Web video of two goofy guys creating a replica of the Bellagio Fountain in Las Vegas out of nothing more than Mentos and bottles of Diet Coke went viral, downloaded by millions, spawning thousands of imitators and attracting intensive media coverage, and it hit Healy. "What could be a better fit than Adam Sandler and Mentos geysers?" he asked himself. "It reflected our personality."

What followed was a marketing coup that has become a textbook example of how a company can harness the power of viral video, where the standard thirty-second TV ad, which is waning in influence, is replaced by the audience. Because in this new world of collective curation, they and they alone decide what's good and what should be watched while the traditional gatekeepers—television networks, movie studios, and the news media—are pushed to the sidelines. As was the case with *Four*

Eyed Monsters, this democratization of content is made possible by the advent of cheap video cameras, camcorders, even cell phones that capture user-generated infotainment, aided by powerful, affordable software like Final Cut Pro and iMovie to shape it, and distributed via a massive digital infrastructure with ample bandwidth. The technological zeitgeist is equal parts human, however, as netizens blog about what interests them or disseminate links to everyone in their email and IM address books. Meanwhile, user communities have sprouted up on people portals like MySpace, Flickr, YouTube, and Digg. There, people share everything from blog posts to news articles, pictures, audio podcasts, and videos in a quest for their own Warholian 15 megabytes of fame.

"It's all about the combination of next-generation content creation and distribution coupled to instant access to your social network community," says Adam Lavelle, vice president of strategy for iCrossing, a digital-marketing agency. "Because distribution is so huge and fluid and easy, your community connects to other communities, which fosters this distribution. If I know you, then I know everyone you know."

As for companies caught up in a viral storm, they have little choice but to let go of their brand. As Procter & Gamble CEO A. G. Lafley once said in a speech at the Association of National Advertisers, "The more in control we are, the more out of touch we become. But the more willing we are to let go a little, the more we're finding we get in touch with consumers." This, of course, frightens executives used to molding their brands to fit their own hackneyed scripts. If consumers start tarnishing their name, and that spreads, it could be disastrous. In the old days, if someone had a problem with customer service, he wrote a nasty letter to a company's complaint department—if he could find it. Nowadays, the Web enables the fluidity of information where consumers enjoy unprecedented power. Commerce has become a conversation. Businesses either talk to their customers or face their wrath, which can echo through the blogosphere and sites like Digg and Slashdot with their legions of snarky users, who tell others, and so on and so on, until millions are mocking a company. Just ask AOL, Dell, and countless others that have learned the hard way, with scorching blog posts by dissatisfied customers becoming the equivalent of hit songs.

On the upside, a company willing to let go of its brand can find its way to great, untapped riches as Mentos did. The Bellagio Fountain video was downloaded 20 million times and more than 10,000 copycat mint-soda videos were posted online, which created a multiplier effect: Mentos tallied a staggering 215 million mentions of its product in TV, print, or radio stories over the next nine months, and estimates the free publicity was worth $10 million to the company, half its annual marketing budget. More to the point, Mentos made a mint: sales climbed 20 percent during the first viral tsunami, and even after the commotion died down, they remained 15 percent higher than they had been.

Coca-Cola also reaped rewards. Before the video, Diet Coke's sales had been flat, while the company as a whole was losing market share. But Michael Donnelly, the soft-drink maker's interactive director, reports that after it went viral there was a "significant spike" in sales of 2-liter bottles of Diet Coke, the ones used on camera. He wouldn't give exact numbers but confirmed it was between 5 and 10 percent. A second video by the original instigators, employing 251 bottles of Diet Coke and 1,500 Mentos in a massive chain reaction, led to a 27 percent increase in traffic to Coke.com.

All of this was a million miles away from the minds of Fritz Grobe, a professional juggler, and Stephen Voltz, a trial lawyer, who were the ones responsible for all of this. In fall 2005, the two heard from a friend that if you drop Mentos into a bottle of Diet Coke, it would explode. Performers at heart—Grobe and Voltz were members of a Buckfield, Maine, regional theater company—the two went out to the backyard to try it. After the pyrotechnics, their first thought was, How far could they take it?

Naturally, they weren't the first. For decades, high school students had mixed vinegar and baking soda to make volcanoes erupt at science fairs, and science educators tossed Wint-O-Green Life Savers into diet soda to demonstrate chemical reactions. (Why diet soda? Cola's brown color makes it easy to see, and diet cola's lack of sugar makes it easier to clean up.) Since the early 1990s, Mentos had been aware of the geyser phenomenon, which would come and go in popularity. Then in September 2005, science educator Steve Spangler demonstrated the Mentos–Diet Coke effect on Denver, Colorado's 9 News, with anchor Kim Christiansen getting soaked in the process. The online video became a minor hit.

As for Grobe and Voltz, they spent the morning playing around with the idea. After corralling as many bottles of Diet Coke and tubes of

Mentos as they could, they constructed a ten-bottle fountain with the aid of some cement blocks and put on a show at the Oddfellows Theater for other members of their troupe. The response urged them to greater heights. They spent about five months experimenting—cutting slits in bottles, drilling holes, adding screens. After settling on the Bellagio Fountain in Las Vegas, the two drafted blueprints, carefully choreographing their effects to match those of their glitzy muse. On April 29, 2006, the two laid out two hundred bottles of Diet Coke in an intricate design and prepped more than five hundred Mentos mints (total cost: $300), then spent eight hours doing walk-throughs. "It felt like blowing up a building," Grobe says. "We had one chance. We had never done more than twenty bottles at a time before that."

While a friend with a digital video camera recorded the action, the two, dressed in white lab coats, crossed their fingers and let it fly. Amazingly it all went off without a hitch. In fact, it went better than they had imagined because it was an unseasonably warm day, so the effects were even more spectacular, especially at the end when the grand crown shot out in different directions and spun. They got soaked, puddles of Diet Coke gathering in their goggles.

They entered a Web video contest sponsored by the E-Channel but didn't win, so the first Saturday in June they posted it to their website, EepyBird.com. Voltz told one person about it: his brother. Within hours, thousands of visitors were viewing "Experiment #137." By the end of the first day, they counted fourteen thousand downloads. Two days later, *The Late Show With David Letterman* called. Grobe told producers they had only done the fountain once and would need a chance to rehearse. Over the course of the next few weeks, Grobe and Voltz grew sufficiently confident they could perform the Mentos geyser live.

Meanwhile the video became a runaway hit. Over nine days, more than 2 million people logged on to their site. There was also downside: enthusiastic viewers kept posting it on YouTube. But Grobe and Voltz had a deal with Revver.com, where they would split ad revenue. Voltz put his legal expertise to work and sent a flurry of letters to YouTube, which automatically stripped the Revver ad from the video, demanding that the site remove their copyrighted material. As soon as one video came down, five would go up. Grobe and Voltz just couldn't keep up. In the end, they earned $50,000 in advertising revenue and estimate they could have made double that if YouTube and other video-sharing sites had proactively blocked users from posting it.

[JOKE CYCLES]

Viral video has many analog precursors and the concept of collective curation has been around thousands of years, it just didn't have as sophisticated a propulsion system as it does today. At first it was verbal, with gossip and information spreading from person to person. Town criers in the Middle Ages called out the news of the day, which was echoed by the townsfolk. Paul Revere spread the message that the British were coming, but it was the patriots who amplified the message and helped save a young nation. Chain letters mailed through the nation's postal system urged recipients to make copies and send to ten other people, or suffer the consequences. Then came the telephone, the first efficient person-to-person mode of communication, which before the rise of the Internet offered an unprecedented level of virality.

A little over a minute after liftoff from Cape Canaveral on January 28, 1986, NASA ground control ordered the commander of the space shuttle *Challenger* to go to full power. Seconds later, the ship exploded, leaving a trail of light and smoke and killing all seven astronauts onboard, including Christa McAuliffe, a New Hampshire schoolteacher whose family witnessed the tragedy from the launch site while her students watched on live television. It was a shocking scene, the worst disaster in U.S. space history. The media reacted in hushed, reverent tones, and President Ronald Reagan, in a news conference, called the deceased "heroes." As the nation mourned, tuning into the "electronic hearth" known as TV, the inevitable cycle of tasteless jokes began.

Q. What does NASA stand for?
A. Need Another Seven Astronauts.

As newscasts replayed the explosion on television in an almost endless loop and newspapers, magazines, and radio covered the inevitable investigation, the joke spread fast and furiously. Almost before the space-ship debris hit the water eighteen miles off the coast of Florida, Wall Street bankers, bond traders, and stockbrokers, plugged into near instant communication were yukking it up, sharing it over the phone with colleagues and clients alike. In *Liar's Poker,* Michael Lewis, who sat with four others at a desk with a hundred telephone lines, reported that six people from six points on the globe called with the NASA "need another seven astronauts" line. "If you ever care to see how all the world's most awful jokes spread, spend a day on a bond trading desk," he advised. Elizabeth Radin Simons, a researcher at the University of California at Berkeley, tracked it to a nearby school, where the morning after the tragedy students were entertaining one another with the joke. Federal employees shared it over government phone lines. It made for water cooler chatter at accounting firms and conversation fodder at bars and cafés, at parties and in hair salons.

Naturally this type of viral humor, known as a joke cycle, was not new. In the United States they date back to at least the late nineteenth and early twentieth century, when a series of "Little Willie" jokes were all the rage.

Little Willie with his thirst for gore.
Nailed his mommy's baby to the door.

Following World War II, there were Holocaust jokes, Jesus jokes, and in the 1950s, bizarre family jokes:

Q. Mama, why is Daddy's face pale?
A. Shut up and keep digging.

Other joke cycles made fun of ethnic groups—Polish people and the Irish, among others. Helen Keller jokes poked fun at blindness and deafness. In the 1960s dead-baby jokes were popular, and the 1970s brought "Yo, Mama" cracks.

As Simons noted in an article titled "The NASA Joke Cycle: The Astronauts and the Teacher," published in *Western Folklore* seven months after the calamity, the jokes aimed to offend in two respects: they attacked targets usually viewed as immune from crass commentary, and they were often gross or violent. The difference between these cycles of mirth, however, and the one involving the *Challenger* space shuttle was the speed with which it traveled. Little Willie jokes took decades to infiltrate large tracts of the country. The others were also slowed by predominantly face-to-face contact. But the *Challenger* disaster spawned almost instantaneous jocularity across all fifty states within weeks. It even took hold abroad—in Australia, Canada, England, Iceland, Scotland, and Switzerland—spread by a combination of one-to-one telephone communication and face-to-face joke telling. Unlike with most sick jokes, there was a catalyst. The explosion was a singular event that virtually every American knew about, while other sick jokes had no news hook, no reason for being told at that particular point in time.

Simons, who collected the jokes from small business owners, company workers, elementary and high school students, college students, and teachers between late February (almost one month after the explosion) through June 1986, called them "a grieving ritual which also served to vent anger and alleviate disillusionment at the failure of NASA—symbol of the USA. And, by chance, because of the presence of a teacher among the crew, it was an opportunity to strike out at teachers, the symbol and perceived cause of the failure of the American public school system."

Mercifully, the *Challenger* joke cycle ran its course in three months. But a decade later, after Mosaic and Netscape seeded the viral plain, jokes, memes, and information of all sorts could be dispatched to dozens, if not hundreds, of people at the click of a mouse, and the pace of virality picked up dramatically. Many early online chain letters involved virus hoaxes, which urged recipients to warn everyone in their address books. One of the earliest warned of the "Good Times" virus, which, the email claimed, could rewrite hard drives and therefore erase every file on users' computers. It urged recipients to alert everyone they knew. The virus warning was itself a virus. By passing on the message, the recipient was unknowingly adding to its viral coefficient, helping to clog email gateways. It wasn't just virus hoaxes that spread far and wide over the Internet. Jokes, quotations, faux health alerts, oddball conspiracy theories, and articles that touched someone's heart, funny bone, or both were commonly dispatched onto the viral plain. It was only a matter of time before businesses began to recognize the benefits of viral campaigns to extend their brands, and in the process increase sales. They just had to figure out how.

The answer came from Burger King in the form of a guy dressed up as a chicken willing to do whatever you wanted. The brainchild of ad firm Crispin Porter and Bogusky in 2004, the "subservient chicken" was one of the first mega-successful corporate viral campaigns. One component involved a series of wacky television spots, starring a man in a chicken suit. In the first, a guy in his living room orders the chicken around; the tagline was "Chicken the way you like it." Another showed a rodeo cowboy riding the chicken before a cheering throng: "The only way to beat it is to eat it." A third featured two man-sized chickens in a cockfight. But it was the ensuing interactive Web campaign that turned it from idle curiosity into a phenomenon.

Crispin launched a website with the chicken in a living room, encouraging visitors to type commands and watch him perform what they asked, as long as it corresponded to one of more than three hundred prerecorded moves. A user could order the bird to do everything from a push-up, a cartwheel, a back flip, or even a moonwalk like Michael Jackson to peck, pee, shake his booty, and turn off the lights. But the chicken would hold the line at anything obscene (such as a sex act). He would respond by approaching the camera and wagging his finger in disapproval. And if told to eat a Big Mac from McDonald's, he would stick his finger down his throat.

Within a week, the chicken hosted more than 20 million visits, with the average user spending an astonishing 5 minutes and 44 seconds on the site. Word spread virally online and off, with the media, particularly broadcast, amplifying the message with some 7 million mentions of the campaign. More to the point, sales of Burger King chicken sandwiches increased 9 percent a week in the month following the site's launch.

[CATCHING THE WAVE]

Pete Healy of Mentos heard about the geyser phenomenon after his marketing director tuned in to National Public Radio, which ran a segment on it. Healy told a *Wall Street Journal* reporter that Mentos was "tickled" by the video. Although he didn't mention it, he did wonder about liability. "You hope people have common sense and won't allow their three-year-old to stand over a bottle of exploding soda," he said. Healy called Grobe and asked if there was anything the company could do to help?

"Send Mentos," Grobe replied.

Healy did more than that. Although he knew there would be risks to involving Mentos in this type of new-media campaign, in the end, Mentos was candy, not a cure for cancer. How much effort would people put in ridiculing it? "As long as we maintained a light touch and were authentic, we figured we would probably be okay," Healy says. "We knew there were parodies of the old Mentos TV ads. It didn't bother us; in fact it showed people were engaged with the personality of the brand."

When Grobe and Voltz appeared on the *David Letterman* show at the end of June, Healy dispatched the Mentos-mobile, a Pontiac Solstice convertible wrapped in Mentos graphics, which was parked outside the theater, while street marketers in Mentos T-shirts toting six-foot rolls of Mentos gave out candy to passersby. At the same time, the Coca-Cola Company, slower on the uptake, didn't know what to think. A Coke spokeswoman told the *Wall Street Journal*, "We would hope people want to drink [Diet Coke] more than try experiments with it." She added that the "craziness with Mentos" didn't "fit" Diet Coke's "brand personality."

Michael Donnelly, the company's interactive director, admitted that Coke wasn't prepared for this. But in July the soft-drink maker relaunched Coke.com with a new focus: consumer-generated media that celebrates creativity and self-expression. Within days of starting his job at Coke, Donnelly contacted "the eepy.com guys," as he called them. This led to a powwow between Coke, Mentos, Grobe, Voltz, and Google, which also wanted in on the action.

The companies agreed to work together to support the performers in a second Mentos-Coke sprinkler video, which Grobe and Voltz dubbed *The Domino Effect.* At the end, there was an advertisement that linked to Coke.com or cocacola.com, announcing a contest. For three months, people could submit their own videos of ordinary objects doing extraordinary things, and Grobe and Voltz were the judges. One that Grobe says he particularly liked involved balloons, Mentos, Diet Coke, and a series of chain reactions. Coke supported the campaign by buying up hundreds of search keywords on Google, MSN, and Yahoo, anything relating to Coke, Mentos, and explosions, and counted 1.5 billion ad impressions from the campaign.

Still, with 5 million downloads on Google Video, Grobe and Voltz's second video wasn't nearly as popular as the first. That's because they can be extremely hard to replicate. On YouTube some videos have been downloaded tens of millions of times—a cat playing the piano, a beauty contestant unable to string together a coherent sentence, a music video set on treadmills at a gym, a kid acting out a fight scene from *Star Wars* with a broomstick, a cackling baby. At first blush there may not seem any rhyme or reason behind their appeal, a secret code that, when deciphered, guarantees a certifiable hit. Yet there are shared characteristics to some viral videos, some of which are created by companies to advertise their products. There was:

• A two-minute Honda Accord web video consisting of one continuous shot of a Rube Goldberg–like contraption made entirely out of car parts.

• A series created for the Sony Bravia HDTV featuring explosions of paint covering whole buildings, thousands of bouncing balls, and giant clay rabbits, all in vivid color.

• A Dove *Evolution* ad of a normal-looking woman instantly transformed into a supermodel before our very eyes. Tagline: "No wonder our image of beauty is distorted."

• The cheesy Blendtec *Will it blend?* series, showing an old guy in a lab coat blending everything from golf balls to hockey pucks to marbles and iPods.

What do they have in common? For one, they are fun to watch and the antithesis of the hard sell. They offer the audience a value proposition. In exchange for entertaining us the companies are afforded the privilege of mentioning their product. The narrative of each video is woven tightly into the brand's message. For Honda, it is the Rube Goldberg device made from car parts, which represents the idea that the Honda Accord simply works. Sony's ad played up the Bravia's color and image clarity. Dove's idea expanded the idea of beauty to encompass more than twiggy supermodels. Blendtec wants everyone to know how powerful its blenders are. The videos are short (less than two minutes), clever—and make viewers want to learn more: the Honda ad sent more than one watcher to the Web to figure out how it was done. So did Dove *Evolution*.

JibJab (jibjab.com), a flash animation studio based in Los Angeles, is one of the few to build a business around replicating viral success. Conceived by Evan and Gregg Spiridellis, JibJab has attracted a worldwide following with its funny, satirical political cartoons. The Brooklyn-born brothers had their first viral success in 2000 with the release of an animated short featuring the Founding Fathers rapping about the Declaration of Independence. Then, during the run-up to the presidential elections, they hit 5 million downloads with a video of George W. Bush and Al Gore slinging dirt at each other—this at a time when the majority of Internet users were on dawdling dial-up modems. To follow up they had fun at the expense of Arnold Schwarzenegger with *Ahnold for Governor*, which got them admitted to the Sundance Online Film Festival. But it was *This Land*, a political parody of the 2004 George Bush–John Kerry campaign set to the classic Woody Guthrie tune, skewering "liberal wienies" and "right-wing nut jobs" alike, that thrust them into the big time. After seeding the virality by sending the link to the 130,000 people on their email list and premiering the video on *The Tonight Show* with Jay Leno (which averaged 5 million viewers per show), the brothers Spiradellis's Web server almost "spontaneously combusted" under the onslaught.

"The more people you can email, the faster you get viral adoption," says Greg Spiradellis, who got his MBA at Wharton. *The Tonight Show* acted as a huge multiplier. Between the two, "this is how we were able to turn 130,000 emails into 80 million streams." Naturally, they released a video leading up to the 2008 election called *Time for Some Campaignin'* that featured Barack Obama atop a flying white unicorn, crooning dulcet tones imploring "change" and John McCain exhorting conservatives to lend him a helping hand, with Hillary Clinton, George Bush, and Dick Cheney competing for screen time. When *Newsweek* asked Spiradellis the secret to JibJab's success, he replied, "It's all about potty humor and politics."

JibJab has been capitalizing on its popularity by embracing the Netscape business model—attracting people to its website with regular parodies and free e-cards, then attempting to monetize a tiny fraction, charging $13.99 a year (or $4.99 a month) for a premium subscription. This gains you access to "content you can use for expression, which has value," Spiradellis says. For example, a subscriber can insert his head on one of the characters and send it out as an e-card to all of his friends, or post it on his MySpace page. Even nonsubscribers can do that, which is what 12 million people did with the Obama-McCain *Time for Some Campaignin'* video. "Traditional TV guys don't get it," he says. "It's a new medium and requires new creative storytelling formats. A twenty-minute sitcom on the Web is precisely the wrong way to go about it. People want to engage in content." Besides, "Why make TV shows when you can make content and distribute it without gatekeepers?"

[WHAT NOT TO DO]

Because the odds of benefiting from a phenomenon like the Mentos–Diet Coke geysers can be less than the chances of winning *American Idol*, some companies have been trying to game the system, with decidedly mixed results. Samsung released a series of videos on YouTube featuring a Saint Bernard named Sam on a plane. The few who actually watched characterized them as "lame," "a stinker," and "zzzzzz." One user summed up: "I would really like to know which agency and production company came up with this uninspired piece of crap."

Dove has also had hits and misses. It scored big with *Evolution*, a Web video that illustrates through makeup and software how an ordinary woman can be transformed into Mischa Barton hot. On YouTube alone, several parodies were viewed a total of 5 million times. (Personal favorite: *Slob Evolution*, in which a male model eats, drinks, and smokes himself into someone who resembles Christopher Hitchens.) Dove also issued a flop when it tried to foist a promo for Dove Cream Oil Body Wash on to the YouTube community. The video received more than ten thousand comments, almost universally negative. FedEx, on the other hand, squelched any viral marketing potential by threatening legal action against a customer who had created furniture out of the air shipper's boxes, then posted the pictures on his website. "The worst thing you can do is act like a grumpy old brand and send out cease-and-desist letters," says Michael Maslansky, president of Luntz, Maslansky Strategic Research. "It makes you look bad." Adds Mentos's Healy: "If I had been FedEx, I would have gone online and created a 'Design Your Own Dining Set Out of FedEx Cartons' contest."

There have been some modest corporate-inspired Web video successes, too. Millions of YouTube users have watched Tom Dickson, the earnest founder of Blendtec, a blender manufacturer, pulverize an iPod. He also stars in several other must-see *Will It Blend?* videos released on YouTube and Blendtec's own website, where he destroys baseballs, rake handles, light bulbs, magnets, marbles, half a rotisserie chicken, and a 12-ounce can of Coke. The month after the videos first hit the Web, Blendtec sold four times as many blenders online as it had over the previous monthly record.

Mentos continued to sponsor Grobe and Voltz, helping them perform with Blue Man Group in Boston. They appeared on French TV and gave performances in the Netherlands, Belgium, Turkey, and Pittsburgh. "We are earning a decent living as performers and it all started with a simple Web video," Grobe says. The company also struck up a relationship with Steve Spangler, a highly caffeinated educator who has made a career teaching teachers how to teach science. A staple at conferences, Spangler, whose father was both a magician and scientist, speaks to roughly 150,000 teachers a year. And at each conference he can't resist but demonstrate the power of Mentos and Diet Coke.

Spangler, who claims to have set off more than five thousand Mentos–Diet Coke geysers over an eight-year period, markets toys based on this theme. The first to hit the market was the Steve Spangler Geyser Tube, which sells for $4.95 and says on the label "powered by Mentos." He also released the Great Geysers Kit for $19.95, which contains a geyser tube, test tubes, chemicals like citric acid and baking soda, macaroni, string, a basic science kit, an instruction book explaining carbonation, and, of course, Mentos. Spangler filed for patents and receives any and all money, since Mentos isn't entitled to any of the revenue. Spangler even paid for the mints.

What's the secret of a campaign like this? "You have to have a light touch and be careful not to act like a guy in his mid-forties trying to be a hipster," says Healy, the fifty-something Mentos marketer. "It doesn't smell right."

III

VIRAL NETWORKS

eBay and the Viral Growth Conundrum

Faster, Pussycat. Scale! Scale! Scale!

At the onset of the tech boom, Pierre Omidyar, a young, French-born Iranian American computer programmer, placed an order through Charles Schwab to purchase stock in 3DO, a video-game maker. He did it shortly after the company announced plans for an IPO, far in advance of the actual date. Yet by the time his buy order went through, the stock had jumped 50 percent. Investment bankers and other insiders got in at the initial $15 per share, while regular people like Omidyar were forced to pay a hidden, variable premium to wait in line. *That's not how a free market is supposed to work*, he thought. Musing over the ideal market mechanism, he came up with the concept of an auction, and the emerging Web, he realized, was the perfect place to hold it. There could be complete transparency, equal access for all, and the price of a good or service would be whatever the highest bidder was willing to pay. Since Omidyar held a full-time job and could only work on his own pursuits in the evenings and on weekends, it took him a couple of years to get around to building it.

Over Labor Day weekend 1995, Omidyar cobbled together freeware he scooped up from around the Internet with his own homemade brew of applications. The do-it-yourself site, with its clunky blue-black letters over a drab, gray canvas, "had all the graphic charm of a Usenet newsgroup," observed *The Perfect Store* author Adam Cohen, who published a history of eBay's early years. Having never attended an auction, Omidyar didn't know what people might sell online, so he based categories on sheer guesswork: antiques, automotive, books and comics, computer hardware and software, consumer electronics, and the like. "The computer code Omidyar wrote let users do only three things: list items, view items, and place bids," Cohen recounted. "The name he chose was as utilitarian as the site itself: AuctionWeb."

Omidyar tacked it onto his existing hobby site, which also had a page devoted to the gruesome Ebola virus, he hosted on eBay.com, short for Echo Bay; he had plucked the name out of thin air because he liked the sound of it. When he learned Echobay.com was taken, he registered what he considered the next best thing. Over the course of several weeks, he publicized AuctionWeb on Usenet groups and in the what's-new sections of websites ("The most fun buying and selling on the Web," he boasted.). He listed a quirky array of items for sale and their respective bids, which included a pair of autographed Marky Mark underwear ($400), a used Superman metal lunchbox ($22), a Nintendo PowerGlove ($20), and a 1989 Toyota Tercel with 64,000 miles ($3,200). As traffic increased, so did the number of auctions, and word-of-mouth satisfaction spread. A week after posting his first list, Omidyar noted a 66 percent increase in the number of items for sale, including a 35,000-square-foot warehouse in Idaho (floor bid: $325,000).

It was so encouraging Omidyar ginned up an informal test. He had purchased a laser pointer for demonstrations that he ended up using to entertain his cat, which gleefully chased the red dot until it went kaput in a couple of weeks. Instead of tossing it in the trash, he posted it on AuctionWeb with the model number, a description of its failings, and an opening bid of $1. A little over a week later someone bid $3. Then $4. By the time the two-week auction ended, the broken laser pointer sold for $14.83 and Omidyar realized he might be on to something.

What he couldn't have known was that his little free-market experiment would soon prove so popular it would outstrip technology's ability to keep pace. Even if he had, there was little he could have done about it.

[THE SCALING CONUNDRUM]

Scaling is a massive challenge that can bedevil any viral loop business. Jeremy Liew of Lightspeed Venture Partners points out that if your viral coefficient is 1—not more than 1, exactly 1, the minimum needed to grow virally—and you have 100 users, the next day you'll have twice as many. On the third day there will be 400 users and on day four, 800. On the fifth day you will have a higher order magnitude of users than you did when you started, and two days means another order of magnitude. Multiply that by days, months, and years and the result is millions of users doubling at an ever-increasing rate. To design and build a system that can scale to multiple orders of magnitude is no trivial engineering accomplishment. Transferred to the material world, what would the city of Los Angeles do if suddenly the number of cars doubled in the next six months, then doubled again six months after that?

An online business that is scaling fast is often faced with the classic chicken-and-egg dilemma. To implement a scalable system before you launch "is frankly a complete waste of time if you don't know if anyone will show up at all," Liew says. People are "doing these lightweight development cycles not planned to scale out that far and that's what causes these scalability problems. Others are building for scalability, but it takes them so freaking long because it's not an easy problem and a lot of times that effort is wasted because they never do get viral." Simply put, it doesn't make sense to plan for massive scaling unless you actually start to massively scale. For his part, Omidyar hadn't given it a thought. He was too busy getting his business off the ground. But there were signs from the beginning.

Five months after he unveiled AuctionWeb, his hosting company, complaining the site was bogging down its entire network, raised his monthly fees from $30 to $250. Omidyar had no choice but to charge for the service, even if it meant an end to his free-market experiment. Wisely, he let sellers continue to post items for free. If, and only if, it concluded with a sale, AuctionWeb would skim 5 percent for items priced under $25 and half that for anything over. He had no way of enforcing payment, but was well aware of the concept of shareware, in which engineers posted software applications on the Web and requested users to send whatever they thought it worth. An inveterate optimist, Omidyar was fine depending on the kindness of strangers.

Soon after, envelopes brimming with cash and checks arrived at his Bay area home. In his first month he took in enough in dimes, quarters, and dollars to cover the $250 hosting fee. "That put his fledgling little website in a category almost all by itself," Cohen noted. "It was one of the very few Internet companies to be profitable from its first month of operation." A month later Omidyar collected $1,000; in April he received $2,500. May's tally was $5,000, and Omidyar, who didn't have time to open all the envelopes, made his first part-time hire. May's revenues doubled again to $10,000, and Omidyar quit his day job to work full-time on his fledgling business.

Throughout history cities sprang up wherever there was trade, people from all over gravitating to wherever buying and selling took place. The more who traveled to these marketplaces, the more who would learn of its existence through word of mouth. AuctionWeb was simply replicating this phenomenon in a virtual space, attracting future power users like Jim Griffith, a middle-aged veteran auction attendee living in Vermont who, in May 1996, built inexpensive computers out of discarded parts that he sold for a small profit. He was hunting a hard-to-find memory chip from IBM when a friend emailed him a link to AuctionWeb. There, among a thousand other doodads and doohickeys for sale, Griffith found what he was looking for. The bid was up to $8. He got it for $10. Right then and there he became an addict.

He spent much of his time over the next few months on the site, bidding for computer parts, offering his own computers for sale and answering questions on the bulletin board, which Omidyar had set up as a way for the growing community to handle the thousands of niggling details that arose daily, everything from settling disputes to fielding technical queries and passing on tips. As a former rock and blues musician with what he describes as an "unquenchable need to perform in front of people," Uncle Griff, with his oddball online persona, quickly developed a cult-like following, dispatching homespun wisdom under an endlessly patient online demeanor, "a cross-dressing bachelor dairy farmer" with a talent and desire to answer questions. When, battling depression, Griffith disappeared off the site for two weeks in the fall, Jeffrey Skoll, Omidyar's first full-time employee, called to check in and offer Uncle Griff a job in customer support.

The site's traffic continued to swell 20 to 30 percent a month, with mailbags stuffed with money arriving at Omidyar's doorstep each morning. In October 1996, AuctionWeb held 28,000 auctions, and over the next four and a half months the number of items posted grew 350 percent, fueled by Beanie Babies, the era's must-have collectible. By year's end the site counted forty-one thousand registered users. Every time Omidyar ventured a projection he would find that his forecast had drastically low-balled it. Meanwhile other auction sites, hoping to ape eBay's success, sprang up, including onSale, which touted millions in venture capital, a far glossier website, and $30 million in transactions. While an auction site, it pursued a significantly different business model. It took possession of the goods it sold and profited on the actual sale, as well as levying a transaction's fee. This meant it had to budget for warehousing and shipping, unlike Omidyar's virtual model, which simply took a sliver from bringing buyers and sellers together. His strategy also offered incentive to sellers to attract buyers, while onSale, though capitalizing on the auction mechanism, was more like an online retailer with a liquid price scheme.

OnSale never did manage to dent AuctionWeb's torrential growth. Later neither could AOL, Yahoo, or more than a hundred other auction businesses. Omidyar had unleashed a viral loop. He had first-mover status, a large and growing pool of enthusiastic users and an insurmountable lead. Soon AuctionWeb's market share hit 80 percent.

[FASTER, PUSSYCAT. SCALE! SCALE! SCALE!]

In January 1997, AuctionWeb held 200,000 online auctions compared to the 250,000 it had hosted the entire previous year. With the spike in traffic and usage, the site, which still chugged along on Omidyar's original mishmash of code, reeled. New listings sometimes didn't post for a full day; it could take a minute between the time a potential buyer clicked on an item and the description appearing. Asking users to list items for sale during off-peak hours did little to ameliorate the situation. Omidyar hired an engineer to re-architect the entire infrastructure and gave him a deadline of Labor Day. Then, desperate to drive away users before the whole site came crashing down, he instituted several measures that

included requiring credit approval for people with less than stellar payment histories and limiting the number of items that could be offered
for sale in a day.

EBAY'S EARLY YEARS

1996   41,000 registered users
$7.2 million in gross merchandise value
$350,000 in revenue
Hosts 28,000 auctions
Receives 100 emails a day
Half a dozen employees

1997   341,000 registered users
115,000 listings a day
138,054 items for sale
$4.3 million in revenue
371 product categories
Receives 1,200 emails a day
41 employees

1998   2.1 million registered users
$700 million in gross merchandise value
$48 million in revenue
6.58 million items for sale
10-millionth item listed
Receives 2,500 emails a day
138 employees

1999   10 million registered users
$2.8 billion in gross merchandise value
1,628 product categories
Receives 4,000 emails a day
641 employees

Source: eBay; *Forbes*; Adam Cohen, *The Perfect Store: Inside eBay* (Boston: Back Bay, 2003).

Yet nothing stanched the flow of users, although AuctionWeb's business didn't seem to be suffering. In fact, in June, when Omidyar tried to pull up the site during a meeting with venture capitalists, it was down. Nevertheless Benchmark Capital invested $3 million, which would sit forever in a bank gaining interest, since Omidyar never saw reason to spend it. Famously frugal, he was adamant about keeping expenses low. The business had only one phone line, which staff were instructed to ignore, and as part of new worker orientation, each employee picked out cheap, often used office furniture. AuctionWeb's headquarters was a study in disorganization, with no receptionist and chairs and desks arrayed in no discernible pattern.

On September 1, 1997, AuctionWeb unveiled its revamped site, renamed eBay, running on an entirely new scalable architecture. Omidyar then turned his attention to hiring a chief executive officer to run eBay with the intent of taking it public. He settled on Meg Whitman, head of Hasbro's Playskool division, who, he believed, with her down-to-earth manner, embodied the eBay ethos. (He didn't hold it against her that when she was first contacted she had never heard of Omidyar's company.) Whitman took the reins in March 1998, and six months later eBay went public, its shares nearly tripling in its first full day of trading, resulting in a market cap of $1.9 billion. By year's end eBay's $48 million in revenue was ten times greater than the previous year's, which itself was thirteen times more than all of 1996.

All of this came at a price. EBay's rebuilt architecture proved no match for the rapidly growing onslaught of users and the computing power that millions of auctions required. For the next year and a half brownouts and outages were frequent. Security was, at best, an afterthought, which was starkly illustrated on March 13, 1999, when a twenty-two-year-old college student who went by the handle MagicFX hacked eBay. He achieved "root" access on its computers, the same kind that the site's own administrators enjoyed, which meant he could change prices or place fake ads, divert traffic to other sites, or even take down the entire network. When a reporter told him to back up his boasts with evidence, the hacker took down eBay's home page for two minutes and replaced it with the message:

Proof by MagicFX that you can't always trust people . . .
not even huge companies. (who woulda known that?)

It's 9:30 PM . . . do you know who has YOUR credit card information?

After figuring out a simple password (eBay had not followed standard password protection schemes), the hacker copied Omidyar's source code governing auctions and took over a Solaris server with a well-known exploit—eBay's technicians had not kept up with the latest patches. From there, MagicFX modified the system's software so he could intercept passwords and log in names. He bragged that he could actually watch everyone's keystrokes and monitored email from users alerting the company to the hacked page.*

Embarrassing as it was, it wasn't nearly as disruptive to eBay as the outages that struck the company on June 10, 1999, following two less severe ones in May lasting several hours each and a half dozen others running from ninety minutes to several hours in the months preceding. While an outage for any company is serious, it was far worse for eBay, which depended on its computer network to conduct business. Twelve hours after eBay's site went dark, engineers still couldn't figure out what had gone wrong and weren't sure they could bring it back.

If they couldn't, all of eBay's data, the lifeblood of its business—its millions of registrations, credit card numbers, feedback, auctions that had been in progress when the machines went down—would be lost forever. The company might never recover.

[IF YOU CAN'T SCALE, YOU FAIL]

All viral loop businesses face quandaries as they spread, at times forced to invent whole new technologies and practices. But not every company is successful. Before MySpace and Facebook there was Friendster, founded

---

* In 2004, Jerome Heckencamp, who worked at Los Alamos after graduating from the University of Wisconsin-Madison, pleaded guilty to two counts of gaining unauthorized access and recklessly damaging eBay's computer systems, in violation of 18 USC Section 1030(a)(5)(B). He also admitted to penetrating computer systems at Qualcomm, Lycos, and others. The following year he was sentenced to eight months in prison and required to pay restitution of $268,291.

in 2002 by a self-proclaimed "Jewish tech-geek poster boy" in his early thirties named Jonathan Abrams, who started the site because his girlfriend had "dumped" him and he wanted to "get laid." Trolling dating sites felt creepy, and he wondered if there was a way to bring "real-life context" to cybercourting. His solution was to lift the user profile page idea from Match.com and add links to friends' profiles, which he believed would encourage people to be as authentic online as they were off. Abrams coded the entire site himself in his apartment, plopped on his queen-size Posturepedic mattress while watching TV. The result was a site that would allow people to conceptualize their social relationships in a completely new way.

After raising $400,000 in start-up capital from a dozen investors, Abrams launched the site in March 2003 by simply inviting twenty friends, who invited others, and so on, until the site took on a life of its own. Every time a profile page displayed, the user's connection to other users was mapped out within four degrees of separation. In some cases this skein of connections could result in a web of hundreds of thousands of people. "The effect was to give users a vivid sense of how they fit into their social groups as well as into the larger world," wrote Max Chafkin in *Inc.* "Abrams, it seemed, had created a piece of software that could tell us who we were."

Within three months Friendster had logged 532,000 visitors, according to Alexa, the rating service. The next month the number rose to 675,000 and Abrams raised $1 million in venture capital. By August, there were 962,000 visitors. Seven months after launch Friendster was one of the top 100 most popular English-language websites and college kids from around the globe were flocking to it. But this frenzied growth led to serious technical snafus. Mapping users' social connections within four degrees of separation was doable when there were ten members, or a hundred, or a thousand, or even a million. But Abrams had in essence created two viral loops and his servers simply couldn't keep pace. The first was the growing number of members, which was growing virally and the second was the four degrees of connections, which were increasing even faster. "Because that feature is inherently not scalable, the scale gets exponentially worse as the number of users grows," says Matt Cohler, a former Facebook executive who is a general partner at Benchmark Capital.

Abrams's servers were required to perform trillions of calculations every time a user clicked, which required a terabyte of pricey RAM. As a result the site became buggy, with pages taking minutes to load at peak times. Frustrated users would email the company to complain but never received a response because Friendster had only a few overworked employees. Others left Friendster because they objected to policies Abrams had instituted governing acceptable language and the kinds of photos that could be posted. In August 2003, Abrams's Friendster profile listed interests including wine, parties, friends, and painting. By late September his profile reported that he was interested in only one thing: sleep. As Friendster sank and rivals like MySpace rose, his investors ousted him. Today Friendster barely cracks the top 15 in social networks in the United States, although it is popular in Asia, especially Indonesia, Malaysia, the Philippines, and Singapore. "All they had to do was keep the damned servers up and running" and Friendster would have been unstoppable, Cohler says. "But there was this one feature they refused to take down," the one that calculated distant connections, which showed how you were socially tied to everybody else. "If they had just made that one change, [Facebook] might not be here today."

A more modernday example of a company that has had major hiccups along the way is Twitter, which at its core confronts a similar computation challenge to the one that brought Friendster to its knees. While a heavily trafficked site like Yahoo burns bandwidth by serving up millions of webpages and images, it faces a known and predictable scaling equation. Social networks engage in more complex issues of interactivity, but they need only to route messages to one user at a time, or at most to a defined group. But Twitter text messages simultaneously go out to hundreds of "followers" (Twitterese for contacts), while each of these hundreds of users are also transmitting messages to hundreds of others. This means that every additional Twitter user and every new connection yields an exponentially greater computational requirement. During peak times—during one of Steve Jobs's keynote presentations at MacWorld, for example—Twitter suffered embarrassing outages. Some weeks it seemed Twitter was down as often as it was up. While the patience and loyalty of its legions of users has been sorely tested, its viral growth has continued unabated.

Twitter code, built in Ruby on Rails, an out-of-the-box software frame-work, offered myriad benefits. It was relatively easy to create a workable prototype—in 140 characters or less you are asked to respond to the question: What are you doing?—and it's straightforward to add additional applications. But it wasn't designed for a mass audience. "We were taken by surprise by the scaling issue," admits Biz Stone, one of Twitter's founders. He points out that Twitter was first a project, a cool idea that blossomed into a real company, which counted more than 6 million users by April 2009.

Union Square Ventures partner Fred Wilson, who invested in Twitter, believes the microblogging outfit was simply too slow in coming to grips with the severity of the scaling issues. "They're playing catch-up now and it's been unnecessarily difficult for them," he says. "But Twitter is what it is because of the people who created Twitter. You could have taken a bunch of people who were the best scaling engineers and put them in a room and they wouldn't have created Twitter. In the best situation, the people who had created Twitter would have figured out the scaling issues and found some great scaling engineers and recruited them onto the team." But top engineers are in short supply and if you were responsible for helping Google scale to 1 zillion queries per second, you're not going to work for Twitter. You'll stay at Google or build your own company. Nevertheless Twitter has gradually improved its dependability. The company experienced 84 percent of its downtime in the first half of 2008, while there were no major outages in the second half.

Some companies limit growth so their systems can handle the exponential rates that come with viral growth. Paul Buchheit, the brains behind Gmail, purposely controlled the rate of adoption by instituting an invitation-only sign-up procedure. Because Gmail offered 1,000 megabytes of storage while others gave users only 4 megabytes, Buchheit chose to drag down Gmail's growth rate so Google could keep the application operational without risking sluggish download times, outages, data loss, or any other performance problem that often emerges with rapid scaling. After all, being able to hit the brake in a speeding car is just as important as putting your foot on the accelerator.

Even then, it's rarely a smooth ride. Even with controlled growth, Gmail coughed up hairballs as it grew. So did Facebook. YouTube has gone dark and so has Ning—and all of them were started by people with programming backgrounds.

[TECH SAVIOR]

As for eBay, which in 1999 was on the verge of losing everything because it couldn't keep the site up, it would need to find someone with the engineering chops to do something that had never been done before: scale a company's infrastructure faster than Moore's law. For almost fifty years Moore's law, named for Gordon Moore of Intel, accurately described the long-term trajectory of computer hardware: the number of transistors on a chip will double about every two years. What that means in real life is that the speed and performance of microchips—the brains of computer hardware—doubles over that same time period while shrinking in size by half. In the case of eBay its existing hardware was no match for its fast-growing needs. It already ran on the largest mainframe Sun Microsystems had to offer and its database servers were approaching their limits of physical growth.

Meanwhile, eBay's legions of users were turning on the company and migrating to other auction sites and the market punished eBay stock. When engineers finally got the site up after twenty-two hours of darkness, eBay shares, which were $180 when the last auction went through, had fallen almost $50 a share to $136 by the time the site came back, slicing $5 billion in market capitalization. Referring to the fiasco as eBay's "near-death experience," CEO Whitman ignored calls for her discharge and ordered her four hundred employees to phone users to apologize for the inconvenience. "It humbled the company," Whitman told *USA Today*. "We were on a rocket ship. . . . It really stopped any idea of 'Gee, aren't we special,' which was really good culturally."

The company had been so focused on growth and user experience that it had neglected its infrastructure. Not only was it not sturdy enough to handle its needs, there were no redundancies—no data backups—built into the network. Now that the site was limping along with scattered brown-outs and glitches, a sleep-deprived Whitman, determined to prevent anything like this from ever happening again, sought a new chief technology officer. A headhunter remarked that there were perhaps ten people in the world who could get eBay out of this mess, but she had just the man: the aptly named Maynard Webb, chief information officer at Gateway, the PC maker.

In some ways the system that Webb oversaw at Gateway was even more complex than eBay. It had to be able to configure a PC made up of two thousand separate components, and then produce and ship twenty-five thousand orders a day, an infrastructure that strung together manu-facturing systems, shop-floor automation, and supply-chain management. Designing and maintaining a website and back end to handle a product that each customer could configure to taste was a major engineering feat. It had to be ready to run at all times and track an order through the system. But there were only so many stages in the shipping process and Gateway could create automatic processes to handle them and give the appearance they were working in real time when they really weren't. While eBay's transactions might have been simpler than Gateway's, it had a far greater volume of interactions that came in bursts. The site had to run in real time with no margin for error. With an auction, a user wanted to know every second when somebody had outbid her. Those had to be true real-time interactions, multiplied by hundreds of millions of users. Adding to the infrastructure's burden was the fact that eBay was doubling in size every six months, on pace to negotiate more daily transactions than NASDAQ.

Whitman wooed Webb with the promise that he could have any and all resources at his disposal to right eBay's ship. She was also willing to pay him more than she was earning: a salary of $450,000 (more than double hers) plus a signing bonus of $108,000, an extra $300,000 if all went well and options to buy half a million shares of eBay stock. While he was house-hunting with his wife three weeks before his start date, the site went down again. Webb left his wife to do the negotiating and jumped into the fray. He ducked an encampment of reporters who were camped outside eBay's San Jose headquarters to reach the engineers who were furiously searching for a diagnosis. Thirteen hours later, Webb and his engineers learned what was ailing them: a software glitch.

A sound infrastructure for a growing e-commerce company should be flexible, scalable, and reliable. EBay's was none of these. The network was a mishmash of Solaris and Microsoft NT servers with numerous single points of failure. If a component burned out, the entire network could blow with it; if the function was tied to the central database, the outage would last for hours. Webb's first move was to identify all single points of failure—what were the bottlenecks and how could he ease them? "Once you're in the soup it's hard to climb out," Webb says. "If you fall behind the scale curve it's very hard to get ahead with all that volume coming in."

Webb quickly moved to manage downtime by having his engineers construct a "warm backup"—a redundant system to take over in the event the main system went down—for each of two hundred NT servers that accepted bids and processed new members and the Sun server database that held the 3 million items listed for auction. Even if eBay experienced a systems crash, it would only be down a few hours, not days. These redundancy systems meant that if the site went down, all he would have to do was flick a switch to get back online while he figured what was ailing them. The number-one rule for any online business was to keep the lights on.

Then he wanted to know how much wiggle room there was in the network. "What are the upper limits that the system can handle?" he asked. "When do we run out of capacity?" While his team worked on the answer, Webb identified the major bottlenecks and architectural blunders and constructed systems to handle them. His crew returned with bad news. The hardware was running at 95 percent of capacity, which meant eBay had about three weeks of life. Because Sun wasn't scheduled to release a new upgrade to the server for eighteen months and eBay would soon enter the Christmas season, its busiest time of the year, Webb threw himself into scaling the architecture to remove the looming thresholds. He divided eBay's gargantuan, nearly maxed-out database into more manageable pieces, relocating functions like accounting, customer feedback, and various product categories to separate machines. This distribution resulted in more room for growth and took away the risk of a single server dragging down the entire system.

At times he found himself working at cross purposes, with the marketing department pushing growth strategies while Webb was trying to slow things down. "The marketing guys would want to do free listing days," Webb recalls, "and sellers would stay up all night posting items for sale. It would drive the volume up a huge amount—a year's worth of volume in one night. It was like 'something's gonna blow!'"

It took time, money, and labor power to install new equipment and port over the code. In his first six months on the job Webb spent $18 million on top of the millions eBay was already budgeting for computer infrastructure. Reflecting this diversion of funds, the percentage of profit eBay accrued from listing fees fell 10 percent from earlier in the year. This led to complaints from the marketing department, which Webb shrugged off. "Demand generation is always easier than demand fulfillment," he told them. By the end of the year most eBay users who had bailed after the blackout returned as the site became more reliable. Soon after, the company was measuring outages in mere seconds per month, as traffic and transactions continued to mushroom. And when eBay's techies didn't catch a glitch, its customers often would, alerting staff within seconds if something went awry. From then on, eBay touted a 99 percent uptime.

It also continued to grow at a fierce rate. In 2001 it counted 42.4 million registered users, 95 million in 2003, and 181 million in 2005. With huge cash reserves it was able to buy two other viral loop companies: PayPal for $1.5 billion in 2002 and Skype for $2.6 billion three years later. Between the three companies, eBay counted half a billion registered users by 2006. Eventually, like all viral loop companies, however, eBay hit a point of ultimate saturation. By March 2008 its revenues and profit were growing in the midteens, compared to the 30 percent growth it had grown accustomed to over the years.

Still it remains a formidable force with a market cap of $40 billion, monthly traffic in excess of 100 million users, and 14 percent of global e-commerce revenue. It's also a primary source of income for some 1.3 million people who are part of an entire economy that sprang up around Omidyar's perfect market experiment.

Perhaps if there's one phrase that sums up eBay, it might be: "Going . . . going . . . going . . . still here!"

PayPal:
The First Stackable Network

Viral Synergy, Greedy Inducements, Scalable Fraud,
and Battle of the Network All Stars

One way to look at the history of the Web is to view it through the prism of viral synergy. The precipitating event was the release of the Mosaic and Netscape browsers, which encouraged the creation of sites. More sites, more reason to venture online, which yielded more sites. But this collection of seemingly disparate sites weren't, when taken together, a single network. Nor was Hotmail, ICQ, or Napster, tools built atop the Internet's viral plain. That had to wait for eBay, which was the first true viral network to spawn its own ecosystem, the millions of sellers who set up shop there. They in turn generated an entire economy: demand for shipping and delivery services, boxes, tape, and a transactions medium, which Pierre Omidyar's brainchild had yet to fill—until PayPal came along.

It was the summer of 1998 and Max Levchin, a twenty-four-year-old Ukrainian-born computer scientist from Chicago, had journeyed halfway across the country to crash on the floor of a friend's place, wondering what to do with the rest of his life. With nothing but time on his hands, he figured he might as well check out a lecture at Stanford on political freedom and the globalization of the world economy. The guest lecturer, Peter Thiel, was a staunch libertarian who was by all accounts a genius. Levchin had always been attracted to people who might be as smart as he, and he had a personal connection to the topic. A Jew from Kiev, he had grown up in the Soviet Union where everybody was equal—except Jews, Christians, gypsies, homosexuals, and anybody who didn't toe the Communist line. While almost everyone else in the crumbling Soviet empire lived second-class lives, the Levchins were relegated to a third-class existence, subject to harassment and denied opportunities, limited in where they could live, work, and attend school.

Fleeing the crumbling Soviet empire most likely saved their lives. When Levchin was eleven, his mother, a physicist who worked as a government research assistant, overheard news of a leak at the Chernobyl nuclear reactor, which was on the verge of a meltdown. Acid rain misted down as the family quietly vacated their home and rushed to the train station in Kiev. After they were onboard, news of the disaster became public, and hours later, as they chugged into Crimea, Soviet guards ordered them to turn back, fearful of contamination. Following an animated discussion, Levchin's mother convinced them to check for radiation. All were clean, except Max, whose right foot sent the Geiger counter into spasms. The guard said the boy's bone marrow was contaminated; his leg might have to be amputated. His mother told Max to take off his shoe and he was tested again. This time he passed and they were let through, *sans* shoe. The culprit was a radioactive rose thorn that had lodged in his sole as they escaped Kiev.

The family arrived in Chicago with $700 in life savings and moved in with a distant relative. Levchin taught himself English by studying reruns of *Diff'rent Strokes* on a busted black-and-white TV he fixed after rescuing it from the trash. His parents somehow afforded a used PC and he continued the coding and cryptography he had pursued as a preteen. After receiving his high school diploma Levchin enrolled at the University of Illinois at Champaign-Urbana. There, he heard the stories about its most famous alum—Marc Andreessen, whose company, Netscape, was taking on the world—and dreamed of following in his footsteps. Levchin earned a reputation as a brilliant and quirky engineer, a guy who never seemed to sleep, coding day and night yet still finding time to launch three start-up companies, including NetMeridian, an automated marketing-tools firm he sold to Microsoft for $100,000 just prior to graduation. While waiting for the deal to close, Levchin, practically broke, high-tailed it to Silicon Valley to figure out the rest of his life. And on a hot summer's eve with the air static and unflinching, he met Peter Thiel, who found himself back at Stanford lecturing to the six people willing to brave the weather.

Born in Germany and raised in California, Thiel, who was in his thirties, was once ranked among the nation's top chess players under

twenty-one. He was so hypercompetitive that after a rare loss he had an-
grily swept the pieces off the board. Thiel stopped playing competitively
because he feared chess had become an "alternate reality in which one
loses sight of the real world." To get to the next level, he calculated, would
have prevented him from attaining success in other aspects of life. Ever
suspicious of crowds and groupthink, he gravitated toward libertarianism
at a young age even though his parents weren't overtly political. As a student at San Mateo High School he read two books that profoundly shaped
his worldview: Aleksandr Solzhenitsyn's *Gulag Archipelago*, which pulled
back the Iron Curtain to expose the brutal, dehumanizing Soviet state,
and J. R. R. Tolkien's *Lord of the Rings*, a parable on the perfidy of power.

At Stanford he majored in philosophy and founded the *Stanford Review*, a libertarian-leaning newspaper that he transformed into a campus
institution that attracted national attention. Thiel also displayed enviable
talents in math and finance: he could calculate square roots to the decimal
point in his head. He graduated from Stanford Law School in 1992 and,
after a spell with Sullivan & Cromwell, moved to CS First Boston to trade
derivatives (he was hired after getting every question right on a math test).
Somehow he found time to coauthor *The Diversity Myth*, a book attacking
the liberalization of Stanford's curriculum. It made Thiel a darling of the
conservative movement, and when he returned to California to start his
own hedge fund, he did it with right-wing backing.

The lecture that Thiel offered that day centered on the dangers of
concentrated governmental power. No one despises totalitarianism more
than someone who fled it, and Levchin was so moved that he worked up
the courage to introduce himself. The first thing he noticed about Thiel
was his blue-eyed intensity, a word that had often been used to describe
Levchin. After chatting a few minutes, Thiel suggested breakfast. They
met the following week at Hobee's, where Levchin pitched a couple of ideas
for start-ups, including one that revolved around cryptography. In college,
he had mastered the art of creating software for handhelds and the ability
to store heavily encrypted data without any loss of performance—a major
feat, since these early PDAs had severely limited power, memory, and
storage. Levchin proposed a company that would create a library of encryption schemes, which they could license. He figured it was inevitable

that everyone would have a Palm-like device and they could capitalize on this emerging technology. Sell the encryption libraries, let others create applications; collect a penny or two per copy and let the money roll in.

Thiel found the idea intriguing enough to continue the discussion over several weeks, and the two became fast friends, challenging each other for hours on end with brain-twisting puzzles, competing to see who could finish first. Eventually Thiel recommended that Levchin start the business and promised his hedge fund would invest a couple of hundred thousand dollars in seed money. But Levchin knew hardly anyone in the Bay area and couldn't find anyone to act as CEO. With no one to run the company, Levchin told Thiel that he might as well start coding and recruit a few programmers from Champaign.

"Maybe I could be your CEO," Thiel said.

"That's a really good idea," Levchin replied.

It was decided. Thiel would run the business and Levchin would act as chief technical officer.

[FALSE STARTS]

They named their fledgling enterprise Fieldlink. In the meantime Levchin's initial idea had been taking on decidedly different contours. After starting work on the crypto library, he learned there was no inherent demand for this level of security, hence no one would create applications. He then proposed that he code the software, package and sell it, but found no takers. Companies saw no compelling need for it. By now Levchin had built much of the underlying technology, which offered the capability to secure almost anything on a handheld device. What, though, could they protect that had value? Changing course again, they chose to address the consumer market and create a digital wallet to enable a user to stash private data like passwords and credit card numbers. But this, they realized, didn't offer a powerful enough value proposition.

That's when Thiel suggested the idea of storing money. This sent Levchin on a mission to create cryptographically secure IOU notes that could be beamed from user to user via the Palm's built-in infrared ports.

The basic premise was to turn that Silicon Valley staple, the PDA, into an electronic wallet to securely store and transfer money, and unlike cash, if you lost your PDA you wouldn't risk a dime. Thiel figured that by backing these IOUs, it would be possible to make money on the float—that is, the interest accruing between the time money was deposited and spent. The idea was similar to the way traveler's check companies profited, by skimming interest from customer accounts between the time checks were purchased and cashed. He suspected most users would keep some money in these Palm accounts instead of directing it immediately into checking accounts or to their credit cards to make it easier to pay people.

In the physical world, gaining access to cash had been getting increasingly easy over the years. By 1999 there were roughly 300,000 ATMs in the United States handling almost 1 billion transactions (compared to 40,000 ATMs in 1983 and fewer than 1,000 a decade earlier). Meanwhile the Web had been co-opted by e-commerce, with virtual stores of all stripes setting up shop, accepting Visa, MasterCard and American Express. The only way to settle a debt with a nonmerchant, however, was to snail-mail a check or money order, which ran counter to what the Internet was all about: instantaneous communication and convenience. That's where their mobile cash concept came in: it filled a void that technology had created but had not yet filled. They named their new venture Confinity, a combination of "confidence" and "infinity," reflecting the brand they aimed to foster.*

To Thiel, however, Confinity was far more than a business opportunity; it was an extension of his entire philosophy. Beginning in the seventeenth century certain enlightened thinkers had been gradually pulling the world away from humans' nature-bound existence toward a new virtual realm where people conquered nature. Value, Thiel believed, existed not merely in manufactured goods but also in imaginary concepts such as relationships between humans. That was, after all, what money was—an agreed-upon transactional medium between people. In a physical sense it had no value. Money was simply paper or digits in an electronic bank account. It made little sense to exchange molecules for digits.

For neocons like Thiel, the Internet was greeted as a promised land that

---

* Apparently Thiel and Levchin didn't realize that "confinity" is an actual (albeit obscure) word that means "community of limits." If they had, they might not have chosen it.

promoted freedom in human relations, business, and laws and was an escape from arbitrary national boundaries. It revealed a world of free trade and laissez-faire expansion, a hedge against corrupt governments. He believed the ability to circumvent currency controls and move funds anywhere in the world at any time equaled no less than liberation from government and multinational conglomerate tyranny. As Thiel and Levinch laid the foundation for Confinity, Neal Stephenson's cyberpunk novel *Cryptonomicon* was published, and in their fantasies they hoped that life would imitate art, that their concept could one day blossom into its own currency system, reminiscent of Stephenson's hero programmers who deploy encryption to set up an offshore data haven to foil governmental control.

Quaint by today's standards, Levchin's prototype quickly generated buzz in Silicon Valley with its legions of PDA-toting professionals. Imagine: three geeks sitting around a table, beaming one another IOUs for $10 to settle their lunch tabs. But to rely on one company—even one like Palm that had carved a respectable market share—would have doomed Confinity to failure. Silicon Valley might be Palm Central, but what about the rest of the country, which was slower to adopt new technologies? What if someone didn't own a Palm? Thiel and Levchin bandied about, then discarded, the idea of creating a platform to run across all mobile phones. For that Levchin would need a minimum of two years to develop it and cell phone makers would have to redesign their equipment to accommodate the beaming function, something the Palm already had. That's when Levchin remarked that a user wouldn't necessarily need a Palm. He could sync the software with email and the Web and use it that way, too. With or without a Palm, a user could transfer money.

[BEAMING MONEY]

They called the product PayPal and on the strength of this futuristic vision Thiel raised $4.5 million in first-round financing from Nokia Ventures and Deutsche Bank. As Levchin readied the product for development, Confinity scheduled a splashy press event for July 22, 1999, when Nokia's $3 million portion of the investment would be beamed to Thiel's Palm organizer. A week before the beaming at Buck's of Woodside, a diner popular with the venture capitalist set, the code wasn't finished and Levchin realized they weren't going to make it. Sure, he could go all Hollywood and fake it for the cameras. "Beep! Transaction complete." But if anyone found out, he swore he would commit seppuku. So Levchin did what he always did when his back was against the wall. Forgoing sleep, he and two other programmers coded five days straight. With crypto, precision is key; off the tiniest bit, nothing works. They crunched the last string of code around midnight, ten hours before the press conference was set to start, and began testing. They fixed some bugs, tried again, and fixed some more. Long after night dissolved into dawn, Levchin was satisfied the path the money followed was secure. But there were memory leaks, enough to crash the software at just the wrong time. Levchin tuned up a stack of PalmPilots to stand by in case he needed to make a switch, jumped in a car, and with minutes to spare arrived at Buck's, where Thiel waited anxiously.

Before a handful of journalists and TV cameras, Peter Buhl, a partner at Nokia Ventures, inputted $3 million in the amount box, tapped *Pay*, and pointed his Palm at Thiel, who sat nearby—not that any of the diners sipping coffee, their forks poised over scrambled eggs and toast, could see anything. Seconds later, the words *Would you like to accept the money?* popped up on Thiel's screen. He tapped *Yes*. "Of course, that's an understatement," Thiel said. "It should say, 'Yes, yes, yes!'"

A group of journalists staggered in five minutes late and asked Thiel to repeat the demonstration. Levchin told them the whole point of security is you can't replicate the transaction because the money has already been transferred. The whole point of a press conference, the journalists countered, is to accommodate the press. So Thiel pretended to receive the $3 million all over again but hid his screen from the camera since it warned against transmitting the same funds twice. Although it didn't make for good TV, Levchin viewed it as a personal triumph. Then things got hazy for the exhausted programmer. A reporter interviewing him left for the restroom and a waiter brought him breakfast. The next thing Levchin knew his head was resting on the table and he was staring sideways at his omelet. Everyone was gone. They had left him to sleep.

Over the next few months Confinity rented office space—the real estate market for office space was so tight that Levchin had to promise shares in the company to his Palo Alto landlord—and went on a hiring binge. Because Thiel's ultimate plan was to create a Web-based currency to undermine government tax structures, which would require taking on powerful interests like commercial banking, the cofounders sought people a lot like them: hypercompetitive, well-read, multilingual workaholics who had, above all, a proficiency in math and an aversion to authority. At first they hired from within their own "concentric circles," as Thiel described it. Thiel tapped his network at Stanford, including those who had worked at the *Stanford Review*, and Levchin reached out to friends at the University of Illinois. They valued talent over experience and would bring in someone to fill a role with which he had no experience. An accountant became a marketing chief. A former journalist ran customer service.

While Google was also known for pursuing Mensa-like minds, there was a distinct difference: Thiel and Levin didn't care a whit about a piece of paper. As Roelof Botha, PayPal's former chief financial officer, told *Fortune*: "Google wanted to hire Ph.D.s, and PayPal wanted to hire the people who got into Ph.D. programs and dropped out." Levchin defined a "great hire" as someone who was introverted, "just as geeky" as he was, willing to sleep under his desk, and didn't "get laid very often." Among those who were unwelcome were jocks, MBAs, and women. Levchin told a story about asking a potential hire what he did for fun. The guy said he liked playing hoops, and Levchin refused to hire him because everyone he knew in college who played basketball "was an idiot." Levchin's game of choice was Ping-Pong, which he used to gauge a candidate's competitive fire. When a female applicant for an engineering position played poorly, Levchin had to be coerced into hiring her. She quit six months later.

For his part the thirty-two-year-old Thiel ruled like one might expect a wonky numbers libertarian to rule. Informal even by Silicon Valley standards, Confinity resembled a college dorm. Almost everyone was in his twenties, wearing the uniform of youth—jeans and T-shirts—the expected detritus of pizza boxes and board games spilling over the floor and furniture. New staff found no desks or computers waiting for them. Sometimes they didn't even know what position they would be assigned. Not all of Thiel's hires were neocons. He appointed a close friend, Reid Hoffman, whom he had met in philosophy class at Stanford, to Confinity's board and, and Hoffman was as liberal as Thiel was conservative. "Take his position, you make a sophisticated negation of it and you get my position, and vice versa," Hoffman says.

Confinity prided itself on being a meritocracy. Underlings were expected to snark it out with superiors, the belief being that the strongest argument would win. Jeremy Stoppelman, who would climb the ranks to become the company's vice president of technology, recalled being a twenty-two-year-old engineer who flamed the entire executive staff in an email. Instead of being fired for insubordination, he "got a pat on the back." Meetings were discouraged. Instead, employees were expected to solve problems themselves. The exception was when Thiel called an all-hands open-book session where he would document the company's progress—revenue, burn rate, fraud, rate of sign-ups. When Thiel called on someone, he had better have data to support his point. People may lie, numbers don't.

[VIRAL SPREAD]

From the beginning Thiel was counting on PayPal to grow virally in the vein of Hotmail, ICQ, and Napster. He focused on viral distribution for both practical and philosophical reasons. First, he wasn't convinced that traditional advertising or business development would work, and he was well versed in the mathematical formulae that explain infectious growth. Then the key wouldn't be the number of people they started with; all that would matter was the rate it spread. Second, Thiel subscribed to a theory of human behavior known as "mimetic desire," propounded by French historian and philosopher René Girard, who believed that people were essentially sheep who, without much reflection, borrowed their desires from others. This theory has been applied to describe financial bubbles and panics, when investors blindly act as a flock and follow what others are doing even if it flies in the face of economic logic, and to war and violence, which arise when two individuals vie for the same possession, leading to antagonism and strife. Pretty soon the object of desire is forgotten and all you're left with is the antipathy.

With PayPal, Thiel was confident that customers would be sufficiently self-similar, and one of the predictable ways they would act would be to spread the technology to other people. Naturally this ran counter to Thiel's entire libertarian worldview, that the individual should reign supreme. In a sense he was about to capitalize on an aspect of human nature he wished to wipe away. And the money he would use came, in part, from his hedge fund, which was backed by conservatives whose values matched his own. Then again, no one was forcing people to act in a mass, predictable manner. Thiel, it seemed, could live with this apparent renunciation of his core beliefs if he could build a company to take over the world, which became PayPal's rallying cry. In fact, Luke Nosek, one of Levchin's first hires, had a counter on his PC monitor labeled World Domination Index to tally the ever-growing number of sign-ups.

The riddle that Thiel and his management team had to solve was how to ensure that people would spread the product. As originally conceived, PayPal was a person-to-person payment system. Quickly an idea took shape that a user should be able to send someone money even if the recipient didn't have an account. The easiest way to do it would be to set up one for him. Instead of two forms of ID, the user could simply use his email address as a unique identifier to claim the funds. Hoffman recalls that Nosek came up with the idea of a financial inducement to juice PayPal's virality. Each sign-up would receive a $10 deposit in his PayPal account just for registering and providing a credit card number, and for every new user he referred, he would get another $10 bounty. Although $20 a head may seem like a lot of money, Thiel and his management team calculated it was a modest amount to spend on customer acquisition for a company with no marketing costs. This was, after all, a time of Silicon Valley excess, when new companies bleeding red on their balance sheets spent millions on advertising, branding, and marketing, upwards of several hundred dollars per person for customer acquisition.

Stories of waste were legendary. Seventeen dot-coms forked over $2 million each for a thirty-second spot in Super Bowl XXXIV in January 2000. CMGI, a dot-com investment firm, contracted to pay $7.5 million to own exclusive naming rights to the New England Patriots home stadium for fifteen years. *The Industry Standard*, a magazine that covered the tech business, burned through $200 million in just a few years. Dot-coms of all sorts spent lavishly on employee perks—the Web business that took its entire workforce to California's wine country for the weekend, the online ad agency that hired Tito Puente to play its Christmas party, CyberNet's collection of fine wine, valued at $108,000. Clearly, none of these wasteful branding schemes generated any measurable return on investment. By contrast, if Confinity spent $2 million on inducements, it could count on two hundred thousand registrants and be on its way to unleashing a net-work effect.

Confinity launched PayPal for the Palm in November 1999, with its twenty-four employees seeding it by sending email to friends and family with the subject box "PayPal User Beamed You Money" and the message holding a Hotmail-inspired link to the PayPal website. Almost as an af-terthought Levchin slapped a website demo online so users could down-load the software and, if they chose, do everything there they could do on the Palm. He put almost no effort in the look and feel of the site, which was there to promote the Palm application. Much to his surprise people began using the website for transactions. It grew on the order of 5 to 7 percent a day, while the Palm application drew merely three hundred new users daily. Eventually Confinity would discontinue the Palm applica-tions, the concept on which their original idea rested, to concentrate solely on the Web. After parsing the data, Thiel and everyone else was surprised to learn that the lion's share of users weren't the young, affluent, tech-savvy early adopters they had been targeting. They were middle Ameri-can auctiongoers on eBay, the sort who trafficked in tchotchkes like Beanie Babies, Pez dispensers, and vintage Tupperware.

Hoffman recalls the general response as, "What the hell? This isn't designed for eBay."

[STACKING PAYPAL OVER EBAY]

Actually it made perfect sense: eBay sellers needed a better way to com-plete transactions online. Most couldn't process credit cards and waiting for a money order or personal check in the mail took time, not to men-tion the inconvenience of cashing a money order at a bank or waiting for an out-of-state check to clear. The process for becoming a credit card mer-chant took several weeks and required several fees—the application fee,

the 1 to 4 percent fee that covered every transaction, the monthly premium that could run hundreds of dollars for maintaining a merchant
account, the additional 20 to 30 cents per transaction the merchant bank
would slice off the top. Then there was the threat of fraud, with the merchant often held culpable for processing a stolen card. Most eBay sellers
believed credit cards weren't worth the hassle or expense. But PayPal was
free and didn't lay responsibility for fraud on its users.

As eBay sellers embraced it, the bulletin boards lit up with discussions.
Can it be trusted? What if the company goes out of business? Does it really pay $10 for each referral? David Sacks, a Confinity vice president, re-
ceived an email query from an eBay seller requesting permission to display
PayPal's logo. On his auction he had embedded an advertisement for the
payment service, which he linked to PayPal's home page. Good for him,
since he collected a fee for every buyer he referred, and good for PayPal—a
win-win all around. But he wasn't the only one on eBay marketing PayPal.
Several thousand auctioneers had embraced it, adding clickable links to
the home page or writing detailed descriptions of the service so buyers
could sign up. By the end of December, less than two months after the
initial email seeding, Confinity tallied twelve thousand PayPal accounts.
With 10 million registered users on eBay and more than tripling each year,
the virtual mega–garage sale site offered almost limitless possibilities.

It was only logical that Confinity drop everything to concentrate on
auctions. "We would build PayPal's payments network on top of eBay's
marketplace," declared Eric M. Jackson, a Confinity marketing executive
and author of *The PayPal Wars: Battles with eBay, the Media, the Mafia, and
the Rest of Planet Earth*. This would be the first time a viral network
would be stacked atop another viral network, and it offered a significant
advantage to going it alone. Everything hinged on PayPal's viral adoption,
but users were spread all over the world. A clump of customers formed
here, another there, a third another place, but they existed as separate sat-
ellites lacking synergy. On the other hand eBay offered a single destination, with users clustered in one space and, on average, processing multiple
transactions with different buyers each day.

In the way that there was little sense in selling on eBay if there were no
buyers (and, conversely, little incentive to shop if there was nothing to

buy), sellers had dual reasons to promote PayPal. It helped streamline business over the Internet and the seller profited from it, multiplying the effect of Paypal's $10 referral fee. In essence, PayPal became a product to hawk on eBay just like any other. To help market it, engineers created a clickable HTML logo that eBay sellers could insert into their auctions, thus closing the viral loop. Not only were sellers pushing PayPal; buyers would, too. "As sellers used their listings to train buyers to look for PayPal, buyers would in turn learn to ask sellers who weren't using PayPal if they could pay with our service," Jackson wrote. "PayPal customers in eBay's community would recruit other users for us—it was viral growth in its most basic form." PayPal could then piggyback on the auction portal as it continued on its merry way to hundreds of millions of users, one viral network superimposed over another.

It didn't take a PhD in mathematics to see the possibilities. A month after doubling down on eBay, PayPal counted the number of auction logos it had on the site and calculated it was accepted on 6 percent of all listings on eBay, up from 1 percent the previous month. At the same time PayPal's user growth began to mirror the classic hockey-stick curve indicating exponential growth. On February 3, 2000, it tallied one hundred thousand registered users, and by mid-April, 1 million. But PayPal wasn't alone in chasing after online gold. Competitors like Dotbank, which launched with venture capital around the same time, touted similar services and a snazzier-looking website, while X.com sought to be a one-stop-shop for financial services.

A third, PayMe, was led by the CEO of a firm that had funded Confinity; this looked to Thiel like an investor partner had used his due diligence to back a rival. Thiel demanded he either sell back his PayPal stake or pull the plug on PayMe, which he rejected in favor of remaining a much despised shareholder. They all duked it out over who could sign up the most users, with Dotbank matching PayPal's referral fee while X.com broke the bank by gifting $20 per new user, and kept tabs on one another, often copying services and strategies. Finally, PayPal raced headlong into auctions and only X.com followed.

As they both grew, the "burn rate"—negative cash flow—reached epic proportions, with every new user forcing them deeper into debt. Thiel believed the one to win would be the first to file for an IPO. He calculated that X.com with its name brand management team had a slightly better chance than Confinity. X.com's CEO was Elon Musk, a young entrepreneur born and raised in South Africa who was fresh off having sold a company to AltaVista for more than $300 million.

[MERGING, BUT NOT OF THE MINDS]

The two companies merged in March 2000, with Bill Harris, a former CEO of Intuit, leading the combined company and Musk, the largest single shareholder, becoming chairman. Thiel was the chief financial officer and went off to the capital markets to raise more money. They agreed that Confinity would drop its name and become PayPal. It would follow its present course on eBay while also being used to sell its users on X.com's premium financial services, which on the surface seemed a nice synergy. To stop the hemorrhaging, X.com ended its $20 referral fee and PayPal sliced its fee in half to $5. The effect on X.com was immediate: its growth stalled, while PayPal continued growing at a frantic pace with barely a ripple.

But, as often happens in mergers, the two companies clashed, with X.com's button-down culture running headlong into PayPal's freewheeling environment. Perhaps telling, it took two full months before email from PayPal could be delivered to X.com users—and they were a technology company. The three-headed hydra of Harris, Musk, and Thiel couldn't agree on strategy. Harris, who came of age in the old economy, proposed charging users to send money, since PayPal's original idea of living off the float wasn't working; users spent money as fast as it came into their accounts. Thiel, however, vehemently opposed this because not only would it stall the company's viral growth, it could drive them out of business. Their disagreements escalated when Thiel learned that Harris had donated $25,000 of company money to the Democratic Party. After a heated exchange, Harris accused Thiel of insubordination and Thiel, who had just raised $100 million in the financial markets, quit in disgust. The real tension, however, arose between the two engineering staffs. Musk wanted to transition to Microsoft NT servers to relaunch the combined site, while Levchin was adamant about sticking with Unix.

Despite its brisk pace of user acquisition (half a million new accounts a month and climbing), the combined company continued to bleed red, unable to fix on any one course. Its infrastructure was overtaxed, the website becoming less reliable under the swarm of new users, and customer service was unable to handle the hurricane of calls that came into the company's switchboard. It got so bad that employees communicated by cell phone, since they couldn't get an outside line anymore. Six days after Thiel's resignation, Musk, responding to concerns expressed by the rank and file, called an emergency board meeting to replace Harris as CEO. Musk was named the new CEO and Thiel returned as chairman, with the board commanding the new management team to solve its cash flow problems. Its margins were negative 3.5 percent because it paid $2.50 for every credit card transaction plus another $1.04 to fraud on every $100 in payments. At this $10 million a month burn rate, the $100 million Thiel raised wouldn't last long.

Meanwhile Levchin was infuriated by Musk's order to transition to Microsoft servers and throw all of his engineering resources into a revamped website while fraud threatened to run them out of business. With Thiel out of the picture, he had resigned himself to the inevitability of the platform change away from Unix. Levchin thought about quitting and bided his time by creating a program to compare Unix to Windows that showed that Microsoft had 1 percent of the scalability of Unix. Then he became interested in looking into the fraud problem, and what he discovered frightened him. While the number of transactions was increasing at a fierce rate, fraud was going up even faster. It was only about 1 percent of company revenue, but when Levchin charted out its growth, he could see that, left unchecked, it was on its way to 5 percent, then 10 percent. By midsummer PayPal was losing $10 million a month to fraudsters, many of them backed by the Russian mob. When he emailed Musk with his findings, telling him the migration to Microsoft and site redesign would have to wait until they did something about fraud, the CEO brushed it aside.

But the final straw was when Musk took steps to phase out the PayPal brand in favor of X.com, a domain name that, despite costing him $1 million, company surveys showed the public had little appetite for, since it was reminiscent of the porn industry. Just before leaving for the Sydney

Olympics, Musk ordered the PayPal name expunged from the website. Levchin gathered his former executive team together and led a PayPal revolt. They took up a petition to demand that the board remove Musk or they would quit. The coup was successful, with the board removing Musk as CEO while he was on a flight to Australia—"That's the problem with vacations," he would later remark—and appointing Thiel as interim CEO, a title he would end up keeping.

Musk, who would later go on to found Tesla Motors, a builder of electric cars, and Space X, which seeks to colonize space, was understandably bitter, blaming his decision to migrate the company's infrastructure over from Unix to Microsoft for the shabby treatment, as well as simply having a different point of view. He told *Fortune*, "Peter, Max, and I are not directly aligned philosophically. Peter's philosophy is pretty odd. It's not normal. He's a contrarian from an investing standpoint and thinks a lot about the singularity. I'm much less excited about that. I'm pro-human."

[FRAUD FIGHTER]

Thiel's first step after wresting control of PayPal was to turn Levchin loose on the fraud problem. The more the company scaled—the more accounts were opened and the more money that coursed through its network—the more bogus charges scaled along with it. In the middle of 2000 one criminal ring stole, over a four-month period, $5.7 million by creating a robotic script to automatically open hundreds of thousands of PayPal accounts at a time. With filched credit cards the ring could send payments through seemingly endless layers of fraudulent accounts until transferring the balance out at the end. Instead of receiving thousands of Beanie Babies or used books and compact disks, the criminals siphoned millions in cold hard cash. Somebody had to pay for it. When a credit card user contests a charge, the merchant is the one left holding the bag, which in this case was PayPal. Around the same time MasterCard added to PayPal's woes by fining the company $313,600 for excessive charge-backs. At fraud's peak, PayPal was losing an average of $10 million a month.

Working with PayPal engineer David Gausebeck, Levchin's first step was to address fake accounts. Whatever system they created would have to complicate the registration process just enough to hamstring automated methods of creating accounts while not driving away legitimate users and disrupting PayPal's viral growth. He realized the key lay in the difference between a machine and a human. In 1950, Alan Turing of the Computing Laboratory in Manchester University created a blind test to demonstrate whether a machine could exhibit human-like intelligence. A man would sit at a keyboard and, without being able to see or hear whom he was communicating with, type out a conversation. If after a time he was convinced he was communicating with a human only to learn that it was a computer, the machine would be deemed to exhibit intelligence. Levchin realized he needed to design and implement a "reverse Turing test."

The solution was ingeniously simple. Levchin simply added a slight wrinkle to the sign-up process. A would-be registrant was instructed to retype into a separate box a random series of hazy letters that sat atop a yellow background etched with slender black lines in a grid—something a person could easily manage but a machine couldn't because it wouldn't be able to decipher the symbols through the slight distortion. Just for fun, Levchin inserted an "Easter egg," a joke or secret message that programmers sometimes leave behind, which he intended for one of his arch fraud nemeses, a Russian who had set up thousands of accounts under the name Gregory Stivinson. Levchin called his code "GSWeb" and when anyone tried to screw with the system, it would taunt back by spelling out *Nice try*. Shortly after instituting the Gausebeck-Levchin test the Russian cybercriminal who inspired it sent Levchin an angry email, cursing the Ukranian-born programmer for taking away his livelihood. Levchin replied in kind: "I have a great job for you, which involves wearing an orange-colored jumpsuit." Shortly after, Levchin's reverse Turing test became a staple in online commerce.

But Levchin was only half done. Now that he had found a way to prevent crime rings from faking accounts on a large scale he needed to stop criminals who were already inside or able to break into PayPal's system. This he accomplished by crunching an algorithm that would drive a software program he named Igor, after another Russian nemesis, to automatically flag suspicious activity and freeze the accounts. Levchin accomplished this by visually mapping out legitimate and illegitimate financial transfers and looking for disparate properties. A human investigator would then review the transactions, contact the registrant, and decide whether to un-freeze the funds. "If you reduce [fraud] down to essentially a picture, you can combine the aggregate suspiciousness into a single image," Levchin says. "Symmetry turns out to be a fantastic predictor of whether some-thing is fraud or not, and you can basically reduce investigation time from several days per scam to several seconds."

Of all the illicit transactions PayPal registered, 75 percent arose from bogus credit cards while the remainder was merchant fraud. After Levchin unleashed Igor, credit card fraud dropped to less than 1 percent.

[EBAY STRIKES BACK]

Fraud was but one problem plaguing PayPal. It also had to deal with a slew of new competitors, with names like PayPlace and gMoney, eMoney-Mail and Yahoo PayDirect, all vying for a slice of the online transactions market. PayPal's most direct threat, however, came from eBay, which viewed it as a parasite sucking money out of its network. Meg Whitman had long wanted to close the loop on transactions and profit from each one. In 1998 eBay purchased Billpoint, a credit-card processing business, which it promptly shut down so it could be rebuilt to handle the kind of volume millions of auctions would bring. As a public company, eBay had to find adequate strategies to manage the kind of fraud that would likely ensue before it dared to release a product. Then came the severe outages that forced the company to focus exclusively on its infrastructure until it became robust enough to sustain its stratospheric growth. Meanwhile PayPal continued to grow. By April 2000 approximately 25 percent of all eBay listings involved PayPal, double the level in March.

Since going public, eBay had moved far from the people-are-basically-good, hippy-dippy ethos with which its founder, Pierre Omidyar, had started. Now it was a cold and calculating corporation with merely the patina of down-home folksiness. EBay's first shot over the bow involved the auction logos promoting PayPal. The new regulation, which eBay claimed was intended to limit distracting third-party ads, mandated logos a quarter the size of PayPal's. Every auctioneer with a PayPal logo had to resize it to meet the new regulation.

EBay was laying the foundation for Billpoint, whose partners included Wells Fargo (handling the back end) and Visa. Billpoint was rolled out in April 2000, with eBay announcing it with large clickable banners that would take users through the registration process. EBay also ensured that its Billpoint logos would have far greater visibility by placing them at the top of auctions, while PayPal's would be relegated to the bottom. Then to further encourage sign-ups, eBay offered a free-listing day so any item a seller put up for auction would not cost the usual 25 to 50 cents. In one day Billpoint jumped from a 1 percent to a 10 percent share of auctions. "To put this gain into perspective, this free-listing day propelled Billpoint to a listing share level that it took PayPal a month to reach after we began focusing our efforts on eBay," *PayPal Wars* author Jackson wrote. "It was utterly demoralizing."

Then a strange thing happened. Billpoint's share slipped to 6 percent over the course of several days. Sellers, taking advantage of the free offer, had flooded their auctions with new items, which sat around longer than usual before being sold. In the interim PayPal continued its surge, gaining a 5 percent share of listings, from 25 to 30 percent. EBay tried again with another free-listing day, with similar results. Billpoint topped out at 14 percent before free-falling to 7 percent. A third free-listing day did little to improve Billpoint's share. Because PayPal continued to grow virally during this spate of free-listing days, which cost eBay millions in lost revenue, it actually increased its lead over Billpoint—from a spread of 20 percent in April to 26 percent in May.

EBay tried another tactic. It introduced Buy It Now, a feature that would enable a seller to fix a price rather than take bids and made Billpoint the default payment option. To use PayPal a seller would have to change the settings, an additional step that could drastically slow PayPal's adoption. This time it was eBay's own community that rose up against the new policy, generating a fair amount of negative press coverage. Soon PayPal was grabbing 70 percent of all transactions on eBay. Clearly it had achieved a point of nondisplacement, and nothing eBay did could knock it off its payment pedestal. Being viral, it grew simply because it had already grown. Simultaneously PayPal transitioned users away from credit cards, which cost PayPal a 2+ percent fee on every transaction, and to interest-bearing bank accounts, and began levying a 1.2 percent fee on sales, which was still far less than Visa charged. Along with a vast reduction in fraud, thanks to Levchin, PayPal's burn rate was slashed. Now, as the company grew, its financial situation improved along with it. While still deeply in debt, PayPal was on the road to profitability, while its competitors crashed and burned. The construction of a call center in Omaha, Nebraska, to handle customer service also alleviated much of the bad press the company had received.

["IF IT'S WAR YOU WANT, IT'S WAR YOU'LL GET"]

With the company on its way to 200 million PayPal accounts worldwide, Thiel and Hoffman agreed it was time to seek a buyer, set their minimum price at $600 million, and approached Google and Yahoo. Both claimed PayPal's reliance on eBay (70 percent of its business took place there) made it too big a risk. What if eBay blocked PayPal? Then a $600 million investment would be worthless. Of course, if eBay did that it would risk running afoul of antitrust statutes, but for Thiel and Hoffman it would be a bullet from the grave; by the time it could be litigated PayPal would be dead. Thiel and Hoffman agreed it was time to prepare for an IPO, even though the economy was mired in recession.

After the announcement became public, eBay approached PayPal about a deal. Hoffman, who had been tasked with dealing with the auction Brobdingnagian from the beginning, told negotiators from Goldman Sachs it appeared to him like the classic we-can-destroy-you-so-we-are-going-to-offer-you-a-pittance ploy. If eBay was serious about acquisition, he wanted a common framework for evaluation. When they met to exchange spreadsheets, PayPal valued itself at $650 million while eBay's estimate was $320 million. After poring over eBay's spreadsheet, he recognized that values they had agreed to beforehand were set too low. Hoffman theorized that eBay had told Goldman its maximum price was $400 million and Goldman fixed the variables to offer haggle room. After they again exchanged spreadsheets, Goldman inserted the original variables, and Hoffman accused the bankers of not bargaining in good faith. EBay responded with what Hoffman calls the "Microsoft lecture": "We are going to make this offer once and then crush you; you should really take this offer." Hoffman walked out.

Subsequently, Hoffman realized that as long as eBay was negotiating with PayPal, it couldn't bad-mouth it in the press during PayPal's quiet period. If investors contacted eBay and it said, "We think the company is built on cards, it's going to fall over, and we are planning on replacing it as fast as possible," PayPal's IPO would sputter. Hoffman gathered the board together to settle on a minimum sticker price they would accept in lieu of going public. They decided on $1 billion. When Hoffman relayed the news to eBay, negotiators countered with $750 million, then, as negotiations dragged on, $800, $825, and finally $850 million, while Hoffman stood pat at $1 billion. After several weeks eBay claimed $850 was its final offer. Hoffman replied: "I have a mandate to sell the company for a billion dollars. I'll be very clear again: You give me a billion dollars, you own the company. At $850 million I don't know if you own the company or not. I'll have to go back to the board to talk about it." Five days before PayPal had its IPO, Hoffman got back to eBay. "Sorry," he said. "The board decided they want to go out. All the investors have already been lined up, so we are going to go public."

There were eleven revisions to the prospectus and a delay caused by a patent infringement suit over its transactions technology (which settled for a "nonconsequential payment"). Finally PayPal's stock debuted at $13 on February 15, 2002, and after a wild ride closed the day at $20.09, giving the company a valuation of $800 million. As the NASDAQ cratered, PayPal's stock continued to edge up, and by the time PayPal and eBay rekindled negotiations, the market valued PayPal at $1.2 billion. By law, PayPal could not sell for less than that, since that would be cheating investors. EBay would have to offer a premium. After some hemming and hawing, eBay agreed to $1.5 billion.

All the documents were finished, the due diligence completed, and all Hoffman had to do was get PayPal's four other top executives—the two cofounders Peter Thiel and Max Levchin, Roelof Botha, and David Sacks—to sign off on the deal. Hoffman and Thiel voted to sell, but the other three balked. The company had heralded its successful IPO with its first quarter or profitability and the future looked bright.

Thiel told Hoffman he didn't want to sell unless everyone agreed.

"Look, I thought we wanted to do this," Hoffman replied. "I went and architected this whole thing, but now we will have a serious problem when we tell them no, because they are going to feel like the bride left at the altar." He reiterated his strong recommendation to sell, which the other three rejected. Fine, Hoffman said, but he was done dealing with eBay. He had burned up all his credibility. "Blame the whole thing on me," he told Thiel. "Tell them I exceeded my mandate."

Meg Whitman's response when she heard the news was, "If it's war you want, it's war you'll get." This was no idle threat. Soon after, Hoffman learned that eBay was in negotiations with Citibank, proposing they join forces to build a PayPal killer, which would be entirely free to eBay users for two years, then Citibank would receive an exclusive contract to build all sorts of other services. The way Whitman was feeling, he wouldn't be surprised if eBay banned PayPal and dared it to sue after launching the new service.

Long ago Hoffman had received the title "Mr. Fix-It," but when the four other executives showed up at his office he only had one solution. One of them—and it couldn't be Hoffman or Thiel—should contact Jeff Jordan, eBay's head of North American operations, who had been the one most vocal about buying PayPal. They dispatched David Sacks, Thiel's coauthor of *The Diversity Myth*, who told Jordan that PayPal would agree to the deal the two companies struck. A few days later they struck a deal. Then, while the companies conducted the required due diligence, Thiel and Hoffman flew to Hawaii to unwind, jet-skiing, paragliding, and touring the islands.

The day that eBay took over, Thiel, Levchin, and Hoffman, who collectively took in more than $100 million, walked away from the viral company they had started just a few years earlier. But PayPal was simply the beginning for these former employees, and the lessons they learned at PayPal would spread virally to other viral concerns. Thiel founded his own hedge fund, Clarium Capital Management LLC, invested $750,000 in Facebook, and joined the board. Levchin created Slide, a widget maker that counts hundreds of millions of installs of its photo slideshow and other applications across social networks. Hoffman is the CEO of LinkedIn, a networking tool for business that counts almost 40 million members and, since it has multiple revenue streams, boasts that it is profitable. Roelof Botha, PayPal's CFO, moved over to the venture capital side and became a partner at Sequoia Capital. One of his first investments was in YouTube, which was started by former PayPal alums Chad Hurley and Steve Chen.

As for eBay, it appears to have gotten a good deal for its $1.5 billion. Revenue for PayPal in 2008 was $2.4 billion, which eBay predicts will double by 2011. Eventually, PayPal's revenues may exceed auctions and become eBay's biggest business.

Flickr, YouTube, MySpace

Spreadable Spreadables, Stackable Stackables,
and the Point of Nondisplacement

When PayPal launched, less than 10 percent of Internet-enabled households in the United States had broadband connections. By February 2004 the number had risen to 30 percent, and it was close to 70 percent by 2008. But high-speed access is not relegated to the domain of the desktop. Mobile devices are the fastest-growing broadband segment, and this has vastly increased the size and reach of the viral plain. It has energized collaboration, interactivity and interoperability in the form of wikis, photo- and video-share sites, social networks and millions of blogs, which have effectively ridden this wave of greater connectivity. Their numbers have grown even faster than broadband penetration, doubling every five months since 2003. Taken as a whole, the blogosphere is a teeming viral network, with every blog that sprouts up offering a testimonial to the ease of self-publishing.

"Blog" (short for "web log") is an unfortunate term that sounds like the noise someone makes after scarfing down a plate of nachos and tipping back one too many tequila shots. It has evolved into a sphere of memes and ideas constantly shaped by the millions of Web users who write, read, and comment on blogs, many of whom followed links there, which were themselves spread virally. In a sense, the blogosphere operates in a similar fashion to open-source code, where a loose confederation of programmers tinkers with software, adding to it and sharing contributions with anyone who is interested. Of course, there are often stark intellectual inefficiencies, as well as a lot of hot-gas rhetoric, vitriol, inane discussions, score settling, and outright buffoonery. Actually the blogosphere can be downright

Hobbesian, with posts that are nasty, brutish, and (often mercifully) short. At its best, though, it is a marketplace of ideas, with the best ones holding sway, a pure meritocracy. Indeed, during the 2008 presidential campaign, blogs—the really good ones from all sides of the political spectrum— competed with the traditional press and not only held their own but were often superior: Nate Silver, Andrew Sullivan, Daily Kos, Town Hall, Politico, and Huffington Post did not just provide analysis but in some cases broke news. Taken as a whole, the coverage was far more insightful than it was in 2004 or 2000 or 1996.

With blogs anybody with an Internet connection can engage anybody else. Concepts are presented, attacked, sliced, diced, added to and subtracted from, mangled, massaged, and molded until what is left is an amalgam of the finest online society has to offer. For the digitally well-endowed, it's akin to free-market capitalism, with information as its currency. And not only do we all get to watch, we can join in—in real time or via asynchronous communication. Before, blogging was largely fixated on the failure of mainstream media. Now it is a necessary supplement and, in rare cases, a substitute. You can trace this back to July 2005 and the London bombings. When former Federal Communications Commission chairman Michael K. Powell watched television coverage, he noticed that most of the significant pictures didn't originate from professional photographers employed by news agencies. They came from witnesses at the scene using cell phones and digital cameras to document the tragedy. "Journalists are trained not to be emotional, like a doctor doesn't fall in love with his patients," Powell says. "But people experiencing a tragedy can convey what actually happened while at the same time express[ing] deep emotion and engag[ing] in spirited storytelling. A photo of someone climbing up through train wreckage is extremely powerful. A reporter rolling up to the scene behind a police line can rarely give you that." To Powell, London proved that blogging had morphed into the art of raw, personalized storytelling. "You really felt as if you were there," Powell says of the blog posts and Flickr photos he surveyed, "as opposed to watching CNN or reading MSNBC.com, which are fine for the facts but stale and a bit removed."

[MY FRIEND FLICKR]

The first viral network to stack atop the expanding blogosphere was Flickr, the popular photo share site and community. As with many Web innovations, it started out as one idea only to end up as something completely different. In 2002 Flickr founders Caterina Fake and Stewart Butterfield married. Two weeks later they started development of a massively multiplayer online game called Game Neverending. Both were early bloggers intrigued by the idea of creating a virtual world ruled by social interactions, a precursor to World of Warcraft and Second Life. The way Fake (her real name) describes it, Game Neverending sounds as if it were divined over a bong. Part whimsy (a player would find a wombat whistle, blow it, and baby wombats would cuddle up against her), part meta-reality: users could work alone or in concert to create a business or product, raise venture capital, hype it, and everyone would grow rich. "You could cheer people up by sprinkling everyone in a crowded room with magic sparkle powder and their mood would go up," she says. Since it was intended for the Web, it wasn't the kind of game you could shrink-wrap and sell at Best Buy, and they couldn't interest financial backers. The young couple had mortgaged their home to partially self-fund the project, together with the money they had raised from friends and family, although not nearly enough to finish development. Discouraged but unbowed, they scaled back their grandiose ambitions.

An important aspect of the game hinged on instant messaging, and Butterfield suggested they develop it with the capability of dropping photos into conversations, which they agreed was "very cool." In early 2004 they stuck it up on a webpage and it went nowhere. The problem was, it wasn't a stand-alone product. For a user to benefit, others had to be on the same instant-messaging client. So they created a primitive social network with photo share capability and incorporated tagging to better organize photographs. Butterfield and Fake recognized the impact that digital cameras, which were getting cheaper and more powerful by the month, were having on the Web. It meant that photography had become, as Fake put it, "delaminated from its delivery mechanisms."

An amateur photographer like Fake, with hundreds or even thousands of pictures on her hard drive, was faced with a seemingly endless list of JPEG files with no effective way to place them into context. She could, of course, organize them into folders, but that was a binary solution to an infinitely more complex organizational challenge. Where would she stash a photo of, say, her best friend on vacation at the Angkor Wat temple in Cambodia at sunrise with a monkey nicknamed "Filch" running off with a tourist's backpack? In a folder labeled Vacation? Angkor Wat? Melinda? Monkey? Tagging allowed the photo to be easily found in all of these contexts. And since anyone could add a tag and a comment, it became a democratic mode of organization that jibed with Flickr's mission—to be public in the way a blog was.

Most photo share sites operated as loss leaders for portals, a strategy to keep users occupied and on the site. Flickr, however, was intended to be part of a larger conversation, where users could share photos with a community, indeed, the world at large, since a blogger could link to an entire album. The first newspapers online imitated the physical form from which they came, as did online magazines, which were called "zines" for a reason, since they all took their metaphor from prior (analog) technology. The same held true for photo share sites like Ofoto, Shutterfly, and Snapfish, which aped the look and feel of predigital picture albums. Flickr, a product of Web 2.0, was different. "The reason jellyfish are designed the way they are is because they live in water," Fake says. "Flickr was designed in the way it was because it is digital."

The earliest members came from the Game Neverending community, and Fake made it a point of introducing everyone who entered the site to someone else. "I see you are into Norwegian metal; here's this other guy who's also into it," Fake would offer. Or, "You live in Pittsburgh? Here's another person from there." "Communities take on a certain kind of character of a party at the outset and you need to be a good host," Fake says. "If you come to a party and nobody offers you a drink, you leave to a happening party somewhere else."

While Flickr was free, it wouldn't always remain that way since photos online soak up a lot of expensive bandwidth. Why not use that to help seed the site? Fake thought. She instituted a viral policy: invite five friends to join and get three months free. The implicit carrot-stick worked better than she could have imagined. For the first few months sign-ups increased 75 to 100 percent month over month, then spiked as bloggers became hip to the site. Like Andreessen, who predicted that Web users would embrace the ability to post pictures, Fake figured that bloggers also wanted to add to their palette of self-expression. As the blogosphere exploded, so did Flickr. Every blogger who used it acted as an advertisement, since to view pictures readers had to click to Flickr. Its growth quickly accelerated to 30 to 50 percent month over month, a product of the social and conversation-fueled viral loop that was created. The more blogs that displayed photos that were stored and shared on Flickr, the more people were exposed to Flickr. This led to more blogs and more blog readers adopting the service.

Soon the site that Butterfield and Fake had started as an afterthought to their multiplayer game had become the fifth most popular site on the Internet, generating revenue by charging a fee to heavy users wanting to store a lot of photos. A year after launching, the formerly debt-riddled couple sold Flickr to Yahoo. Six months after that, the site hosted its millionth photo. Five years later, it was approaching 3 billion images.

Although Flickr might be a billion-dollar business today, Fake says she has no regrets selling out for $40 million: "If you throw a rock in Silicon Valley, you can find somebody that could have been a contender," she says. "I think it's a waste of time to sit around and think of what could have been."

[MYSPACE: GLITTER AND SMILEY FACES]

After the blogosphere propelled Flickr's viral loop, the next stackable ecosystem to arise was MySpace, launched from the seamy side of cyberspace six months after Flickr. Initially it was devised as a last resort to save eUniverse, a lowbrow net-based entertainment company that trafficked in adware and recycled printer cartridges and was about to go under. As *Wall Street Journal* reporter Julia Angwin relates in *Stealing MySpace: The Battle to Control the Most Popular Website in America*, MySpace cofounder Chris DeWolfe was a notorious spammer having trouble selling ill-gotten ads to advertisers, a brash gambit even for him. After the United States invaded Iraq in 2003, he peddled free software to turn a PC user's cursor into an American flag. Alas, such patriotism was merely a Trojan horse, a way for DeWolfe to spread spyware that would log an unwitting user's online movements and fire ads based on his Web-viewing habits, burying the poor schmuck in a blaze of pop-up ads. Visit an auto site and ads for car insurance would plaster the screen.

His partner, Tom Anderson, was spending a lot of time at home logged into Friendster—more time than he would have liked, since the site was buggy and slow. The famously antisocial Anderson had been a notorious teen hacker who, under the *nom de hack* Lord Flathead had broken into a Chase Manhattan Bank data center, that, according to a *New York Times* article held "much of Chase's data processing and record keeping," including mortgage records and the "portfolios of major customers such as pension funds." Once inside, he allegedly altered passwords to prevent bank officials from accessing their own system. The *Times* reported that Anderson threatened to erase bank records unless he was given free use of the system, which led to a massive FBI raid. The fourteen-year-old Anderson was given probation. After graduating from the University of California at Berkeley, he performed in a band called Swank in San Francisco, did a brief stint in Taiwan, returned to the United States to attend graduate film school at UCLA, then took a job as a copywriter at a company called XDrive, a digital storage company where he met DeWolfe. When the company declared bankruptcy, he and DeWolfe formed a new company called ResponseBase that would eventually merge with eUniverse.

Sensing Friendster's vulnerability, Anderson suggested they build a competitor, an idea that DeWolfe first ignored. Then he received three friend requests from Friendster the next day, and with his company withering on the vine, DeWolfe figured they didn't have much to lose. Friendster had raised $1 million in venture capital and Google offered $30 million to buy it outright. If they could achieve a fraction of that success, they would be in business.

On August 15, 2003, MySpace went live. Reflecting the scammy background of its creators, it had what Angwin characterized as "a freewheeling ethos" that ignored conventions like copyright and allowed users to post under whatever persona they chose, unlike Friendster, which was all about user authenticity, with one's social network of friends offering a way to truly judge someone's character. A conflusion of happenstance changed the course of both companies. As Friendster struggled to scale with server bottlenecks and suffered backlash among users who complained about tight policing of the site, MySpace emerged as a wild and woolly alternative, partly by accident.

A coding glitch made it possible for MySpace users to insert their own HTML code onto their profiles, making them customizable. Profiles became vehicles for self-expression, adorned with colorful wallpaper and patterns, hearts, bubble dots, glitter, and smiley faces; users could also post MP3s of their favorite bands, photos, and video. This led to MySpace being discovered by a powerfully viral segment of the population: teenaged girls, who joyfully shared coding tips with one another. Because it drained bandwidth and slowed down the site, MySpace engineers proposed putting a stop to this, but DeWolfe overruled them. He realized that fighting users was a useless exercise that would only limit their growth. Let Friendster alienate its user base. MySpace would out-friendly Friendster. "Much like you could walk into my house and listen to what music I had playing in the background, see photos of my family, notice what taste I have in furniture, read my diary to find out a lot about me, a person's profile would be the same thing," DeWolfe says.

Not only that, but MySpace would offer users the tools of self-expression to accomplish this. The former spyware peddler, who had essentially tricked users into downloading nefarious applications, was suddenly reborn. Now he was all about transparency. This was less a philosophy for DeWolfe than simply good business. On MySpace the users would be in charge; if he didn't provide them with what they wanted, they would simply go somewhere else. If he could retain them, the company had the potential to grow to obscene levels. "People are going to go and socialize where their friends are, and once you have a person's friends list in a social community locked in, viral growth really happens," he says. To foster this, DeWolfe ordered programmers to concoct as many programs for self-expression as possible. They would release an application. If it stuck, they would finetune it; if it flopped, they'd kill it. Such pragmatism also extended to Anderson, who ended the memory-gorging practice of plotting out people's friends of friends of friends networks, that is, Friendster's four degrees of separation. As he wrote on his blog, which he used to communicate with the MySpace community, at the beginning "we used a 'network' concept to show you how you were connected to friends. If Dave knows John and John knows Amy, then Dave could see Amy in the network. When you'd view someone's profile it'd show if you were friends, or how you were connected to a person."

But Anderson and his engineers could see this made it virtually impossible to scale, since "the site was slowing down trying to process this relationship each time you viewed a profile." His solution was to become everyone's "first friend" by default. "If a user wanted to only see a network of people they actually knew, they could just remove me as a friend." Inserting this extra step diminished the demands on MySpace's already taxed servers, and helped MySpace pages download ten times faster than Friendster's. Most users didn't care about not being able to track out degrees of separation anyway.

[TASTEMAKERS]

Taken with all of their other gripes, Friendster users began a steady exodus to DeWolfe and Anderson's upstart start-up, famously illustrated by the life and virtual times of Tila Tequila, a self-described actress, model, rapper, and singer, who *Time* called "the least lonely girl on the Internet." A twenty-two-year-old bottle-blond Vietnamese bombshell from Singapore who was transplanted to the States as a baby, Tequila (real name Tila Nguyen) was Playboy.com's Asian Cyber Girl of the Month who shook her assets at car shows and in hot-rod magazine spreads. When Friendster took off, she recognized the marketing possibilities and quickly took to viewing maintenance of her online self as a full-time job. This ran smack into Friendster's ethos, which expected that each user would actually know their friends. Not Nguyen, who collected thousands of admirers, mostly men, who visited her page to view photos of her wearing next to nothing or read her profanity-laced musings. As a result Friendster kept suspending her, which prompted Anderson to invite her to join MySpace.

At first she was reluctant. There were millions of people (read: fans) on Friendster and perhaps a few thousand on MySpace. But after being booted off Friendster a fifth time, Nguyen finally decided she would

rather switch than fight. She signed up for MySpace in September, feeling, she told *Time*, "like a loser while all the cool kids were at some other
school." To remedy that, she emailed "between 30,000 and 50,000" of her
closest friends (who could keep track?) and invited them to the party.
"Everybody joined overnight," she boasted. Well, not everyone, but she
did add juice to MySpace's virality. Aber Whitcomb, an engineer who was
there from day one—and was the third person to sign up on MySpace—
recalls that for the first month the site counted roughly a thousand sign-
ups a day, but by mid-September linear growth had become geometric.
"The more users we got, the more invites they sent," he says. "It was completely blowing up faster and faster."

In October, nearly two months after going live, MySpace counted
100,000 members, and soon more than 10,000 people a day were registering. DeWolfe knew MySpace had turned a corner three months after
launch. "I remember being at a dinner party, maybe three months into
MySpace, and someone asked me what I did, and not only didn't I have
to explain what MySpace was, the person actually said, 'I am on it,'" he says.
"That started to happen more and more. I remember specifically going
out and hearing people talking about MySpace three or four times a week."

Because DeWolfe and Anderson took pains to seed the site with taste-
makers in fashion and music, they noted certain fast-growing pockets. Los
Angeles was one, New York another, and a third one, which surprised
them, was Hawaii. Soon the site surpassed a million users, adding 20,000
more members daily. By May 2004 there were 2 million users, and four
months after that the number doubled to 4 million. While Friendster stumbled, MySpace thrived, tripling its user base six months later to almost
12 million. When Rupert Murdoch's News Corp. bought MySpace for
$580 million in July 2005, it counted 22 million registered members, many
of whom were spending hours on the site every day. But Anderson and
DeWolfe weren't done, not by a long shot. A year later MySpace was
home, by *Fortune* magazine's count, to more than 2 million bands, 8,000
comedians, and thousands of filmmakers, performance artists, poets, rappers,
models, photographers, and 100 million other social (network) strivers.

It didn't take long for other viral businesses to glom on to MySpace,
creating applications to help users more easily customize their pages. But
the first true viral network to take hold was Photobucket, a photo share

site similar to Flickr. While Butterfield and Fake's fortunes were aligned with the blogosphere, Photobucket, founded by a couple of engineers from Colorado, became indispensable to MySpace because it offered space for photos the social network couldn't handle. That's because all of this free expression and user customization came at a cost—bandwidth—which led MySpace to severely limit the number of photos users could post on their profiles. Photobucket solved this by allowing users to link to their stash of photos. By September 2006, 60 percent of MySpace's pages connected to Photobucket as the number of visitors it served jumped to 17 million a month. It was as much a curse as it was a blessing, as bandwidth consumption consumed most of its revenues and, finding no other suitors, sold to MySpace in 2007 for $250 million.

[YOUTUBE: A VIDEO VERSION OF HOT OR NOT]

But the viral network to eventually outdo the viral network it launched from was YouTube, which was initially conceived as a video version of Hot or Not. Cofounder Steve Chen teamed up with Chad Hurley and Jawed Karim to create YouTube. Until the site officially went live in November 2005 after six months of public beta testing, viewing video clips on the Web was often frustrating and inconvenient. It required a user to download one of the various players available, such as Apple's Quick-Time, Microsoft Windows Media, or Real Networks. If a video was encoded to run in QuickTime but the user only had Real Networks, he was out of luck. Because YouTube ran on Flash, an animation software, it provided a faster, one-click video experience even if the quality was low. MySpace members immediately gravitated to the service to embed links on their pages, which played the video clip YouTube hosted. These links not only spread the idea of posting a video clip on a MySpace page; it expanded YouTube's reach across the social network, exposing its millions of members to the site itself, creating a viral loop.

Since it had been planning to distribute video across MySpace, News Corp. viewed YouTube as a threat. First, citing security concerns, MySpace disabled MySpace links, saying it couldn't vouch for third-party applications. Its users howled and MySpace backed down. As eBay had learned, a viral network is dependent on its community of users. When they band together, they become a force that can influence company strategy. Behind every community uprising is the implicit threat that people can go elsewhere, and there can be a fine line between balancing their needs with those of a company looking to capitalize on its aggregating power.

Then in early 2006 MySpace released its own video player, which showed promise early on but then lost steam. Google and Yahoo also tried to play catch-up with YouTube. All of them would learn what eBay had learned. Once a viral network achieves a viral loop and a point of nondisplacement, it can't be stopped. By midyear, YouTube's reach surpassed MySpace's, even though YouTube was largely dependent on it, with 60 percent of its videos streaming from MySpace pages. Then came the coup de grâce. News Corp. made numerous overtures to buy YouTube, but its founders claimed it wasn't for sale until Google walked away with the year-old site for $1.65 billion in October 2006.

DeWolfe and Anderson could not have been happy. After all, YouTube, which had been stacked on top of their network, not only became bigger than MySpace; it sold almost three times as much. But YouTube's viral loop was even more potent than MySpace's.

Once YouTube had set down viral roots, there was little they could have done to stop it.

10

Tweaking the Viral Coefficient

Bebo, Patterns in Virality, and Critical Mass

While books, magazine features, newspaper articles, online news pieces and endless blog posts have been written about Facebook and MySpace—the Hertz and Avis of the social networking world—one social network you may not have heard as much about is Bebo, started by Michael Birch, a Brit living in San Francisco. After he built it into the third-largest social network in the world and a few years later sold it for more money than Rupert Murdoch paid for MySpace, some believed that Birch was an overnight success. Far from it. The first three start-ups he launched failed miserably.

A long-haired Brit with a ponytail, he was raised in Hertfordshire, England, and studied physics at Imperial College in London, where he met his future bride, Xochi, a California native, in a pub. Graduating into a tight job market in the early 1990s, he took what he assumed would be the most boring job imaginable—as a database programmer for an insurance company. Although right about the insurance part (he found corporate bureaucracy particularly irksome), he discovered that not only did he enjoy programming, he had a gift for it. Later he would wonder what he would have done with his life if computers hadn't been invented; he didn't think he would have been good at much else. After he had spent six years of working for someone else, Birch and his wife set out to become entrepreneurs, remortgaging their modest home, which had doubled in value during Britain's housing boom. With little chance they could raise funding, he decided to create a viral business, something that would propagate from friend to friend without requiring a dime in marketing money. His model: Hotmail.

His first idea was to create tests for tech professionals at job interviews, but he quickly discarded that. Then the Birches began work on Lemonlink, a Web-based self-updating address book, which went live in January 2000. The viral hook consisted of users entering their friends' and acquaintances' contact information. Each person added to a user's address book would be notified by email and asked for contact details. Lemonlink grew slowly. Having a science background, Birch sifted through the data to analyze why. He calculated the viral coefficient was barely .5: each person led to only a quarter of an additional person signing on to the service, which was too low to result in exponential growth. One reason for the laggard growth was that Lemonlink depended on prospective users downloading an Active X application, something many were loath to do. Another hurdle was Lemonlink's reliance on email notifications. With spam a growing irritation, people were less likely to respond to these kinds of clickable entreaties. Birch coded a plug-in for Outlook, a popular Microsoft email program, and this pushed the viral coefficient to .7. Not bad, but not good enough.

The young couple now had a baby and moved on to a second business that hit closer to home, Babysitting Circle, a subscription service they believed would be inherently viral since parents of young children often know one another. The Birches hoped to rely on word-of-mouth endorsements as a viral mechanism to attract families to the service, but it was a hard slog. It was simply too niche. Families were willing to pay, but not in sufficient numbers to make a profitable business. The Birches resorted to spending money on advertising, which brought in a wider pool of members but not enough to get them over the hump. Any additional revenue went straight into paying for more marketing. Eventually they concluded the business would never be viral enough to sustain itself. With cash running low, Birch partnered with his brothers on a do-it-yourself online family-wills business. "I didn't particularly want to do it," Birch says, and wasn't surprised when it proved to be a bust. All along the way, however, he was learning what worked and what didn't, vowing not to repeat mistakes.

[TWEAKING THE VIRAL COEFFICIENT]

Finally, they hit pay dirt in 2001 with their fourth business, Birthday Alarm, which began as a way to remind people of their friends' birthdays. "It was incredibly simple, an incredibly short viral loop," Birch says. "Everyone has birthdays, so there is no reason you wouldn't email everyone you know to ask them when it is." To seed the site, Birch paid $99 to the Cool Site of the Day, and on the first day five hundred people signed up. The site grew slowly, with Birch tweaking things until he could get it right. Initially he had plastered the site with privacy notices (promising not to sell users' emails, etc.) but found it slowed page load times. Faster down-loading led to an uptick in virality, and no one complained about the missing privacy notices anyway. Simplifying the instructions also helped. In fact, the rule seemed to be, the simpler he made things, the more viral the site became. People, it seemed, were turned off by anything that re-quired them to think.

The big breakthrough came when he added a cut-and-paste function. That way, users didn't have to type in friends' email addresses and birth-days; in two keystrokes they could transfer them from other programs. This pushed the viral coefficient above 1, with ten thousand people a day joining. The site generated revenue from banner ads through advertising networks that took a 30 percent cut, and the Birches added e-cards, since it was natural that users would want to send greetings to their friends. By the time the couple relocated to San Francisco to be closer to Xochi's family, the site was bringing in $10,000 a month, enough to rent an apart-ment and a tiny 20-square-foot office in the Valley's bubbly real estate market.

Two years after Birthday Alarm's birth, the site practically ran itself, and Birch sought other viral business ideas. One day he came across Friend-ster. After clicking through it for about half an hour and marveling at its simplicity, he sat down to create a copycat site on top of his Birthday Alarm code base. Thirteen days later he unveiled Ringo.com, named after the former Beatle. The Birches blasted an email to 3 million Birth-day Alarm users announcing the new site, which resulted in 30,000 sign-ups—a conversion rate of 1 percent, decent for any email campaign.

They also incorporated an invitations mechanism for users to bring in their friends, and in the span of three months Ringo.com grew to 400,000 users, making it the second most popular social network on the Web. Most users were American, but Birch found it interesting that a viral cluster had also formed in Australia, where a quarter of the site's traffic originated.

While thrilled to have cracked the formula for a successful viral loop business, Birch didn't have the resources to scale. It was just he and his wife squeezed into a box of an office, swamped with customer support questions and service outages. The site, which was pulling in $30 a month in revenue, was becoming slow and buggy. He couldn't afford more hardware, hire engineers, or move into a larger office space. Birch had a choice: either find angel investors or sell Ringo.com. In December 2003 he received three offers in one week, and sold to online quiz purveyor Tickle .com for a couple of million dollars in private stock. No cash, just shares. In fact, the Birches wouldn't see a dime for eighteen months, when Tickle (known for the classic online IQ test and the silly What Kind of Dog Are You?) sold Ringo.com for even more to Monster.com, where it became a photo-sharing site. Part of the deal required Birch to agree to a noncompete clause, which meant he couldn't start a social network site for eighteen months and agreed to work at Tickle for three months. He enjoyed being around other engineers and stayed half a year.

[VIRAL PATTERNS]

After going solo again in mid-2004, he tried another virality experiment on Birthday Alarm, which was reminding more than 1 million people a day about their friends' birthdays. While he was at Tickle, the engineers had tried email scraping, a program that would automatically import a person's contacts, but it didn't work. Birch figured if he could create a program that would make it even more convenient for Birthday Alarm users to list their friends' emails—the site still employed his simple cut-and-paste function—it would improve the site's viral coefficient. He targeted Hotmail and ten hours later finished the code. At the time, Birthday Alarm was getting 10,000 new sign-ups a day. Now that Hotmail users could easily import their address, membership spiked. Twenty-four hours later he counted 100,000 new members.

Birch kept on experimenting. He returned to his very first idea: a self-updating address book, applying everything he had learned along the way. He called it Bebo, a name he chose because it was short, snappy, and utterly nonsensical, like Yahoo. Users could project their own meaning onto it, which was well worth the $8,000 the domain cost. Later he turned it into an acronym for "blog early, blog often." He put the link up on Birthday Alarm, seeding it with just a few members, and it "went ridiculously viral," so much so that he took the link down after seven days. The viral coefficient: 2.5. One million people signed up, three hundred thousand of them on day nine alone. By the end of a month, he had a few million members. But the concept wasn't sticky; no one was coming back. After signing up, people didn't bother to update their address books, and what good was an address book if only 10 percent of your friends were in it?

Eyeballing the data, Birch noted another pattern. Those with the biggest address books—say, five hundred names—were the first to sign on, and they tended to spread it to others with similarly large virtual rolodexes. That, he saw, accounted for the initial viral spike. Over time, the sign-up rate decreased as people with leaner address books joined. But someone with ten addresses was virtually impossible to reach because he was part of the small-is-beautiful flock, included in other less-connected people's address books. "So you end up exploding within all these well-connected people and filtering down to less-connected people," Birch says. "Your viral growth diminishes to the point you end up getting a viral factor of 1," which was where it remained, decreasing to thirty thousand new members a day. Nevertheless, he had built a network of 6 million users. At the time, Friendster had already imploded and MySpace registered 9 million unique visitors.

While his noncompete prevented Birch from combining pictures with profiles, which was the definition of a social network in his noncompete agreement, nothing prevented him from adding photo share to an address book. That, too, proved reasonably viral. After the clock ran out on his noncompete, he and his wife, excited about the possibilities, spent three months redeveloping Bebo into a full-blown social network with profiles, pictures, blogs, and an invitation system. It would be, at its essence, a community enabler, helping people to get to know one another without the societal constraints that characterized public interaction. Because MySpace was quickly cornering the market on American teens and Facebook was roaring through college campuses, Birch targeted urban thirty-somethings who, he believed, needed a means to widen their social networks. As people aged, they became mired in their own cliques, rarely venturing outside their established networks, even though the ideal future friend might be sitting on the next bar stool. Friendships were often predicated on similar interests, but to learn what interests someone had required getting to know him.

Bebo would streamline the process, and it would do it through electronic mail. Not email per se, which, while virtually universal, was two-dimensional. Its mail would be far richer, three-dimensional communication, because everything a user sent and received would be purely personal. Not like a fantasy video game or immersive virtual world either. It would be tethered to reality, a person's existing social relationships transported to the digital realm, which would foster other relationships that could seep into the offline world. A recipient could click on the name and encounter a kind of Rorschach test—a page devoted to human expression—and learn about the person who sent it. Bebo would pull together media that previously functioned separately in the way that mobile phones combined phones, SMS texting, and email. Birch envisioned a day that Bebo would do all of this while adding blogs, chat, photos, quizzes, and any other product of the human mind, which together would become a multimedia channel.

[CRITICAL MASS]

When Birch unveiled the revamped site with all of the new functions, he expected it would take off. It didn't. Traffic stayed flat. Although it occurred to him that Bebo might simply be too late to the social network party, he didn't panic. MySpace was grabbing the kids and Facebook was targeted to college students. Bebo, on the other hand, by virtue of starting out as an auto-updated address book, was keyed on an older demographic. But teens and twenty-somethings are always the earliest adopters.

They have a lot more time on their hands than adults, less money to spend, and social networks are free. It would take time to bring in the over-thirty crowd. He also suspected that repositioning the Bebo brand had sapped momentum. While he counted more than 6 million members, most had simply inputted their names and the names and addresses of their friends. When he browsed the network, he encountered a sea of bare-bones profiles. It was like stepping in to your local pub and encountering only a few customers. "We needed a critical mass of people who had filled out their profiles to make it interesting," Birch says. In the interim he kept tweaking the site, making it run faster, trying to improve the user experience. For two months Bebo treaded water. Then profiles began to fill up with photos, comments, and overlapping conversations between friends.

Bebo, Birch realized, had finally attained a viral loop. From a base of 6 million users, the site was increasing page views by 10 percent a week. The steep course correction had proven the right move, but it was growing in a surprising direction. Another teen population had discovered Bebo: British youth, who took to the site with the enthusiasm American teens had when the Beatles first crossed the Atlantic. Over the next several months it spread to Ireland, Scotland, New Zealand, and Australia. As one British commentator remarked, teenagers were "taking to Bebo quicker than they can pop a can of paprika-flavoured Pringles."

Birch focused new member recruitment on universities and high schools across the UK, Australia, and New Zealand, listing them on the welcome page. To sign up, new users had to state where they attended school, and this acted as a magnet for others. As a result, Bebo outpaced MySpace in England and proved so popular in Ireland that several colleges banned access before the start of summer exams when students complained they couldn't get near a computer terminal to work on their theses with so many peers logged onto Bebo. One college estimated half its bandwidth was consumed by students on Bebo, while another found more than half of its computer terminals were logged onto the site at any given time. Birch estimated that five hundred thousand Irish youth were members, which, as one newspaper pointed out meant "virtually every teenager in the country has their own page on Bebo." It ended up the largest trafficked site in all of Ireland, passing Yahoo, MSN, and Google.

Within ten months, Bebo counted 24 million members leafing through 2.5 billion monthly page views.

He found it ironic that he had left Britain for San Francisco to start a social network that took off in Britain. Perhaps he had imbued Bebo with his own personality. There were places his British sense of humor came through, like when someone didn't post a picture, a big question mark would appear. The more likely explanation, he decided, was that no social network had achieved penetration outside of the United States. Britain was largely virgin territory, largely because it tends to adopt trends and technologies after Americans. Bebo was there when MySpace arrived and was in a prime position to take advantage.

Birch and his wife maintained a clear division of labor, he acting as chief executive and programmer, she handling the money and dealing with customers. Every dollar Bebo earned from advertising they plowed back into the site, adopting the grow-at-all-costs network effects model. They kept overhead low, adding minimal staff. For the first year the Birches funded Bebo with income generated by Birthday Alarm, which by this point was bringing in a few million a year. Nevertheless they raised $15 million in venture backing from Benchmark Capital. Barry Malone, a Benchmark partner, learned of Bebo from his daughters, who had become hooked on the site. But the Birches would never touch that money, since they were able to keep Bebo afloat with the income the site generated. If they didn't have to plow huge resources into development, Bebo would be profitable.

Borrowing concepts from MySpace, its larger competitor, Birch also learned from its mistakes. One was themed, user-generated skins in cus-tomizable patterns that Bebo members used to decorate profiles. Birch extended them to advertisers like Nike as a way to extend their brands. Instead of allowing users to fiddle with a page's HTML (as MySpace did), Birch required Photoshop. HTML was a security risk, and because it was complicated, beyond the technical level of many users, MySpace was lit-tered with broken pages. Photoshop was easier and Bebo-ites happily shared their art, with their creators earning cred when their skins were on twenty thousand other profiles. Because snap-happy teenagers spiced up pages with images, Birch lifted restrictions on uploading photos, which resulted in even more user engagement. It came at a price, though, with

Bebo burning through a few gigabits of bandwidth a second, requiring 120 servers and technical finesse to keep the site up and running.

Another MySpace initiative that translated well to Bebo centered on music, with Birch launching a campaign to attract bands to the site. Each group was offered a home page that enabled musicians to interact with fans and upload unlimited music and videos. Birch designed it so users could share songs and spread the word about bands they like. There was a playlist function for users to create lists of favorite tunes, shareable with their network of friends. The most popular lists were promoted on the site and to ensure a steady supply of music, Birch signed agreements with several record labels and independents. Within two weeks more than twenty-five thousand groups and individual artists had signed up.

One area where he wouldn't copy MySpace was the way News Corp. was layering in advertising, which Birch believed had the potential to alienate his user base. The classic banner ad that had been driving Internet marketing for a decade would eventually die off, because on social networks it wasn't about throwing ads like confetti at users—it was about integrating product experience. And the demographic that first tuned into social networks—teens, "twenteens," which was how some in their early twenties not ready to graduate to adulthood referred to themselves, and young working stiffs—were the consumers of the future. They were pulling away from TV, didn't buy newspapers or magazines, and were intent on setting up house on the Web. As Birch's own data showed, they were online a lot, much of it spent on social networks. To reach them, companies would have to come to social networks, but on users' terms. Although Birch didn't have all the answers, one experiment showed promise. Instead of trying to divine what kinds of ads would be most effective, through a complex relevance algorithm, Birch opted for an explicit targeting strategy that let users choose the types of ads they wanted to see. He wasn't concerned about revenue anyway. Right now he was focused on growth, and to accomplish that he had to continue providing an enjoyable user experience. Once he had a large enough base, he was confident he would be able to monetize. As it was, the site was reaping millions a month in revenue.

[SOCIAL PROBLEMS PLAYING OUT ON THE WEB]

While Bebo grew at a fantastic rate overseas, Birch's family life in San Francisco remained downright normal. He woke up at 6:30 a.m. to help his children get ready for school; then, after dropping them off, he and his wife would arrive at the office at 8:00 a.m., and Birch would spend half the day programming. The few meetings he held were with suppliers and prospective partners or advertisers. With Bebo adding ten thousand new members a week, either he or his head programmer was always on call, since they were the only ones who knew the site's architecture. Since his co-coder got his kicks from skydiving, Birch would stress whenever he took to the sky. Then he would leave around 7:00 p.m. to see his kids for an hour before they went to bed. A few times a week he attended networking events, for instance, a website launch, and he traveled to England, where he and his wife would combine business with pleasure.

Things were humming along, with Bebo the subject of fawning press coverage in the UK, until a spate of articles on bullying, a scourge of British society transplanted to Bebo, hit the media. One of the first, appearing in an Irish newspaper, began: "She's such a stupid, ugly bitch. I can't stand being in the same classroom as her. Everybody hates her. I'd kill myself if I was her." The reporter pointed out this wasn't even one of the most offensive posts about the girl. She called Bebo "a forum for bullies to attack their victims," with pupils "being bullied remorselessly about their perceived weight, poverty, appearance, intelligence and promiscuity, among many others." One Dublin school suspended ten students for bullying on Bebo, with teachers among the victims. Then came death threats against two men suspected of being linked to the murder of a teenager. There was the man who used Bebo to disseminate porn to teenage boys and mobile phone video of rugby fights.

Birch found himself confronting the broken-window syndrome. When bad profiles proliferated, he blocked them; others took their place, and the cycle continued. Because he couldn't prevent anonymous users from creating new profiles, Birch enlisted the community to police the site, vowing to shut down abusive sites within twenty-four hours of being contacted. After an *Irish Times* report, Birch pulled all ads for gambling sites and dating services and appointed an expert in online pedophilia to work toward helping make Bebo safer. Then came a disturbing rash of teen suicides in Wales in which members of an Internet cult communicated through the site. The more popular Bebo became, the more it attracted controversy.

While MySpace fetched more than $500,000 in 2005, Birch long maintained he wasn't looking to sell, even when Bebo became the third biggest social network in the United States and secured its popularity in the UK. Techcrunch, the gadget blog, claimed investment bank Allen & Co. began shopping Bebo in 2007 with a suite of potential buyers—News Corp., Microsoft, and Google—declining to make an offer. Viacom reportedly made a run for Bebo, and Yahoo took a long hard look. But it was AOL that stepped up, offering cash, and lots of it. After six months of hard negotiations, with Bebo growing to 40 million users spending an average of forty minutes a day on the site, the Birches sold the site on March 13, 2008, for $850 million.

The young couple that nine years earlier had mortgaged their home to finance their viral dreams walked away with $595 million, which was more than News Corp. paid for MySpace.

11

Viral Clusters

Facebook, the Social Graph, and Thingamajigs

Facebook, MySpace, and Bebo are but three of more than a hundred social networks around the world. Almost anyone with ties to business has a profile on LinkedIn, Ecademy, Ryze, Spoke.com, or XING. Twitter has become its own medium, with passionate adherents keeping tabs on one another in short, haiku-like bursts, while Yammer taps workers in a corporate setting. Imeem is a social music service with millions of members streaming millions of songs and videos. TravBuddy and Travellerspoint connect inveterate travelers. Ning is, at its essence, a social network for those who create social networks, while hi5, with 60 million users worldwide, has a decidedly international twang and is *numero uno* among Spanish speakers. Blackplanet's membership is primarily African American. Buzznet focuses on celebrities, media, and music, while CafeMom connects mothers. Care2 appeals to green activists, Gaia to those who want to change the world, and DeviantArt to artists. Eons.com has created a community for baby boomers, while Elftown is for science fiction fans. Many of Tagged's users are married but looking for friendship and discreet hook-ups, Adult Friend Finder makes an uninhibited play for sex, fubar touts itself as "the Internet's only online bar and happy hour," and FetLife is, according to the site, "similar to Facebook and MySpace, but run by sexual deviants like you and me."

Social networks have become a global online phenomenon. Orkut is tops in Brazil, Biip is big in Norway, and the anime-like Cyworld is South Korea's most popular online community, with 90 percent of Koreans in their twenties joining (and social ostracism awaiting those who don't).

CozyCot is limited to Southeast Asian women, Dol2day is a platform for politically interested German speakers, and Grono.net lives in Poland. Cloob is an Iranian virtual society, Xiaonei a clone of Facebook in China, Wretch is big in Taiwan, and Mixi is popular in Japan. Iwiw.hu holds sway in Hungary, the Finns go gaga over IRC-Galleria, Skyrock hails from France and has been exported to Senegal, and VKontakte rules Russia. The world map is constantly evolving, with competing networks making inroads and sometimes passing entrenched communities. Some are American transplants like Orkut, hi5, and Friendster, which all failed to take off in the United States but have thrived abroad. Like Bebo, each experienced a viral growth pattern that transplanted it far away from its home market.

For example, Friendster. According to *Inc.* reporter Max Chafkin, as the social networking site was melting down in early 2004, one of its engineers noticed that traffic shot up around 2:00 a.m. He checked the logs and discovered that most of these night owls were actually logging on during the day from the Philippines, fifteen hours ahead of California. Seeking the first member to friend a Filipino, he backtracked through the data until he came to Carmen Leilani De Jesus, the ninety-first person to join Friendster. A marketing consultant and part-time hypnotherapist from San Francisco, she was connected to dozens of Filipinos. They in turn joined with thousands of others, spreading Friendster across Southeast Asia. Because they surfed the network during off-peak hours, they hadn't experienced the slow page-loading times, brownouts, and outages plaguing Americans. Soon more than half of Friendster's traffic originated halfway across the world.

[FACEBOOK'S VIRAL CLUSTERS]

Then there is Facebook, which has sustained a major global push, overtaking MySpace in the United States, Canada, Austria, Italy, and Libya and, after AOL ran Bebo into the ground, wresting control of the UK, Australia, and New Zealand. From the beginning Facebook targeted college campuses, and because students are friends with other students across national boundaries, a viral spurt at, say, an American university led to one in India, France, or Japan. Wherever there are students, there is the potential for Facebook to grow. If you find the global map reminiscent of the classic board game Risk, with social networks acting the part of conquering armies, then perhaps you wouldn't be surprised to learn that Facebook's founder was such an avid player that he coded an online version of it when he was in the ninth grade.

The tale of Mark Zuckerberg has been told so often it's become part of geek folklore. Raised in a New York City suburb, Zuckerberg earned a reputation at Harvard as a prodigiously talented programmer. One application, which he named Coursematch, let students learn who had signed up for which classes. Another parsed the campus newspaper to find people mentioned in its pages and link them through different articles. His biggest splash came with Facemash, which aped Hot or Not, inviting students to upload pictures for peers to rate. Zuckerberg raided an online cache of Harvard student ID photos, posted them side by side, invited users to vote on who was better looking, and tabulated the results into a top 10 list for each campus house. Facemash proved popular and controversial— the administration charged him with violating students' privacy. (He got off with a warning.)

Shortly afterward, three seniors hired the precocious freshman to finish coding a social networking site they hoped would compete with Friendster. Zuckerberg never got around to it, instead concentrating on another project.* He contends the small, extracurricular programming projects he had undertaken set the foundation for an all-purpose tool that would bring together all of those elements. The vehicle, he decided, would be the traditional college facebook, the directory that for each freshman included a photo and brief identifying information like name, hometown, high school, and date of birth. It took about two weeks for Zuckerberg to code Thefacebook.com, which debuted on the evening of February 4, 2004.

It was a simple, streamlined site. A Harvard email address was required for registration, with profiles consisting of a photo, the student's major,

---

* After Facebook became an iconic company, the three seniors sued Zuckerberg in March 2007, alleging a smorgasbord of misdeeds, including copyright infringement, breach of contract, misappropriation of trade secrets, and fraud. The case settled out of court in 2008 for a reported $65 million, more than two-thirds of it in private stock that cannot be sold without board approval. Most of the $20 million in cash went to lawyers and taxes.

favorite books, movies, music, and a place to share pithy quotes. Students could friend other students by linking to their profiles and "poke" someone to indicate they had dropped in. After creating a few test profiles, Zuckerberg made ones for himself and his roommates, Dustin Moscowitz and Chris Hughes. Someone suggested they post an announcement on the dorm mailing list, and dozens joined. Inside twenty-four hours, more than twelve hundred students registered. Five days later the *Harvard Crimson* ran a story on Thefacebook.com, and by the end of the month three-quarters of the undergraduate population (about seven thousand students) had signed on.

Zuckerberg was surprised it took off so quickly. He and his roommates had "a sense that the type of dynamics we were tapping into were pretty universal," he says. "The thing that was surprising was that our implementation, specifically, was so efficient at doing it." Soon other schools asked whether Thefacebook.com would launch outside of Harvard. While enrolled in challenging courses, including an operating systems course that he says is one of the hardest classes at Harvard (a friend tutored him so he could pass), Zuckerberg, Moscowitz, and Hughes spread Thefacebook.com to Yale, Stanford, and Columbia, which they selected because each school had a popular existing community website.

Their reasoning was simple and audacious. To ensure Thefacebook .com was worth their time and effort, they wanted to be sure "we had an implementation that was so efficient that even though everyone already had something they were using, they would just switch and start using ours," Zuckerberg says. Within two weeks there was a mass migration from the existing campus site to Thefacebook.com. Encouraged, the three roommates over the course of the semester expanded to twenty-five more schools—most without entrenched community sites—tacking up on their walls pictures of S curves representing the adoption rates on various campuses.

The bigger the school, the longer it took to arrive at full inflection. At Cornell a couple of weeks passed before exponential growth kicked in. As with smaller schools, however, eventually a critical mass was achieved; then there arose the social expectation that everyone had to be on it. Since students communicate with those attending other colleges, there was significant pentup demand for Thefacebook.com elsewhere, with campus newspapers trumpeting its arrival. This drove the site through the early sign-up phase, when the landscape was particularly barren and there was little utility for early adopters. "The value that people get is tied to how much information everyone is sharing," Zuckerberg says. He and his roommates encouraged the first wave of registrants in the ramping-up period to share information through pictures. The second wave would see the information and attract the first wave back, which helped Thefacebook.com "gel as a network."

Not that it was easy. The faster the network scaled, the more resources had to be thrown at it, which necessitated building new infrastructure on the fly. It wasn't always a smooth ride, but they avoided disaster by controlling the rate of scaling. "We weren't structured as a company, and we didn't have a lot of money, and we were running ads to make money to buy more servers to launch at more schools," Zuckerberg says. "Because we knew we were going to be constrained, we built into the system that not everyone at the system could sign on at once." To accomplish this they required each sign-up to have a valid college email address. It helped Thefacebook.com become "exclubiquitous," to walk the line between being exclusive and ubiquitous on any given campus. "In a lot of ways we slowed down our growth," he says, "but the flip side of that was that as we were growing, we were able to not fall over."

While Facebook's scorching growth appears reminiscent of eBay, there is a stark difference. Through network effects, eBay locked up auctions, making it virtually impossible for a competitor to take root. It's different for Facebook, which eventually dropped the "the" from its name. "Its not like social networking by itself is an activity," Zuckerberg says. It's simply a platform for various social activities expressed through different applications. So "network effects aren't as clearly aligned as they are with auctions. By offering a superior and more efficient product, you can pretty predictably displace any competitor even if they have network effects."

Comparing Facebook to MySpace is perhaps less about being superior and more a matter of taste, but one trend over the past couple years is indisputable. In 2007 both sites appeared to have hit a point of ultimate saturation, their growth slackening. Then Facebook made two changes that spurred on a new wave of sign-ups, leaving MySpace, stuck on 100 million users, in the dust. Facebook calculated that when a new user made ten friends, she would likely shift into becoming active on the site, and her networks of friends would continue to expand. To encourage this, the company added the feature "people you may know," which immediately began to pay dividends. This small change led to a big uptick in Facebook's viral coefficient.

With growth once again jump-started in the United States, it then applied its original college growth strategy globally. Zuckerberg notes the growth curves abroad are "very similar, except instead of colleges we have countries." As with Ivy League colleges' part of Facebook's initial expansion, some nations, like Canada, have reached a point of slow growth since 40 percent of its Internet population is already on Facebook, while others just starting out are in the vertiginous ramping-up phase. As Facebook is translated into more languages, growth has been accelerating in non-English-speaking countries in Europe and Latin America, which makes calculating its global growth rate more complex. In 2007, when Facebook was spreading fast and furiously, it grew 3 percent a week, but that didn't mean it experienced equal growth rates in every nook and cranny of the world. Saturated markets flattened out, while new ones whirled upward. "It's really a combination of markets that are more saturated with other new markets that are just starting to grow exponentially," Zuckerberg says.

His ultimate goal: to attract so many people around the world on Facebook it becomes not only the global standard for social networking, it becomes the new operating system. He takes his lead from Microsoft, which controlled the desktop in the 1990s. Whoever controls the standard wins. Then you can leverage your control with greater numbers of products and applications, giving you a decisive advantage over competitors. With the trend toward cloud computing and the mobile Internet, however, Microsoft's operating system is fast turning into an albatross. Competitors like Google are bypassing it to offer applications in the cloud and there's nothing Microsoft can do to stop them.

[GOOGLE: FACEBOOK'S FUTURE FOE?]

Even Google, with its $100 billion plus market capitalization, is vulnerable, because social networks, which count on user engagement, are, for many people, their first stop on their Web journeys. Why click to Google to find out where you should take your next vacation, what kind of computer you should buy, what the best recipe for chocolate cookies is when you can query your expanding social network—people who are your friends because, in part, you trust them. Instead of being faced with hundreds of thousands of results, you can engage in a dialogue until you arrive at the answers. This doesn't mean Google will go out of business any time soon, but if Zuckerberg gets his way, Facebook will become the portal for half a billion people. (Approaching 200 million users, he is more than one-third of the way there.) This could conceivably help him skim significant amounts off the top from Google's search action. And if Facebook were to incorporate its own trusted network search within the vast informational grid of its members, where users tap the expertise and knowledge of those outside their cliques, Facebook might not only become the Microsoft of Web 2.0; it could become Google, too.

FACEBOOK BY THE NUMBERS . . .

5: number of years that have passed since launch

120: number of friends the average user has

15,000,000: number of users who update their status at least once a day

24,000,000: number of pieces of content (applications, blog posts, messages and chat, news stories, photos, and Web links) shared each month

850,000,000: number of photos uploaded to the site each month

Source: facereviews.com.

There is another perhaps more perplexing problem that Google faces: trust. In other words, it can be gamed, its results skewed by various digital ne'er-do-wells. "Black-hat" search engine optimization (SEO) has been an ongoing problem for Google. Dave Dittrich, a senior security engineer and researcher at the University of Washington Information School, says a typical approach is to create thousands of web pages running on hundreds of servers that cross-link to one another. Each file contains text that includes a word and strings that result from doing a search for that word. It can then push a product or service onto the first page of results, and that is by far the most valuable search engine real estate, because studies show that 90 percent of people don't bother to venture past the first page. (And 97 percent don't read past page three or the first thirty results.) This means there's a lot of money at stake. The difference between appearing on page one of results versus page four can be worth millions of dollars. But it's more than just a question of money. It involves security, too.

As far back as November 2007, cybercriminals have been borrowing black-hat SEO techniques to target popular keywords on Google, everything from "how to teach a dog to play fetch" to terms relating to Easter, March madness, Barack Obama, and in the weeks leading up to April 15, IRS forms. Their goal: to disseminate destructive payloads. This malware, as it's called, can, if downloaded, cause serious harm to a PC—like surreptitiously installing adware, spyware, malicious programs to turn it into a zombie and unleash billions of spam, or even wipe out the hard drive. Google boasts that it uses "more than 200 signals," including its patented PageRank algorithm, to rank sites. Yet, by one count, more than a million links point to a single poisonous domain that has been churning out billions of pages that seek to fool Google's spiders. In response Google created a filter to counter this malware frenzy, which once went haywire, blocking every single site that turned up for almost an hour and freaking out some users. If Google search isn't democracy incarnate, which is how it advertises itself, then what is it? In some instances a rigged system that rewards not the sites that have earned placement on the most valuable real estate—the first page or two of results—but one in which scammers can profit.

And what if these cybercriminals, like those behind the mysterious Conficker worm that penetrated millions of computers around the world, were to deploy more damaging payloads? For the most part they have stuck with basic PC-busting malware, which is often sniffed out by anti-virus products. If these hackers were to switch to more damaging Microsoft

PC "0days" (pronounced "oh-days" or "zero days," it generally refers to unknown, or zero-hour, software threats that are easily attained on the hacker black market), Google could become a most inhospitable place to search. A 2009 report identified a vast cyberespionage campaign dubbed GhostNet that infected 1,295 infected computers in 103 countries, including embassies, international organizations, ministries of foreign affairs, news media, and NGOs. It, too, relied on malware to disseminate an application called Gh0st Rat that transformed PCs into spy devices, pilfering confidential documents and turning on cameras and microphones without users' knowledge. Less than a third of antivirus products on the market provided protection.

[FAILED SOCIAL NETWORKS]

By offering a trusted (and trusting) environment, social networks like Facebook may be direct beneficiaries of what ails Google. But while you hear about the ones that make it big (Facebook, MySpace, Bebo, LinkedIn), you rarely hear about those that don't. Yet they offer equally valuable lessons. Tribe, for one, which its founder, entrepreneur Mark Pincus, dubbed a "social marketplace," is a cross between Craigslist and Friendster, with the inspiration coming from the book *Urban Tribes*, by Ethan Watters. Launched in 2003, Tribe was an attempt to nichify people's interests within a hyperlocal context. Because if you think about it, when you go about your life, you become linked, based on your interests, hobbies, and needs, to smaller niche communities. You might live in New York, work on Wall Street or in a Soho art gallery, play tennis, love jazz, prefer a Mac to a PC, take Pilates classes, shoot your own video that you post on your blog, collect wine and take bicycle trips over the weekend. To some you are a colleague, to others a fellow tennis player (with perhaps some crossover with your job), and to an entirely different group a blogger, and so forth. Each of these interests is, in and of itself, the foundation for a niche community that can act as a filter.

"So much of what we do around the Internet is about personal lead generation," Pincus says. "You have this close-knit tribe and there'll be value in a community level with you connecting with that group." Want

to improve your topspin backhand in tennis? Canvass more advanced players? Look for a new job? "The best possible place for lead generation is a
cocktail party," Pincus says, with Tribe, in a sense, an online version of that,
with cliques collecting around specific interests and vocations. Over the first
six months, it scaled to five hundred thousand members, then stagnated.
(MySpace, in contrast, had 1.4 million users at the end of its first month.)
Tribe was beset by growing pains, which affected site performance. The
coup de grâce, however, was its attempt to broaden its appeal. In 2006 Tribe
underwent a redesign to make it more mainstream, which pulled it away
from its original grass-roots mission and alienated its core user base, many
of whom had joined because they were into alternative lifestyles and the arts.

But Pincus believes his big mistake was that Tribe wasn't naturally
viral. Because it focused on cities, communities were geographically fixed
and grew separately with little synergy. A New Yorker wouldn't bother to
invite a friend from San Francisco since his community revolved around
being in New York, and vice versa. Pincus also found it nearly impossible
to gain critical mass in urban areas. "Once you penetrate fifteen to twenty
percent of an online community, the value is so massive that you get the
other eighty percent, but a city is too big," Pincus says. "Even if you had
fifty thousand in San Francisco, you're not even at ten percent, whereas at
Harvard you get two thousand kids" to sign on to Facebook, "you're done.
Then you have grounds for word of mouth from school to school."

Another early social network was LiveJournal, a virtual community
centered on interests from celebrity gossip to TV shows to rakish science
fiction and Harry Potter porn. Started in 1999, users created blog journals
they could push to their friends. The site employed a paid subscription
model, didn't allow advertising, and counted on the support of volunteers
and open-source software to keep the site up and running. While it grew
to several million members, LiveJournal wasn't inherently viral either,
which limited its growth. That was fine by Brad Fitzpatrick, the founder.
He was exhausted from keeping the site afloat and had considered pulling the plug. Instead, he sold to Six Apart, a blogging platform company,
which in turn unloaded it to a Russian media company.

Predating all of them was SixDegrees.com, the first online social network. Started in prebroadband 1995 by Andrew Weinreich, a freshly

minted Fordham law student, the site had users list friends, colleagues, family members, and acquaintances, both on the site and off, with those who weren't members invited to join. They dispatched messages or posted comments on bulletin boards to anyone within their first, second, or third degrees of separation. While it grew to 3 million members from 165 countries, the site was a money loser. In 2000 YouthStream Media Network bought it for $125 million in stock and promptly shut it down.

The one thing of value it retained was a patent: no. 6,175,831, "method and apparatus for constructing a networking database and system," which Weinreich was awarded in 2001. The patent covers the software platform for an online service that enables users to build relationship networks, that is, the viral invitation system that goes to the heart of online social networking. Andrew Katz, an intellectual-property attorney with Fox Rothschild, told the *New York Times* that it "is probably the pioneer patent out there," and warned that "it should be taken very seriously by everybody in the industry."

Just as Friendster was picking up momentum, YouthStream announced it would auction off the "six degrees patent" in September 2003. Six months earlier, Reid Hoffman, a former SixDegrees employee flush from the sale of PayPal, had started LinkedIn. Weinreich tipped him off about the impending sale, and Hoffman worried that whoever possessed the patent could potentially prevent everybody else from starting social networks. He teamed up with Tribe's Mark Pincus to form Degrees of Connection LLC, a Delaware limited liability company they used to bid on their behalf. They contacted Friendster to see if Abrams might be interested in splitting the cost three ways, but never heard back. It crossed their minds that Friendster's main backer, Kleiner Perkins, might bid against them in a quest to stamp out competitors.

It was a blind auction, so all that Hoffman and Pincus know is they won with a bid of $700,000. Hoffman says his share, $350,000, "is not that much money and it also became an asset of [LinkedIn], which we could figure out later." They could conceivably assert their intellectual-property rights and hold Facebook, MySpace, Bebo, and all the others hostage. Hoffman concedes as much but claims they have no plans for the patent. Buying it was simply a "defensive posture."

[THINGAMAJIGS]

With perhaps a billion people, which is a fifth of the planet, on social networks, an entire ecosystem has been stacked over them. These are the so-called widgets: mini software applications that range from the sublime to the silly—a photo slideshow, video, a map of the places you've traveled, a pop quiz to measure your intelligence, empathy, or what kind of dog you're most like. They can be used to toss virtual sheep at friends, decorate pictures with stickers and graffiti, or add glitter, games like Speed Racing ("mod your car to get more horsepower" then "race your friends"), social interactive pleas for attention like Hug Me ("Do more stuff to your friends: hug, slap, tickle, give beer to, throw Britney at . . .") or your horoscope. Nonprofit organizations release social network applications for fundraising, and media companies for brand extension.

The first social network widgets popped up on MySpace. Teenage girls took advantage of a coding glitch to customize their pages. One of them, Sandi Sayama, a pretty, outgoing seventeen-year-old high school student in California, spent a lot of time on MySpace and had picked up enough HTML coding to personalize her page with sparkling stars and pictures. But she was having trouble creating a slideshow so her photos could rotate because HTML was far from the ideal way to do it. After school, the five-foot, one-inch Sayama played in a volleyball league. Her position: setter. "It's not about height," she says, "it's about heart." She played with a family friend, Lance Tokuda, a computer programmer from Hawaii and told him about her problems with getting her slideshow to work. Tokuda became fascinated with MySpace, which was emerging as the next big thing. Sayama had been the most popular girl in her middle school, and Tokuda figured if he could build a slideshow she liked, a lot of others would, too. Coming from the drab world of enterprise software, he didn't trust himself to know what kinds of applications would have mass-market appeal.

Not long after, he showed her a basic slideshow he coded in Flash, which he had never worked in before. "Oh, that's cool," she said. She would definitely use that on MySpace.

But?

Needs glitter, she said.

Tokuda went back to the drawing board and, in addition to glitter, added the option of snowflakes. While she liked the snowflakes, they were too dark and obscured the picture behind. They should be more see-through, she advised.

Shortly after, Tokuda, along with a colleague from work, Jia Shen, founded RockMySpace, which they soon changed to RockYou, a company to distribute social network applications. The first app was the photo slideshow, which they posted on the MySpace forum six times. The first day only four people downloaded; the second, twenty. Then it went to forty, to eighty, to crashing their servers (see Fig. 9). It proved so popular that Tom Anderson of MySpace emailed the two entrepreneurs to congratulate them. The skyrocketing demand forced them to move to a new host, but within three weeks RockYou's traffic took down the entire network. Despite shutting down the site for seventeen days out of the first thirty while they waited for new servers to arrive, they registered sixty thousand users in the first month.*

Soon MySpace figured it would get in on the action and released its own photo slideshow player. Too late. RockYou had already hit a point of nondisplacement. And MySpace wasn't the only platform anymore. Facebook opened up to outside developers, and others joined Open Social, which meant an application coded for, say, Orkut would also work on Bebo and the others, which offered a tremendous boost to companies like RockYou. To stay ahead Tokuda and Shen hired Sayama, who had enrolled at San Jose State, studying to be a parole officer, as their official arbiter of taste. They thought of their target audience and realized that they—and the engineers they were hiring—were out of touch. Most people at Stanford didn't use MySpace. They thought it was a joke. So before they would release an application, one of them would say, "Let's hear what Sandi says," and she would offer her impressions.

Sayama told them to clean up their website because she felt it was too cluttered and loud, like they were trying too hard. She also created the

---

* Scaling wasn't their only hitch. Before RockYou, Tokuda and Shen had been working on a photo slideshow for software developer Iconix, which accused the two of stealing intellectual property. The case quickly settled.

METRICS FOR VIRAL LOOP

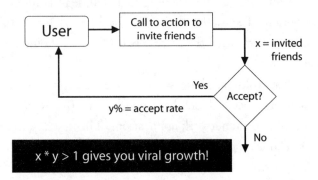

FIG. 9. In this formula, *x* is the average number of friends that a user invites to try an application. In RockYou's case, *x* = 5 while *y* is the acceptance rate, which is 22 percent. The viral coefficient (also known as viral factor) is arrived at by multiplying *x* times: *y* 5 x 0.22 = 1.1. Since it is greater than 1, the application is viral. (*RockYou.*)

greeting cards in RockYou's SuperWall, which was a viral channel that could hold photos, video, and other content and picked the icons for the social app game Hug Me. In exchange, Sayama received shares in the company and was paid handsomely for thirty hours a week of work—which made her feel guilty. She compares herself to a game tester versus someone actually making the game. "My friends always say that I have a really cool job," Sayama says. "I just sit there and work on this, work on that and give my opinions. I feel like somebody making the game is contributing more than somebody testing it."

While Sayama advised on the aesthetics, Tokuda and Shen became expert at designing for the viral loop, with several applications among the Web's most popular applications. Within twenty-five months RockYou registered 50 million users (in contrast, 99 percent of applications don't achieve 1 million installs), and over four years it raised almost $70 million in funding. They want to become one of the highest-trafficked websites in the world, a portal "like Yahoo," Tokuda says, for social applications. By early 2009 RockYou.com was handling more than 100 million users a month.

[SLIDE: NUMBER ONE NEMESIS]

But they have stiff competition, namely, in the former PayPal founder, Max Levchin, who followed Tokuda and Shen to MySpace but was ahead of them in coding widgets. His muse: James Hong, the "Where's Waldo?" of the viral loop business world. Not only had Hong created Hot or Not, one of the early viral loop businesses, he was friends with Levchin, lending him photos so the master programmer could build a "babe ticker," another product of Hong's fertile imagination. This way, guys could stare at an endless loop of beautiful women strolling by on their screens.

While most people would be content to clear $30 million from the sale of their first company, Levchin could not have been more miserable. He simply didn't know what to do with himself. He bought a mansion, then promptly forgot about it. Not only did he not bother to furnish it, he didn't even sleep there, preferring to crash in his office in a sleeping bag. He was deeply afraid that, like a physicist or an athlete, he had already peaked, and now that he was entering his late twenties, life would be a long downward slide into mediocrity. Hong's cheeky girlie project was just the thing he needed to keep him occupied. Then he thought about moving beyond ogling girls and making it a more conventional product.

By August 2005 Levchin turned the concept into a Kodak Carousel–like slideshow that allowed a user to load any photos he liked and offered it as a free download for websites. Not many bothered. Disappointed, Levchin thought of his next move and glommed on to MySpace just as PayPal had once barnacled itself to eBay. His slideshow projector took off in the virality sea of MySpace users, and by the time he sought venture funding, he was able to report that the application had been downloaded hundreds of millions of times. In one six-month period he had streamed 10 billion images across users' screens. He formed a company, Slide, to take on RockYou and any other comers.

The two companies became entrenched in a pitched battle for supremacy, with each claiming the other had ripped off an idea or application. Both pushed the boundaries of acceptable behavior by pushing the virality factor, building hooks into their products to spread faster than the other guy's. Users were caught in the middle, and some complained mightily when an application would hijack his address book and automatically invite all his friends to install an application. At conferences attendees would accuse both companies of spamming social network users. Each blamed the other for the bad behavior, claiming it was necessary to keep up. By June 2006 Facebook had seen enough and began clamping down on these wayward social applications makers, banning them for being too viral or having security holes.

The big question is, how will any of these companies, both applications makers and the social networks they sponge off, make money? Skeptics, and there are many, point out that while social networking has attracted a huge user base, which the apps makers tap into, no one has figured out a viable strategy to monetize. That's because the more people are online, the less likely they are to click on an ad. To attract a large user base, social networks give away their products. They can't charge users, otherwise they will go elsewhere. Advertising doesn't work either. The click-through rate on banner ads on social networks is barely 0.02 percent. Even spam can have a higher conversion rate. That's because the longer someone is online—and social network users are online a lot—the less likely they are to click on an ad.

Comparisons to the dot-com bust are inevitable. As with social networking and widgets, companies seemingly sprouted up overnight and, by dint of their popularity or because they promoted a promising idea, were rewarded with fat valuations even as they reported puny revenues. Potential is well and fine, critics say, but show me the money. Look at YouTube, for which Google paid $1.65 billion: it has yet to generate much revenue. Or Facebook, which makes more than $300 million a year in a deal it struck with Microsoft that gave it a valuation of $15 billion. Ning makes a pittance on Google Ads, and even though it has other revenue streams (premium services, etc.), it doesn't have to spend much time counting the money it collects. Friendster is big in the Philippines and Malaysia, but an also-ran almost everywhere else. RockYou and Slide, despite appearing on millions of pages around the world, don't generate much cash. And Netscape is dead and buried.

The usual strategy for viral companies is to get big and get bought, and on that the record is also mixed. Hot or Not continues to draw oglers. Hotmail is a healthy complement to Microsoft's suite of online offerings. PayPal has become a cash cow for eBay; Skype less so, since the company hasn't been able to incorporate it. AOL bought Bebo only to ruin it. Google's Orkut may have a ringside seat at Carnival in Brazil but it's a nonentity almost everywhere else.

The naysayers claim that Facebook and all its friends in social network land—from competitors like MySpace to widget makers like Slide and RockYou—will never figure out a way to make money.

If history is any guide, they are wrong.

12

The Search for a New Ad Unit

Death to the Traditional Banner Advertisement,
the Arms Race Between Marketers
and Consumers, and Time (Not Clicks)

If there is one constant through time, it's that conventional wisdom often misses the mark, especially in the early days of technological transformation. In 1876, the president of Western Union brushed off Alexander Graham Bell's telephone as little more than an "electric toy," and the company called Bell's proposal to put one in every home "utterly out of the question." Oxford University professor Erasmus Wilson predicted that when the 1878 Paris Exhibition closed, the electric light would "close with it and no more will be heard of it." A Michigan banker advised his client not to invest in Henry Ford's company in 1903 because "the horse is here to stay, but the automobile is only a novelty." And Microsoft founder Bill Gates was years behind in seeing the promise of the Internet.

When the Web exploded in the early 1990s, most people believed there was no way to make money on it. At a conference in December 1996, Nicholas Negroponte, founding director of MIT's Media Laboratories, felt the need to combat the no-money-on-the-Web meme, calling those who held that belief "off their rocker."* One challenge would be to convince people it was safe to share their credit card information over the Web. That didn't mean that Negroponte, an astute observer of all things digital, had clearly developed ideas of how businesses could thrive online, other than to predict that one day transactions—the selling of goods over

---

* One of those adherents was none other than Bill Gates, though he did eventually come around. Or as Negroponte put it: "Bill has an extraordinary ability of being wrong . . . then suddenly changing his mind . . . and being right at exactly the right time."

the Internet—would be a trillion-dollar market and that "digital money" would proliferate. Then came blue chip companies like eBay, PayPal, Yahoo, Google, and Amazon, which, save for eBay, lost money for several years before becoming companies with billion-dollar market caps. EBay spawned an entire ecosystem of sellers that earn their living by selling goods. So has Amazon through its Marketplace. To this day, millions of small businesses have staked a claim online and the "there's no money on the Internet" meme has dissipated into the ether.

In the mid- to late 1990s experts claimed that the Search function was not a stand-alone product because there was no way to monetize it. As a result, Yahoo, Alta Vista, Lycos, and others vied to become super-portals where a user's every need was made available on one supersite. Search, the thinking went, was only good for drawing users, who would stay to sample a variety of other services like news, horoscopes, financial information, chat rooms, the weather, and so on. Then Google flipped conventional wisdom on its ear. As the portals put their re-sources into adding more choices to their menu of offerings, they gave short shrift to the underlying search technology, since they believed there was little differentiation. They became cluttered with content and ads, in contrast to Google, which maintained a simple interface with a lone search box.

Google subsequently introduced a new ad unit: keyword search.* In-put, say, "coffeemaker" in Google's search box and above and to the side of the free results would be basic text advertisements that marketers and indi-viduals could bid on. Because these advertisements were based on intent, catching a searcher at the very moment she was looking for information, they were extremely powerful. What's better: Running car commercials on TV or banner ads on Internet sites in the hopes that a tiny fraction of people might be in the market for a new car? Or hitting her with a highly targeted ad at the moment she looks for one? The keyword ad unit revolu-tionized the search industry, and Google, by skimming nickels, dimes, and quarters off each one, rode it to a multibillion-dollar fortune.

---

* Google didn't invent keyword search. A company called Overture did, and had a patent to prove it. In 2002 Overture, which was subsequently bought by Yahoo, sued Google, which settled the case for $300 million in stock in 2004.

Social networking companies like Facebook and others are also seeking a new ad unit. The problem is that advertising on the traditional banner ad doesn't work anymore. In the Web's early days, click-through rates were as high as 50 percent, simply because users had never encountered them before. ("Hmm. What's this button do?") The rates steadily declined, but even a decade ago they were 6 percent. Now they hover around 1 percent and are far lower on social networking sites. That's because people on Facebook or MySpace spend a lot of time on the Internet, and the more time someone spends online, the less likely he is to click on an ad. In retrospect, it's amazing to think that an entire industry was built on the notion of clickable ads when most people would be hard-pressed to name a single person they knew who actually clicked on them.

[THE ARMS RACE BETWEEN MARKETERS AND CONSUMERS]

But this dynamic is simply the latest round in the battle between marketers and consumers. When there were just three TV networks, radio, and a handful of magazines and newspapers, marketers had a captive audience. One ad on *I Love Lucy* could reach more than a third of the television audience in the 1950s. Today marketers use words like "fractured" or "fragmented" to describe this new media landscape, where there are hundreds of channels, thousands of publications, websites and blogs and social networks, and a million places to put ads. It is, in short, the niche-ification of content, a premise put forward by *Wired* editor Chris Anderson in *The Long Tail: Why the Future of Business Is Selling Less of More.* Specifying media, tech entrepreneur and Dallas Mavericks owner Mark Cuban dubs it the "long-tail marketing effect": "As the number of media and entertainment alternatives grows, so does the competition and cost of moving to the head." The question is: How can marketers cut through the clutter to get their message across to consumers who are increasingly hostile to having their time interrupted?

This sturm und drang has been ongoing for decades, and it is, maintains David Schwartz, founder of Radius Marketing, completely natural. "How many times have you gone home from a commute, left your office after interacting with tons of people, and have no idea what you just did?" he asks. "Your mind is good at canceling out what is not germane to your life." That tendency might explain why many people don't even see banner ads on websites. They just see what they want to see: the news story they want to read, the video they want to view, the information they need to get the job done. It's a form of selective vision, a way of filtering information when the senses are overloaded. Schwartz believes this dynamic is part of an evolutionary process. Advertisers advance the science of advertising, discovering all manner of ways of reaching us, then consumers become expert at shedding messages they don't want to hear. In essence, it's a media version of an arms race.

First, advertisers broadcast TV commercials considerably louder than the shows they interrupted, but the mute button circumvented that ploy. Then the networks added commercial time to television programs, up from three minutes per half hour sitcom (and six minutes per hour) in the 1960s to eight minutes per half hour today. When the commercials were bunched at the ends of shows, consumers used their remotes to surf to other channels, so broadcasters started to run shows right into one another in the hopes of holding on to their lead-ins. Viewers got TiVo and digital video recorders and began fast-forwarding through shows. Marketers responded by making TV commercials more engaging, the kind that make viewers stick around. So far it's been working, according to some recent studies, which found that TV watchers were less likely to hit the fast-forward button if a commercial appealed to them within the few sentences, and if it touched them emotionally. In other words, the ad has to offer a value proposition.

The battle has moved into different media. Marketers littered cyberspace with pop-up ads. Web-savvy consumers responded by learning to use pop-up ad blockers on their browsers. Radio stations packed more commercials into each hour of programming, and as playlists on commercial radio grew mind-numbingly repetitive, listeners migrated to iPods or satellite radio. Sleazy marketers turned to spam. Internet service providers deployed spam blockers—catching billions of spam messages in their nets every day—while consumers tweaked their own email filters.

Today's buzzword is "engagement." Give people a reason to interact with ads and promotions on TV, or to click on or download them via the

Web. "Anything that causes the audience to be grateful for entertainment means they are more likely to pass it on," says Colby Atwood, a newspaper analyst and a president of Borrell Associates. "Everyone likes to be the one to share something interesting with their circle of friends." This value exchange isn't limited to providing cheap entertainment thrills. Because creating a connection with a product takes a commitment, what people really want is for marketers to reach them at the moment they are ready to buy something and leave them alone the rest of the time. Think of it as the consumers' version of the just-in-time delivery supply chain deployed by the tech, retail, and manufacturing sectors. Done right, it's a tremendous business opportunity, as Google showed with keyword search ads. In fact, an entire industry has popped up around the concept: behavioral marketing, which amassed $2 billion a year in spending by 2009.

[THE PRIVACY SHIBBOLETH]

People devote only 5 percent of their time online on search engines. The rest is spent on social networks and browsing other sites. If marketers could follow us without actually eavesdropping, they would be able to compile comprehensive dossiers based on the types of sites we visit, the things we read, the videos we watch, the products we shop for. It sounds spooky, of course, and people claim they do care about the lack of privacy. A UPI–Zogby International poll from 2007 found that 85 percent of respondents claimed privacy of their personal information was important to them as consumers, and 91 percent said they were worried about identity theft. In another UPI-Zogby poll, 50 percent of participants expressed concern over the privacy of their medical records. Most, however, aren't concerned enough to do anything about it.

If privacy is, as Supreme Court Justice Louis Brandeis proposed eighty years ago, "the right to be left alone—the most comprehensive of rights and the right most valued by civilized men," which he included as part of a set of conditions "favorable to the pursuit of happiness" laid down by the Founding Fathers in the Constitution, how would he view our current surveillance society? Over the course of a day the typical American is caught on camera two hundred times: at traffic lights, paying highway tolls, walking the dogs, taking money from ATMs, shopping in convenience stores, and a tiny fraction are caught committing crimes. Within a twenty-block radius of New York University, there are more than five hundred surveillance cameras, which catch students and professors doing everything from buying a falafel, racing past the iconic fountain in Washington Square Park on the way to class, or purchasing allergy medicine like Claritin-D, for which they are required by law to show their driver's licenses because it contains a common substance used in meth.

It's not just New York's Greenwich Village, where NYU is located, with its own 24-7 reality show starring . . . everybody. Dozens of states have set up traffic light cameras that ticket drivers for running red lights or speeding. Casinos in Las Vegas zoom in on players' hands at the blackjack table. Cameras are mounted on police cars, they hang from trees in public parks, they're affixed to the walls in sports stadiums and shopping malls. David Brin, author of *The Transparent Society*, postulates a "Moore's law of cameras." He sees them roughly "halving in size, and doubling in acuity and movement capability and sheer numbers, every year or two." Look out a decade and nano-cameras as small as grains of sand may create a world in which the wind has eyes.

If privacy is "the state of being free from unsanctioned intrusion," which is the *American Heritage Dictionary* definition, what about the Department of Motor Vehicles, famous for peddling personal information to anyone who will buy it? Or the credit-rating agencies like TransUnion, Equifax, and Experian, which profit by selling access to our financial histories? Or the most brazen of all, the government, which stiff-armed companies such as AT&T to record our phone calls and sniff our email, all in the name of fighting terrorism? Or if "privacy is the power to selectively reveal oneself to the world," a view tendered in the essay "A Cypherpunk's Manifesto," what's the deal with Gmail, which keeps carbon copies of all our email correspondence forever, so Google can barrage us with more ads? Or American Express, which collects the details of billions of customer transactions, weaves them into models of behavior, and sells this data to junk mailers of all stripes and sizes?

The truth is, the battle over privacy (no matter how it is defined) has already been lost. As Sun CEO Scott McNealy infamously put it, "You have no privacy. Get over it." Since we consumers have been complicit in this postprivacy smack-down, however, it's not necessarily bad either. In fact, it could be good, and not just for the corporations that profit from it or the government that taps into it to control its citizenry.

"Information wants to be free" is the hacker's credo. In reality, information has a price in the form of convenience, cash, or security. It's why we shop with credit cards, even though they lead to mailbox-cramming junk mail, and sign up for loyalty cards with Barnes & Noble or CVS's ExtraCare program, which has enrolled tens of millions of Americans who receive 2 percent back on every purchase and an additional dollar for every two prescriptions they fill in exchange for tracking every purchase. It's the reason we use cell phones when we are out of the office, global positioning services (GPS) when we are on the road, and OnStar for the few who buy GM cars, all of which can pinpoint our location. We still surf the Web, despite our Internet service provider (ISP) knowing what sites we visit and how long we stay, and search with Google, which maintains lists of all the terms we've queried. Remember that late-night tequila binge and that curiously odd sexual . . . never mind. None of these are spy technologies, but they might as well be.

Donald Kerr, principal deputy director of national intelligence, said in a speech in October 2007 that Americans would have to change their view of privacy, which "no longer can mean anonymity," he said. "Instead, it should mean that government and businesses properly safeguard people's private communications and financial information." He added, "Protecting anonymity isn't a fight that can be won," which is creepy coming from one of our nation's top spies. No surprise that the blogosphere squealed. After all, a staggering 127 million sensitive electronic and paper records were lost or pierced by hackers last year, while identity theft runs rampant, affecting one in eight Americans (and growing every year). The idea of the government safeguarding our information is laughable. Naturally, we can blame technology and the greater interconnectedness of our world, since it replicates our personal information and spews it far and wide in cyberspace, stashing it in far-flung databases outside of our control. We don't just have Big Brother to contend with, we have a series of little brothers—your Googles, DoubleClicks, and ISPs, the credit-rating agencies, social networks like MySpace and Facebook, and marketers who want to know everything about you. With advanced data-sifting techniques, the rise of massive databases and the permanence of the Web, once your information is out there it can never be taken back, our deepest, darkest secrets instantly available to anyone with the desire and know-how to learn them.

If Eric Schmidt, CEO of Google, can't keep secret his home address, the value of his house, date of birth, net worth, value of Google stock, hobbies, quotes he'd just as soon take back (like "Evil is what Sergey says is evil"), what chance do the rest of us have? With Google Earth it's even possible to view his home and property. (It's amazing what $3 million will get you.) If you recall, in 2005 Google briefly blacklisted CNET because a reporter Googled Schmidt, then published what she found (things like he wandered the desert at Burning Man and earned $140 million dumping Google stock). The company didn't like the fact that CNET published the Google CEO's private information, which the reporter found using the company's own product.

It's easy to find people to gripe about privacy, laying blame at the feet of big business and big government, but what to do about it? Talk to the privacy hawks at the Electronic Privacy Information Center and they'll tell you what the problem is, decrying the actions of the credit agencies, Google, and the government, but not how to fix things, other than to offer consumers bromides like "pay with cash where possible," "don't share any personal information with businesses unless it is absolutely necessary," and "choose supermarkets that don't use loyalty cards." But companies have a powerful profit motive. Our information, the more personal the better, is worth billions. The better they know us, our likes and dislikes, the easier it is for them to induce us to buy buy buy and the more money they'll make. The only way to keep our personal information personal is to unplug from the grid: pay with cash, don't surf the Web from home or your job, don't go out in public without a mask, don't drive a car, don't maintain a checking or savings account, don't use a cell phone or PDA, and under no circumstances take out a mortgage. Good luck.

Yet this doesn't mean we are heading toward some William Gibson-esque techno-dystopia. Since we can't parry the privacy hounds, we need to embrace the idea of a more transparent world. Realize for all the brouhaha surrounding the issue, there's little tangible harm that arises from your personal information being used to target more relevant advertising at you. Google knows you have a taste for mud wrestling or midget tossing? So what? They're not talking, unless the government subpoenas them. Facebook told your friends you rented a slasher flick from Block-buster? They might simply ask, which one? Yahoo has proof you've been using webmail to conduct a hot, tawdry affair? Yahoo is the least of your worries.

Looking on the bright side, the wide dissemination of our personal information—that's the unintended by-product of social networks—could lead to a more tolerant, less judgmental society. Because shame is largely generational. If you are in your forties or older, your parents didn't talk about their feelings; today you can barely stop people from telling you their life stories. And today's youth, congregating on social networks, share the most intimate aspects of their lives, hewing to an ethos of kar-mic bulimia. If they don't announce something on Facebook it's, like, it never happened. And they are shaping the privacy debate as profoundly as the corporations that mine our data, the banks that sell it, the credit agen-cies that profit from it, and the government that vacuums it up.

Because what is blackmail but information arbitrage: exploiting dif-ferences in markets for financial gain. Being divorced reflected poorly on a woman fifty years ago and affected her job status. If you went into re-hab, you were shunned in some circles. If you came out of the closet as a homosexual, you might have ended up a pariah. In 1975, Oliver Sipple became a hero for helping prevent an assassination attempt on President Gerald Ford. In the ensuing media coverage, he was outed as being gay, a secret he had been desperate to keep, and his mother disowned him, he was ridiculed publicly and privately, and moved to sue seven different papers for breach of privacy. Can you imagine that happening today?

Part of the cultural change over the past three decades is due to the emergence of media as a daily part of our lives, spreading information on how our politicians, athletes, celebrities, friends, and neighbors live their lives, often focusing on their foibles (which are usually deemed more news-worthy). Now this process of tolerance is sped up exponentially as we be-come even more interconnected, because we are all vulnerable to having our secrets shared and there is little point in pretending to be holier than thou. As people spend more and more time online, their lives become broadcast fodder. Of course, identity theft is a real threat, but it's not the information that commits the crime. The credit card companies and banks cover most of your losses (passing it on to the merchants). It can be a headache to clean up the mess but usually not disastrous. Because banks and credit card companies have a vested interest in preventing fraud, identity theft victims have powerful allies (that profit motive again). Among the ironies here, of course, is that these measures were put in place to protect the public and there are those who feel safer because of them.

It's easy to cry about the loss of our privacy, but what can we do about it realistically? Boycott Google and other search engines? Won't happen. Stop using credit cards and opening bank accounts? Get real. Protest stores and businesses that install surveillance cameras? Fat chance. And you weren't expecting the government to step in, were you? On that bright side, the loss of privacy could mean the opportunity to build a better society.

[TIME, NOT CLICKS: THE NEW AD UNIT]

What does all this have to do with finding a new ad unit for social networking? Plenty, if you talk to Andy Monfriend, founder and CEO of Lotame, a social media advertising and marketing firm. He believes he has already found the Holy Grail. It's not based on cost or price per click, as with banner ads. It's time, as in how long a user interacts with a certain ad. Here's how it works: A social network that deploys Lotame's flagship product, Crowd Control, would furnish a user's age, gender, and zip code. It is barebones data, not personally identifiable information that could be used to find out a person's true identity. Lotame then dispatches a cookie, which is a piece of software that can track movements online, to the user's machine and notes his online behavior. If a client, say, Clinique, wants to target women in their twenties and thirties who have either blogged, uploaded, rated, or shared content that indicates they are looking for beauty tips, Lotame can reach a million of them across twenty or more different sites.

First, Monfried looks for "influencers"—in Malcolm Gladwell parlance, "connectors"—people who affect the buying habits of others. Social media, he points out, has no content. It is solely the by-product of users.

But what are the markers or identifiers that are critical for brand advertisers? It's not what they write, it's what they do. "There are ways consumers use the platforms," Monfried says. "They email, they blog, they comment, they post, they share, they link, they upload, they friend, they stream, they write on a wall, they update a profile. There are one hundred and sixty verbs that we currently track that become a huge identifier." Lotame identifies the influencers—those who add, join, upload, blog, or post—cross-references these actions with entertainment, health, fitness, beauty, then overlays all that with women eighteen to thirty-four. Suddenly you have a robust way of targeting. You can even limit your target to people who have uploaded videos in the last two days or who purchased makeup online in the past week. Lotame then sells an advertiser a block of time (say, four minutes) spent interacting with an advertisement over a certain period (forty-five days), covering a specific number of women (two million) that represent a demographic (aged twenty-four to thirty-five). It brings a level of granularity never before seen in marketing.

For example, Lotame ran a promotion for a new chick flick. An advertiser retained Monfried to reach 1 million American women aged fourteen to twenty-four who in the last twenty-four hours had uploaded, blogged, raided, shared, or commented on entertainment content. The advertiser bought four minutes per user over a three-week period with the understanding that the clock would freeze whenever the user stopped interacting with the ad, which in this case was a trailer for the movie. First, Lotame identified the influencers and targeted the trailer at them. A few thousand of them embedded the video in their social network profiles or blogs. Then Lotame tracked the visitors, the legions of friends and acquaintances who swung by and viewed the trailer. Every person who fit the demographic profile was tallied and timed. Meanwhile the video spread virally since a certain percentage of those who saw it on their friends' sites decided to embed the video themselves, which spread it further. Others were commenting on the trailer, telling their friends or blogging about it. All of this counted as ticks against the clock. The result: a click-through rate as high as 0.63, which is thirty-one times greater than the average rate on social networks, and it cost far less than a traditional banner ad approach to reach 1 million women.

And this takes us back to the conventional wisdom that there is no way to reach the 1 billion users worldwide on social networks. If you think the marketer-consumer seesaw is over, that the end of history is here and marketers will never crack this nut, then you believe that Facebook, MySpace, and the one hundred other social networks around the world are doomed. But if history is any guide, they won't fail. The difference between the dot-com boom and bust and the social graph is that many of the dot-coms were not victims of too much popularity; they were run out of business because they weren't popular enough. The silly poster boys of the era (Pets.com, eToys, Webvan, Kozmo.com) could not entice enough people to use their services to come anywhere near covering their overhead. Social networks have the opposite problem: they have too many users sucking down bandwidth. But it also gives them tremendous leverage.

[MONETIZING THE SOCIAL GRAPH]

If Facebook, with its hundreds of millions of users, were to follow Craigslist's model and monetize a fraction of its site—worth, say, on the order of $1 per month for each user—that would yield around $2.5 billion a year in revenue. Simply by placing ads on its home page it could probably generate $1 billion a year. PayPal focused completely on growth, its burn rate so severe that it teetered on the verge of bankruptcy before breaking even. Now it is on the way to $3 billion in revenue a year. Is Facebook, with its stratospheric viral growth, more like PayPal or Pets.com?

For his part, Mark Zuckerberg believes the answer is neither. He has big dreams and even bigger aspirations. His whole vision revolves around what he calls the "social graph," a diagram illustrating all the interconnections between people, groups, and organizations. You are friends with Charlotte who is connected to Lila, Sophie, and Charlie, and they pal around with Emily, Benjy, Lin, and Jennifer. Each is represented by a node on a graph, and the ties that bind them may be diverse and have many levels. They may be family or just friends, be connected by age, education, or interest, work in the same industry or in different jobs at the same company, share the same gene pool or an interest in politics. Where you see a complex diagram too large and unwieldy to sit on a single page, Zuckerberg sees a business opportunity. That's because he, like Monfried, recognizes there is a phenomenon in peoples' interaction. "The message you get, in a lot of ways, is actually less important than who you get it from," he says. "If you get it from someone that you trust, you'll listen to it. Whereas if you get it from someone you don't trust, you might actually believe the opposite of what they said because you don't trust them. I think that's the basis of the value that people get on the site."

The first hint of Zuckerberg's grand plan occurred in November 2007 with the release of the controversial Beacon, an advertising scheme "to socially distribute information on Facebook," as the company defined it, "a core element of the Facebook Ads system for connecting businesses with users and targeting advertising to the audiences they want." For instance, if a user viewed a video, her friends would learn about it through the news feed. If she bought movie tickets online, her friends would know about it, and this, Zuckerberg hoped, would lead to a discussion around people's tastes in movies. Fandango for its part would gain traction and social distribution on Facebook. EBay sellers would be able to share items for sale with their network of friends, which would widen the pool of potential bidders. The more bidders, the more likelihood the price would rise and the more money eBay would be able to skim off the top.

But things didn't go as planned. Beacon turned into a public relations fiasco. It launched with forty-four partner sites, including eBay, Fandango, the *New York Times*, Blockbuster, and Sony Online, with each partner embedding a piece of Facebook javascript on their sites. This enabled Facebook to follow the user and report back. This was all well and fine except it was virtually impossible for a user to opt out. Users had no choice but to participate unless specifically opting out, and even then the information was still dispatched back to Facebook, even after a user had logged off. To many it felt like the social network was spying on them. Users, joined by the liberal activist group Moveon.org, revolted, calling Beacon "an invasion of privacy." The bad PR drove partner sites to pull out and Zuckerberg to (eventually) apologize.

Badly executed, "but the basic idea was sound," says Bebo founder Michael Birch. It was an attempt to find the new ad unit for social networking, and down the road it will likely reemerge. In fact, a year later the company toyed with another approach, called Social Ads. Beacon informed users' friends of their activities off Facebook; Social Ads could track what they do on it. If a user buys a book on Amazon or downloads a movie from Hulu.com, Facebook would figure out which of his friends would, based on their profiles and activities on the network, be most interested. Amazon would pay Facebook for the right to send an ad across all the friends' news feeds. Vasanth Sridharan of the blog Business Insider, suggested that users should receive a commission for acting as referral marketers, on the order of 5 to 10 percent on any purchases their friends make. This would offer users a financial incentive.

And maybe therein lies part of the answer. Treat users as partners. According to network theory, each has value to Facebook, and the more active a person is and the more active his network of friends is, the more valuable he is. The user then becomes a willing participant in this marketer-consumer game. If Facebook shared some of the bounty of advertising, users would gladly interact with the new ad unit no matter what form it came in. It would be truly innovative, and a worthy extension of the social graph.

That is the premise of the viral loop application that you will find on Facebook, MySpace, and other social networks, or at http://www.viralloop .com. Download it and it will tell you what your viral coefficient is and your value—in dollars—to Facebook et al., based on the company's current valuation, your level of activity, and the activity of your friends.

Then ask for your fair share. After all, Facebook wouldn't be Facebook without the hundreds of millions of users like you.

Viral Creatures on Viral Planet Earth

Language, Religion, Money, and Other Viral Phenomena

While the Internet has become humanity's greatest viral canvas, where within all digital phenomena there is the potential to grow, virality characterizes many human traits, from the cultural to the biological. Language is viral, with toddlers learning from ten to twenty new words a day, which they pick up from conversations taking place all around them; then, when children interact with one another, they spread language. A mini-subset of that is slang, which spreads by word of mouth (and nowadays through email, texting, chat, and on social networks), with a percentage of these new words assimilated permanently into the lexicon. Money deploys elements of network effects: if I have dollars, or gold coins, or scrip of some form, I want you to accept them. So does religion, which may be the ultimate viral loop. A true believer can't be content with saving his own soul. He wants to save yours, too.

But the greatest viral realm of all is Earth. And the modern, post-Internet definition of viral—a replication pattern transmitted from user to user—can even be retrofitted to describe how life took off on the planet. Because all life forms, whether they are humans, wombats, or fire ants, are bred to spread. In essence, virality is imprinted into our DNA. In 10,000 BC, approximately one million people roamed the planet. By 5,000 BC there were 15 million and by 1 AD perhaps 300 million. If there had been one woman wandering the Earth in 10,000 BC, she would have been responsible for producing 300 people in the span of 10,001 years. As such, our growth rate was fairly flat and humans' viral coefficient barely exceeded 1.

Through the Middle Ages it took a millennium to add just ten million people to the planet—the population of a state the size of Michigan. Famine, war, poor living standards, and pestilence prevented humans from scaling. Not until 1700, when the population reached 610 million, did the growth rate pick up, inching past one billion in the early 1800s and doubling within a century. Industrialization, trade, and advances in agriculture and shipping all increased our viral coefficient. Today the world population exceeds six billion and continues growing.

It's possible to apply many of the same analytical tools used to characterize viral-loop companies to human population growth:

Online Viral Loop Companies

- **Web-based:** Better suited to the Internet
- **Free:** Users consume the product at no charge
- **Organizational technology:** They don't create content, their users do
- **Simple concept:** Easy and intuitive to use
- **Built-in virality:** Users spread the product out of own self-interest
- **Exponential growth:** That is, the virality index is above 1.0, which creates predictable growth rates
- **Network effects:** The more who join, the more who have an incentive to join
- **Stackability:** A viral network can be laid over the top of another, helping both grow
- **Point of nondisplacement:** Becomes virtually impregnable
- **Ultimate saturation:** A point of maturity when growth slows

Human Population Growth

- **Earth-based:** Only possible in the real world
- **Free:** It costs nothing to create a child (college tuition is a different matter)
- **Organizational technology:** People create people
- **Simple concept:** What could be simpler than sex?

- **Built-in virality:** People breed out of biological self-interest
- **Exponential growth:** That is, the virality index is above 1.0, which creates predictable growth rates
- **Network effects:** The greater the civilization, the higher the survival rate
- **Stackability:** The fate of one species affects others
- **Point of nondisplacement:** Becomes virtually impregnable, barring catastrophe (a meteor or nuclear war)
- **Ultimate saturation:** A point of maturity when growth slows

   The human population growth rate also mirrors the curves for companies like Skype, Hotmail, Ning, Facebook; peer-to-peer networks; and other viral-loop phenomena.

   Humans appear to have achieved a network effect around 1600, the result of advances in medicine, agriculture, and periods of peace and prosperity. We reached a point of nondisplacement long ago, with many nations (in Europe, Japan, etc.) hitting a point of ultimate saturation as their birth rates fell below replacement levels (immigration is another matter), although the populations of other countries, especially in the developing

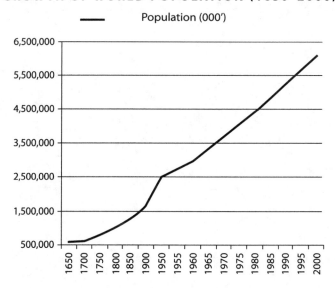

GROWTH OF WORLD POPULATION (1650–2000)

—— Population (000')

FIG. 10

world, continue to grow. Stacked atop this human network are the fates of other species, which are tied to our own. We grow vegetables and cultivate fruits, raise cattle and pigs, and domesticate dogs and cats. Global warming, a product of man, which threatens the survival of polar bears and pollution, may be killing off species of birds and frogs. Whole rain forests are burned to clear land for farmers in Brazil, which affects flora, fauna, insects, and animals.

At our essence we are viral creatures. Creating viral-loop businesses is just a small part of what we do and who we are.

The Viral Loop Company Index

Viral loop companies spread a few different ways. The most basic is "organic," when users, with little or no prompting, like something enough to share it with others. A referral model depends on users bringing others on board and viral growth via "invitation" occurs when users invite friends and others to join, as with social networks. Finally there is "viral spam," when users are hoodwinked or forced to spread something without their consent (as when a product hijacks a user's address book.) This method is unsustainable, hence the fact that no company deploying viral spam made it onto this list.

[VIRAL LOOP COMPANIES]

HOT or NOT

FOUNDERS: James Hong, Jim Young

ESTABLISHED: 2000

PRODUCT: Site that allows users to rate the attractiveness of photos submitted voluntarily by others. Also a matchmaking engine (Meet Me).

VIRAL STRATEGY: Organic

REVENUE: Advertising; paid subscriptions for matchmaking site

http://www.hotornot.com

HOTMAIL

FOUNDERS: Sabeer Bhatia, Jack Smith

ESTABLISHED: 1996

PRODUCT: Free webmail

VIRAL STRATEGY: Organic, marketing tag in each message

REVENUE: Advertising

http://www.hotmail.com

NETSCAPE

FOUNDERS: Jim Clark, Marc Andreessen

ESTABLISHED: 1994 (as Mosaic Communications Corporation).
    Purchased by AOL in 1998.

PRODUCT: Free Web browser

VIRAL STRATEGY: Organic

REVENUE: Premium services

http://www.netscape.aol.com

(No longer supported as of March 2008)

TUPPERWARE

FOUNDER: Earl Silas Tupper

ESTABLISHED: 1946

PRODUCT: Home products line that includes preparation, storage,
    and serving products for kitchen and home

VIRAL STRATEGY: Referral

REVENUE: Direct sales

http://www.tupperware.com

AMWAY

FOUNDERS: Jay Van Andel, Richard DeVos

ESTABLISHED: 1959

PRODUCT: Company that sells a wide variety of products, including home
    care products, jewelry, electronics, and dietary supplements

VIRAL STRATEGY: Referral

REVENUE: direct selling, multi-level marketing

http://www.amwayglobal.com

[VIRAL NETWORKS]

EBAY

FOUNDER: Pierre Omidyar

ESTABLISHED: 1995 (initially called AuctionWeb; renamed eBay in 1997)

PRODUCT: Online auction and shopping site

VIRAL STRATEGY: Organic

REVENUE: Fees

http://www.ebay.com

FACEBOOK

FOUNDERS: Mark Zuckerberg, Dustin Moskovitz, and Chris Hughes

ESTABLISHED: 2003 (as FaceMash) and as The Facebook in February 2004

PRODUCT: Social networking site

VIRAL STRATEGY: Invitation, organic

REVENUE: Advertising, premium services

http://www.facebook.com

MYSPACE

FOUNDERS: Tom Anderson, Chris DeWolfe, Josh Berman, Brad Greenspan

ESTABLISHED: 2003

PRODUCT: Social networking site

VIRAL STRATEGY: Invitation, organic

REVENUE: Advertising

http://www.myspace.com

LINKEDIN

FOUNDER: Reid Hoffman

ESTABLISHED: 2002, launched 2003

PRODUCT: A business-oriented social networking site

VIRAL STRATEGY: Invitation, organic

REVENUE: Premium services, advertising

http://www.linkedin.com

NING

FOUNDERS: Marc Andreessen, Gina Bianchini
ESTABLISHED: 2005
PRODUCT: Users create and operate their own social networks
VIRAL STRATEGY: Invitation, organic
REVENUE: Ads, premium services
http://www.ning.com

TWITTER

FOUNDERS: Evan Williams, Jack Dorsey, Biz Stone
ESTABLISHED: 2006
PRODUCT: Social networking, micro-blogging site
VIRAL STRATEGY: Organic
REVENUE: None
http://www.twitter.com

BEBO

FOUNDERS: Michael and Xochi Birch
ESTABLISHED: 2005 (sold to AOL in 2008)
PRODUCT: Social networking site
VIRAL STRATEGY: Invitation, organic
REVENUE: Advertising
http://www.bebo.com

IMEEM

FOUNDERS: Dalton Caldwell, Jan Jannink
ESTABLISHED: October 2004
PRODUCT: Social media service
VIRAL STRATEGY: Invitation, organic
REVENUE: Advertising
http://www.imeem.com

TAGGED

FOUNDERS: Greg Tseng, Johann Schleier-Smith
ESTABLISHED: 2004
PRODUCT: Social networking site

VIRAL STRATEGY: Invitation, referral

REVENUE: Advertising

http://www.tagged.com

[STACKED NETWORKS]

PAYPAL

FOUNDERS: Max Levchin, Peter Thiel, Luke Nosek, Ken Howery
(of Confinity) and Elon Musk (X.com)

ESTABLISHED: 1998 as Confinity; merger with X.com in 2000
(acquired by eBay in 2002)

PRODUCT: Online transactions

VIRAL STRATEGY: Paid inducements, organic

REVENUE: Fees

http://www.PayPal.com

YOUTUBE

FOUNDERS: Steve Chen, Chad Hurley, Jawed Karim

ESTABLISHED: 2005 (purchased by Google in 2006)

PRODUCT: Video share site

VIRAL STRATEGY: Organic

REVENUE: Advertising

http://www.youtube

PHOTOBUCKET

FOUNDERS: Alex Welch, Darren Crystal

ESTABLISHED: 2003 (acquired by Fox in 2007)

PRODUCT: Photo share site

VIRAL STRATEGY: Organic

REVENUE: Premium services

http://www.photobucket.com

FLICKR

FOUNDERS: Caterina Fake, Stewart Butterfield

ESTABLISHED: 2004 (acquired by Yahoo 2005)

PRODUCT: Photo share community site
VIRAL STRATEGY: Organic
REVENUE: Premium services
http://www.flickr.com

[SOCIAL NETWORK APPLICATIONS ("WIDGETS")]

SLIDE
FOUNDER: Max Levchin
ESTABLISHED: 2005
PRODUCT: Third-party applications
VIRAL STRATEGY: Invitation
REVENUE: Advertising
http://www.slide.com

ROCKYOU
FOUNDERS: Jia Shen, Lance Tokuda
ESTABLISHED: 2006
PRODUCT: Third-party applications
VIRAL STRATEGY: Invitation
REVENUE: Advertising, paid installs for other apps
http://www.rockyou.com

ZYNGA
FOUNDERS: Mark Pincus, Michael Luxton, Eric Schiermeyer,
    Justin Waldron, Andrew Trader, Steve Schoettler
ESTABLISHED: 2007
PRODUCT: Third-party applications
VIRAL STRATEGY: Invitation
REVENUE: Advertising, virtual goods
http://www.zynga.com

[SOCIAL MEDIA AD FIRMS]

LOTAME
FOUNDER: Andy Monfried
ESTABLISHED: 2006
PRODUCT: Advertisements
VIRAL STRATEGY: Targeted users
REVENUE: Fees
http://www.lotame.com

SOCIALMEDIA
FOUNDERS: Seth Goldstein, David Henderson, Dave Gentzel
ESTABLISHED: 2007
PRODUCT: Advertisements
VIRAL STRATEGY: Targeted users, engagement ads
REVENUE: Fees
http://www.socialmedia.com

MEKANISM
FOUNDER: Tommy Means
ESTABLISHED: 2000
PRODUCT: Online marketing
VIRAL STRATEGY: Engagement ads
REVENUE: Fees
http://www.mekanism.com

[PEER-TO-PEER]

SKYPE
FOUNDERS: Janus Friis, Niklas Zennstrom
ESTABLISHED: 2003
PRODUCT: Phone, video chat, instant message, and transfer files
REVENUE: Premium services
VIRAL STRATEGY: Invitation, organic
http://www.skype.com

NAPSTER

FOUNDER: Shawn Fanning

ESTABLISHED: 1999

PRODUCT: File-sharing service to distribute MP3 files.
Now a paid online music service.

VIRAL STRATEGY: Organic

REVENUE: Premium services

http://www.napster.com

KAZAA

FOUNDERS: Janus Friis, Niklas Zennstrom, Priit Kasesalu

ESTABLISHED: 2001

PRODUCT: File-sharing service to distribute MP3s, videos, applications,
and documents. Now a paid music subscription service.

VIRAL STRATEGY: Organic

REVENUE: Paid subscriptions

http://www.kazaa.com

[NONPROFITS]

CAUSES

FOUNDERS: Sean Parker, Joe Green

ESTABLISHED: 2007

PRODUCT: Site where users can mobilize their social networks to raise
money for a cause; integrates with Facebook as a widget.

VIRAL STRATEGY: Organic, invitation

REVENUE: Donations

http://exchange.causes.com

SIXDEGREES.ORG

FOUNDER: Kevin Bacon

ESTABLISHED: 2007

PRODUCT: Social networking charity

VIRAL STRATEGY: Organic

REVENUE: Donation

http://www.sixdegrees.org

JUSTGIVE

FOUNDERS: Kendall Webb

ESTABLISHED: 2000

PRODUCT: Charity

VIRAL STRATEGY: Organic

REVENUE: Donation

http://www.justgive.org

MICROGIVING

FOUNDER: John Ferber

ESTABLISHED: 2007

PRODUCT: Charity

VIRAL STRATEGY: Organic

REVENUE: Donation

http://www.microgiving.com

SOCIALVIBE

FOUNDERS: Joe Marchese

ESTABLISHED: February 2008

PRODUCT: Social networking charity

VIRAL: Organic

REVENUE: Donation

http://www.socialvibe.com

Acknowledgments

I first heard of viral loops while interviewing Marc Andreessen for a cover story for *Fast Company*. If it weren't for Marc, and his estimable sidekick Gina Bianchini, I probably would never have written this book. The more time I spent with them, the more impressed I was with the sheer wattage of their brains. They generously let me tap their social networks of entrepreneurial contemporaries who are doing fascinating things inside and outside Silicon Valley.

It's a privilege to write for *Fast Company*, which would be one of my favorite magazines even if I weren't listed on the masthead as a contributing writer. My editor, Will Bourne, is one of the best in the business and makes every writer better. A special shout-out to Bob Safian for all his support, and props to David Lidsky, Ellen McGirt, Charles Fishman, Noah Robischon, Jocelyn Hawkes, and everyone else at the magazine.

Kate Lee at ICM is everything an author could want in an agent, and her assistant, Larissa Silva, always gets things done. Jon Furay of Vigorous Pictures offered his usual sage-like counsel and was an ideal first reader. Paul Johnson and Elizabeth Brown at StudioE9 in New York run a cutting-edge Web design firm responsible for my website (http://www.viralloop.com), the viral loop social networking application and iPhone app. Brooke Hammerling of Brew PR put me in touch with interview subjects and offered spirited lessons in Silicon Valley etiquette.

I'm fortunate to work at the Arthur L. Carter Journalism Institute at New York University. It sports a world-class faculty and facility, which creates a stimulating intellectual environment that foments the exchange of ideas. My colleague, Stephen Solomon, head of the Business and Economic Reporting (BER) program—easily the finest program of its kind in the world—often covered for me as my deadline loomed, and Brooke Kroeger, NYU Journalism's director, kept things organized so nothing fell through the cracks. Charles Seife offered tips and resources on math and Mike Napolitano made sure technology didn't detonate. Orli Van Mourik and Carolyn Kormann, former graduate students of mine, crafted detailed dossiers on most of the companies and people included in these pages, while Melissa Malka performed yeoman's work in transcribing hours upon hours of recorded interviews.

While writing is largely a solitary pursuit, every book is collaborative. It's all too rare, I think, for an author to be treated with the kindness and respect I've received from my publisher. I owe a debt of gratitude to Will Balliett, who acquired *Viral Loop* for Hyperion and championed it within the company. Brendan Duffy provided valuable editorial guidance and made the book better, and Katherine Tasheff is one hip digital marketing guru. Ellen Archer runs a classy organization that deserves credit for throwing its weight behind quality projects. Thanks also to Mindy Stockfield and Carolyn Grill of Hyperion in New York and to Jack Fogg in London at Hodder, which publishes *Viral Loop* in the UK.

One of the best things about researching a book is that I get to interview whip-smart people like James Hong and Jim Young, founders of Hot or Not; Rick Goings, CEO of Tupperware; venture capitalists Fred Wilson of Union Square Ventures, Steve Jurvetson and Tim Draper of DFJ, Jeremy Liew of Lightspeed Venture Partners, and Howard Hartenbaum, an early investor in Skype; Peter Thiel, Reid Hoffman, and Max Levchin formerly of PayPal; Chris DeWolfe and Aber Whitcomb, who were at MySpace from the beginning; Mark Zuckerberg of Facebook and Matt Cohler, who left there to become a venture capitalist; Michael Birch of Bebo; Lance Tokuda, Sandi Sayama, and Jia Shen of RockYou; Greg Tseng and Johann Schleir-Smith of Tagged; Mark Pincus from Zynga; Seth Goldstein and David Gentzel of Social Media; Michael Jackson, Skype's former director of operations, and Kelly Larabee, who once handled media for the VoIP company; Jack Smith and Sabeer Bhatia of Hotmail; blogger and entrepreneur Andrew Chen; Mary Hodder, who practically lives inside the digital realm; Charlene Li and Jeremiah Owyang—astute technology analysts; the very real Caterina Fake; Andy Monfried of Lotame; the aptly named Maynard Webb, who saved eBay from death by a thousand glitches; Konstantin Guericke, who once led Jaxtr; Hans Gieskes of H3.com; Jonathan Glick of Gerson Lehrman; Kakul Srivastava of Flickr/Yahoo; and Jason Calacanis, CEO of Mahalo.

But the biggest credit goes to my wife, Charlotte, for so long putting up with my "mistress" (as she called it). As challenging as any book is to any writer, it can be equally daunting for the people in his life—for Charlotte, who had to do without her husband for long stretches of time, and my little girls, Lila and Sophie, who missed their daddy. I'm also grateful to my extended family: Nana Lin, Nana Bacon, Auntie Me, Uncle B, Charlie Boy, Nana Tina, and everyone else who pitched in while I pounded out words on my now-battered Apple MacBook Pro keyboard (certain letters have even worn away). Here's also to the memory of Barbara and Arnold. I miss you.

Notes

Transcripts of interviews and more detailed endnotes with hyperlinks available at http://www.viralloop.com. Quotes in text originate from interview with subject unless otherwise noted.

PROLOGUE
Events and descriptions: Interviews with James Hong and Jim Young.

Additional background: "Idea of rate-a-person site gets a perfect 10," by Janet Kornblum, *USA Today*, November 28, 2000; "Cyber Digest: A Weekly Spin on the Web," by Noah Robischon, *Entertainment Weekly*, December 1, 2000; "A New Web Site Asks, 'Who's the Fairest?'" by Joanna Weiss, *The Boston Globe*, December 4, 2000; "These Men Want to Know... Am I Hot?" by Mary Huhn, *New York Post*, December 5, 2000; "Hot Stuff or a Bit of Rough? The World Decides," by Molly Watson, *Evening Standard*, December 5, 2000; "Ego Boost or Bust," by Daniel J. Vargas, *Houston Chronicle*, January 11, 2001; "'Am I Hot?': Popular Site Burning to Know," by David Plotnikoff, *Denver Post,* February 5, 2001; "Digits": Technology News and Insights, *Wall Street Journal*, August 2, 2001; "The Hot or Not Guys," by Adam Green, *The New Yorker*, July 8, 2002; "Facing the World with Egos Exposed," by Gary Rivlin, *New York Times*, June 3, 2004; "Hot or Not?" by David Momphard, *Taipei Times*, July 3, 2004; "You Gotta Love the Enthusiasm of Jim and James," by Alan T. Saracevic, *San Francisco Chronicle*, September 12, 2004; "Hot or Not? Meet the Guys Behind the Popular Rating-and-Dating Web Spot," by Jessica Yadegaran, Knight

Ridder, November 7, 2005; "He Hopes Flush of Embarrassment Leads to Flush of Success," by Kevin Maney, *USA Today*, November 23, 2005.

p. 8   *Salon.com* was planning an article: "Am I Hot Or Not?" by Janelle Brown, *Salon.com*, October 11, 2000.

INTRODUCTION

p. 12   Within ninety minutes: Interviews with James Hong and Jim Young.

p. 12   Peter Thiel, whose $500,000 investment in Facebook: Facebook Factsheet http://www.facebook.com/press/info.php?factsheet

p. 13   Ning raised $104 million in venture capital: "Marc Andreessen Dings Google's Friend Connect," by Dan Farber, *CNET*, May 13, 2008.

p. 13   Slide, which creates photo slideshow tools, attracted $50 million: "Are These Widgets Worth Half a Billion?" by Jessi Hempel and Michael V. Copland, *Fortune*, March 25, 2008.

p. 13   joked that he's considered changing his form's name to "Viral Ventures" and "You can create a crappy application": Interview with Fred Wilson.

p. 13   "is worth a lot of money" and "the most advanced direct-marketing strategy": Interview with Andrew Chen.

p. 14   "One of my fundamental beliefs": "The Facebooker Who Friended Obama," by Brian Stelter, *New York Times*, July 7, 2008.

p. 15   The campaign brought in $750 million from 4 million donors: "Final Fundraising Tally for Obama Exceeded $750 Million," by Alec MacGillis and Sarah Cohen, *Washington Post*, December 6, 2008.

p. 15   Obama's campaign raised $55 million online: "Obama raises $55 million in February, sets new record," *CNN*, March 6, 2008: http://www.cnn.com/2008/POLITICS/03/06/democrats.campaign/index.html

p. 15   "Since most have not donated anything like the maximum amount": "Barack Obama is master of the new Facebook politics," by Andrew Sullivan, *Sunday Times*, May 25, 2008.

p. 16   "I have the record and the scars to prove it": "McCain: End 'the constant partisan rancor,'" by Alex Johnson, *msnbc.com*, September 4, 2008.

p. 16   "After nearly a year on the campaign trail": *Michelle Obama*, by Elizabeth Lightfoot, The Lyons Press, 2008.

p. 16   "Don't walk away thinking that you can talk to only one customer": "5 product management lessons from the Obama campaign," by Gopal Shenoy, productmanagementtips.com, November 7, 2008.

p. 17   "The Wright brothers," while Obama's "skipped Boeing, Mercury, Gemini": "The Facebooker Who Friended Obama," by Brian Stelter, *New York Times*, July 7, 2008.

p. 18   "The viral adoption model": Interview with Fred Wilson.

CHAPTER 1

Material on Tupperware: Interview with Tupperware CEO, Rick Goings; *Tupperware: The Promise of Plastics in 1950s America*, by Alison J. Clarke, Diane Pub Co., 1999; *Tupperware Unsealed: Brownie Wise, Earl Tupper, and the Home Party Pioneers*, by Bob Kealing, University Press of Florida, 2008; "Tupperware," *Time*, September 8, 1947; "Tupperware Sales Up 115 Percent," *New York Times,* August 20, 1953; "Is the Party Over? Has America Heard the Last Burp out of Tupperware?" by Charles Fishman, *Orlando Sentinel*, Mar 15, 1987; "Tupperware the Housewives' Choice," by Alison Clarke, *The Guardian*, September 27, 1990. "Going Stale: Families Have Changed but Tupperware Keeps Holding Its Parties," by Laurie M. Grossman, *Wall Street Journal*, July 21, 1992; "Brownie Wise Sealed Tupperware's Future," by Philip Martin, *Arkansas Democrat Gazette*, February 10, 2004; *Tupperware: An American Experience*, documentary by Laurie Kahn-Leavitt that aired on PBS in December 2003.

Material on Charles Ponzi: *The Rise of Mr. Ponzi*, by Charles Ponzi, Inkwell Publishers (American edition), 2001; *Ponzi's Scheme*, by Michael Zuckoff, Random House, 2005.

p. 24   "Open Mouth Container and Nonsnap type of closure": U.S. Patent # 2487400.

CHAPTER 2

Events and descriptions: Interview with Marc Andreessen; *Netscape Time: The Making of the Billion-Dollar Start-Up That Took on Microsoft*, by Jim Clark, St. Martin's Griffin, July 16, 2000; *Dot.con: How America Lost Its Mind and Money in the Internet Era*, by John Cassidy, Harper Perennial, 2003; *Marc Andreessen: Web Warrior*, by Daniel Ehrenhaft, 21st Century, April 1, 2001; "Architects of the

Web," by Robert H. Reid, John Wiley & Sons, 1997. "What It's Really Like to be Marc Andreessen," by Rick Tetzeli, *Fortune*, December 9, 1996. "Netscape Knows Fame and Aspires to Fortune," by Peter H. Lewis, *New York Times*, March 1, 1995. "High Stakes Winners," by James Collins, et al., *Time*, February 19, 1996. "The Man Who Invented the Web," by Robert Wright, *Time*, May 19, 1997.

p. 44   In 1992, 4.5 million people were plugged into the Internet: *The Affluent Consumer: Marketing and Selling the Luxury Lifestyle*, by Ronald Michman and Edward Mazze, Praeger Publishers, 2006.

p. 44   1 million people had downloaded Mosaic: *Nerds 2.0.1—A Human Face*, PBS documentary, 1998. Text at http://www.pbs.org/opb/nerds 2.0.1/wiring_world/mosaic.html

p. 45   Number of Internet Users, 1992–2007: Data from http://www.inter networldstats.com/emarketing.htm and http://www.allaboutmarket research.com/internet.htm

p. 45   Number of Websites, 1992–2007: http://royal.pingdom.com/2008/04/ 04/how-we-got-from-1-to-162-million-websites-on-the-internet/ and http://www.pandia.com/searchworld/2000-39-oclc-size.html and "Web reaches new milestone: 100 million sites," by Marsha Walton, CNN, November 1, 2006; and interview with Marc Andreessen.

p. 45   *New York Times* article on the front page of the business section: "A Free and Simple Computer Link," by John Markoff, *New York Times*, December 8, 1993.

CHAPTER 3

Events and descriptions: Interviews with Ning cofounders Marc Andreessen and Gina Bianchini.

Additional material: Interviews with Jeremy Liew, Mary Hodder, Nicholas Economides, John Manzo, Greg Tseng, and Johann Schleir-Smith; *The Long Tail: Why the Future of Business Is Selling Less of More*, by Chris Anderson, Hyperion, 2006; *The Wealth of Networks*, by Yochai Benler, Yale University Press, 2006; *Mathematics in Medicine and the Life Sciences*, by F. C. Hoppenstadt and C. S. Peskin, Springer-Verlag, 1992; *The Power of Identity (Vol. II)*, by Manuel Castells, Blackwell, 1997.

p. 57   Viral Coefficient charts: Data provided by Jeremy Liew, partner at Lightspeed Partners, in a blog post, "Viral Marketing, Randomness, and the Difficulty of Controlling Growth in Social Media," September 13, 2007 (http://lsvp.wordpress.com/2007/09/13/viral-marketing -randomness-and-the-difficulty-of-controlling-growth-in-social -media/).

p. 59.   Birthday Alarm, which generated $3 million a year in revenue: Interview with Michael Birch, Birthday Alarm cofounder.

p. 59   "Web 2.0 Hottie": "Return of the Ning," by Chris Mohney, *Valleywag* (now posted under *Gawker*), February 27, 2007.

p. 60   "Ning RIP?" and "Everyone wants a social network": Posts on *Techcrunch.com*, by Michael Arrington, January 20, 2006 and September 23, 2007.

p. 62   Pareto's Law: *The Long Tail: Why the Future of Business Is Selling Less of More*," by Chris Anderson, Hyperion, 2006.

p. 66   MySpace, which News Corp. bought for $580 million; Murdoch estimates is worth close to $6 billion: "$6 billion MySpace: Will this Levinsohn cash in?" by Donna Bogatin, ZDNET blog, November 17, 2006.

p. 69–80 Material on the commoditized Internet, digital me, hooked on the speed of Web life inspired by articles I published in *Media* magazine, including: "The Speed Squeeze," by Adam L. Penenberg, *Media*, September 22, 2006; and "At the End of the Paper Trail: Why Ink on Pulp May Soon Become an Artifact," by Adam L. Penenberg, *Media*, October 1, 2007.

p. 70   "We know of no people without names": *Social Theory and the Politics of Identity*, by Craig Calhoun (ed.), Wiley-Blackwell, 1994.

p. 70   The United States has essentially become a "multitrillion-dollar brand," and "Brands, products, fashions": *Culture Jam: How to Reverse America's Suicidal Consumer Binge—And Why We Must*, by Kalle Lasn, Harper Paperbacks, 2000.

p. 71   "as human beings we are social creatures": Interview with John Manzo, sociology professor at the University of Calgary in Alberta.

p. 71   scanned the brains of fiction readers: "Readers Build Vivid Mental Simulations of Narrative Situations, Brain Scans Suggest," by Gerry Everding, *Physorg.com*, January 26th, 2009.

p. 72   "are scarcely able to lead": *Improvement of the understanding: Ethics and Correspondence of Benedict de Spinoza*, by Benedictus de Spinoza (ed.) Robert Harvey Monro Elwes, Universal Classics Library, 1901.

p. 72   helps us live longer; get fewer colds and flu: "Friends 'help people live longer,'" BBC News, June 15 2005.

p. 72   A research project by Paul J. Zak; "The stronger the signal of trust;" Trust works as an 'economic lubricant'": Interview with Paul Zaks by Corante, December 23, 2004. http://brainwaves.corante.com/archives/neuroeconomics/

p. 73   It's actually closer to 6.6: "Six degrees of Kevin Bacon? Microsoft finds 6.6 in massive data bank," by Matt Asay, CNET, August 4, 2008.

p. 74–75   Mary Hodder material: Interviews with Mary Hodder. Published in part in "Her So-Called Digital Life," by Adam L. Penenberg, *Wired News*, December 2, 2004.

p. 77   Al Gore keynote speech at We Media conference in NY: October 6, 2005.

p. 78   Intel Atom design and production: Interviews with Pankaj Kedia, Intel's ecosystems manager, Mooly Eden, general manager of Intel's mobile platforms group, and Martin Reynolds, vice president at Gartner Inc., who covers semiconductors. Published in part in "Intel Atom: Intel Makes Its Smallest Chip Ever," by Adam L. Penenberg, *Fast Company*, October 2008.

p. 80   "These things are powerful": Interview with Charlie Miller.

p. 80–83   Crushlink material: Interviews with Crushlink founders Greg Tseng and Johann Schleir-Smith.

p. 82   Federal Trade Commission fined the viral duo $900,000: "Ad Firm Pays $900,000 for CAN-SPAM Violation," by Donna Higgins, Andrews Publications, March 29, 2006.

CHAPTER 4

Events and descriptions: Interviews with Sabeer Bhatia, Jack Smith, Tim Draper, and Steve Jurvetson. "What Is Viral Marketing," white paper by Steve Jurvetson, May 1, 2000; "Hotmail Case Study," by Steve Jurvetson and Sabeer Bhatia, created for an MBA class at Stanford Business School; transcription of interview with Sabeer Bhatia, published in *Founders at Work: Stories of Start-*

ups' Early Days, by Jessica Livingston (ed.), Apress, 2007; "HotMale," by Po Bronson, *Wired*, December 1998.

p. 102   Hotmail growth figures provided by Draper Fisher Jurvetson.

CHAPTER 5

Events and descriptions: Interviews with Arin Crumley, Susan Buice, Chris Kentis, and Ethan Marten. Some articles that helped form the basis of this chapter include "Revenge of the Nerds," by Adam L. Penenberg, *Fast Company*, July 2006; "Cue the Computers: How Star Circle Pictures Is Remaking Moviemaking," by Adam L. Penenberg, *Fast Company*, September 2006; "Boom, Bust & Beyond," by Adam L. Penenberg, *Fast Company*, March 2006; "Song Pirates," by Adam L. Penenberg, *Forbes.com*, July 11, 1997.

p. 108   "Just imagine trying to shoot," etc: Interview with James Longley.

p. 109   "The typewriter didn't make better writers": Interview with Ronald Steinman.

p. 109–110   *Open Water* material: Interview with Chris Kentis.

p. 110–111   Star Circle Pictures material: Interviews with Ethan Marten and Kimball Carr.

p. 111   "fascinating," and "deliberately smudges the line between fiction and nonfiction": Review by Robert Koehler, *Variety*, February 22, 2005.

p. 111   "spry," etc: "Barbecue, bummers, and Boston: Our man at South by Southwest," by Gerald Peary, *Boston Phoenix*, March 25, 2005.

p. 113   between 1825 and 1826 and 40 percent of American railway bonds, 45,000 miles of track, etc.: *Engines That Move Markets*, by Alasdair Nairn, John Wiley & Sons, 2002.

p. 114   our exuberance, irrational or otherwise: "Irreplaceable Exuberance," by Henry Blodget, Op-Ed in *New York Times*, August 30, 2005.

p. 114   Amazon founder Jeff Bezos has likened the impact of the Internet to the Cambrian era: Q & A with Jeff Bezos, published in *Businessweek*, September 16, 1999, among many others.

p. 115   U.S population grew by 15 percent between 1910 and 1920, but the number of personal servants fell 25 percent: *Electrifying America*, by David Nye, MIT Press, 1990.

p. 115 "as the beginning of neural pathways": Interview with Wes Craven: "Electroshocker!" by Adam L. Penenberg, *Forbes.com*, November 29, 1999.

p. 115–116 "The Lair" material: Interview with "The Lair," an underground music pirate. "Song Pirates," by Adam L. Penenberg, *Forbes.com*, July 11, 1997.

p. 118–119 It would cost about $3 billion to convert, "You have a $9 billion domestic box office," and cost to offer digitally: Interview with Bud Mayo.

p. 119 "The studios are afraid," etc.: Interview with Ira Deutchman.

p. 119–120 "If a theater pulls," etc.: Interview with David Zelon.

p. 123 Research shows that in 1910, there were 2,600 daily newspapers . . . by 1990, there were 1,600: *The Power of the Press: The Birth of American Political Reporting*, by Thomas C. Leonard, Oxford University Press, 1986.

CHAPTER 6

Events and descriptions: Interviews with Pete Healey, Michael Donnelly, Fritz Grobe, Stephen Voltz, Greg Spiridellis, and Steve Spangler.

p. 127 "It's all about the combination": Interview with Adam Lavelle.

p. 127 "The more in control we are": A. G. Lafley speech at the Association of National Advertisers, December 4, 2006.

p. 131 "If you ever care to see": *Liar's Poker: Rising Through the Wreackage of Wall Street*, by Michael Lewis, Penguin, 1990.

p. 131 tracked it to a nearby school: "The NASA Joke Cycle," by Elizabeth Radin Simons, *Western Folklore*, October 1986.

p. 133 subservient chicken: http://www.subservientchicken.com

CHAPTER 7

Events and descriptions: Interviews with Maynard Webb and Jim Griffith. "Running the World's Hottest Company Is a Lot Harder Than It Looks," by Patricia Sellers, *Fortune*, October 18, 2004; "What Makes eBay Invincible," by Brad Hill, *E-Commerce Times*, March 4, 2003; "Webb Master," Julie Pitta, *Forbes*, December 13, 1999; "The People's Company," by Robert D. Hof, *Businessweek*, December 3, 2001; "Exit Interview (with Meg Whitman)," by Amy Wallace, *Portfolio*, May 2008; "Behind the Scenes at eBay," by Kathleen Melymuka,

Computerworld, January 13, 2000; "eBay Knocked Out by More Tech Problems," by Troy Wolverton, *CNET News.com*, November 2, 1999; "Sun's Bid to Rule the Web," by Peter Burrows, *Businessweek*, July 24, 2000; "Webb Puts a Spin on EBay's Woes (Q&A with Maynard Webb)," *The Age* (via *Salon*), September 28, 1999; "New-Media Companies Come Calling—Dot-Coms Are on the Prowl For IT Talent, and That's Changing the Career Landscape," by Teri Robinson, *Information Week* (reprinted from *ITWeek*), November 1, 1999. Offer Letter from Meg Whitman to Maynard Webb (Source: eBay), July 17, 1999.

I relied extensively on *The Perfect Store: Inside eBay*, by Adam Cohen, Back Bay, 2003, for material on eBay's early years. For anyone interested in learning more about eBay's history, this is a must-read text.

p. 144 If your viral coefficient is one and explanation of scaling: Interview with Jeremy Liew.

p. 149 MagicFX hack of eBay: "Going, going, going . . . hacked!" by Adam L. Penenberg, *Forbes.com*, March 19, 1999.

p. 150–152 Friendster material: "How to Kill a Great Idea," by Max Chafkin, *Inc.*, June 2007; "Friendster, Love and Money," by Gary Rivlin, *New York Times*, January 24, 2005; "Wallflower at the Web Party," by Gary Rivlin, *New York Times*, October 15, 2006; "Friendster Moves to Asia," by Ling Woo Liu, *Time*, January 29, 2008; "Social Networking Is Not a Business," by Bryant Urstadt, *Technology Review*, July 1, 2008; Friendster lost steam. Is MySpace just a fad?" by Danah Boyd, *danahboyd.com*, March 21, 2006; "Friendster Gets $10 Million Infusion for Revival Bid," by Vauhini Vara and Rebecca Buckman, *Wall Street Journal*, August 21, 2008.

p. 152 "All they had to do": Interview with Matt Cohler.

p. 153 "We were taken by surprise": Interview with Biz Stone, cofounder of Twitter.

p. 153 "They're playing catch-up now": Interview with Fred Wilson.

p. 153 Gmail scaling: *Founders at Work* (interview with Paul Buchheit, Gmail creator), by Jessica Livingston (ed.), Apress, 2007.

p. 154 "It humbled the company": "10 Years Ago, eBay Changed the World, Sort of by Accident: Auctioneer Grew by Trial and Error into a Phenomenon," by Kevin Maney, *USA Today*, March 22, 2005.

CHAPTER 8

Events and descriptions: Interviews with Max Levchin, Peter Thiel and Reid Hoffman. *Once Your Lucky, Twice You're Good: The Rebirth of Silicon Valley and the Rise of Web 2.0*, by Sarah Lacy, Gotham, 2008. "Meet the PayPal Mafia," by Jeffrey M. O'Brien, *Fortune*, November, 26, 2007; "The Paypal Exodus," by Rachel Rosmarin, *Forbes*, July 12, 2006; "Technology Is at the Center," by Ronald Bailey, *Reason Online*, May 2008; "New software will allow users to beam money to each other," by Martha Mendoza, Associated Press, July 23, 1999.

For additional behind-the scenes action at PayPal (outside the scope of my interviews with PayPal's founders and early employee Reid Hoffman) I relied extensively on *The PayPal Wars: Battles with eBay, the Media, the Mafia, and the Rest of Planet Earth,* by Eric M. Jackson, World Ahead Publishing, Inc., 2004. For anyone interested in PayPal, it's an excellent resource.

p. 165   "Google wanted PhDs," "great hire," "was an idiot," etc: "Meet the Pay-Pal Mafia," by Jeffrey M. O'Brien, *Fortune*, November, 26, 2007.

p. 173   "Peter, Max, and I are not directly aligned philosophically": ibid.

p. 179   "If it's war you want, it's war you'll get." Recounted by Reid Hoffman.

CHAPTER 9

Events and descriptions: Interviews with Caterina Fake, Chris Dewolfe, and Aber Whitcomb. *Stealing MySpace: The Battle to Control the Most Popular Website in America*, by Julia Angwin, Random House, 2009; "Smiles, Everyone; Online hookup site MySpace is beginning to look a lot less like Facebook and a lot more like MTV," by Erika Brown, *Forbes*, December 10, 2007; "The Battle for Your Social Circle," by Josh Quittner and Jesse Hempel, *Fortune*, November 26, 2007; "MySpace Strikes Back," by David Kirkpatrick, *Fortune*, October 1, 2007. "The MySpace Generation; How a project to feed burritos to the hungry in L.A. spread all the way to Damascus," by Chris DeWolfe, *Forbes*, May 7, 2007; "MySpace Cowboys," by Patricia Sellers, *Fortune*, September 4, 2006; "Look Who's Online Now: It took a while, but Rupert Murdoch has a case of Internet fever. A real-time portrait of a legendary mogul remaking his media colossus," by Adam Lashinsky, *Fortune*, October 31, 2005.

p. 182 "Journalists are trained not to be emotional," etc.: Interview with Michael K. Powell and published in "Technorati: A Public Utility," by Adam L. Penenberg, *Wired News*, July 14, 2005.

p. 183–185 Flickr material: Interview with Flickr cofounder, Caterina Fake.

p. 185–191 MySpace material: Interviews with Chris DeWolfe, Aber Whitcomb, who headed MySpace's IT, and *Stealing MySpace: The Battle to Control the Most Popular Website in America*, by Julia Angwin, Random House, 2009, which offers delicious detail on MySpace and key information on Photobucket and YouTube.

p. 186 notorious teen hacker who, under the *nom de hack*, Lord Flathead: "Chase Computer Raided by Youths, Officials," by David Sanger, *New York Times*, October 19, 1985.

p. 188–189 "the least lonely girl on the Internet": "Tila Tequila," by Lev Grossman, *Time*, December 16, 2006.

p. 190 Photobucket . . . sold to MySpace in 2007 for $250 million: "MySpace owner to buy Photobucket," by Kenneth Li, Reuters, May 30, 2007.

p. 191 Google walked away with the year-old site for $1.65 billion in October 2006: "Google to Acquire YouTube for $1.65 Billion in Stock," Google Press Release, October 9, 2006.

CHAPTER 10

Events and descriptions: Interview with Michael Birch. "Making a mint as the laidback king and queen of gossip central: Profile Michael and Xochi Birch," *Sunday Times*, March 16, 2008; "On the Face of It," by Emily Bell, *The Guardian*, March 17, 2008; "AOL to 'supercharge' Bebo revenues," by Andrew Edgecliffe-Johnson, *Financial Times*, March 13, 2008.

p. 201 "She's such a stupid": "Social networking websites such as Bebo were set up for entirely innocent purposes. But the scourge of teen bullying has now found a new playground in cyberspace," published in *Independent.ie*, April 26, 2006.

p. 201 Dublin school suspended: ibid.

p. 201 death threats: Death Threats Posted on Net, by Jilly Beattie, *Mirror*, May 11, 2006.

p. 201 To disseminate porn: "Bebo evil or innocent?" *Irish Times*, May 20, 2006.

p. 201 *Irish Times* report: ibid.

CHAPTER 11

Events and descriptions: Interviews with Mark Zuckerberg, Matt Cohler, Jia Shen, Lance Tokuda, Sandi Sayama, Mark Pincus, Max Levchin, James Hong, and Jim Young. *Dot.con: How America Lost Its Mind and Money in the Internet Era*, by John Cassidy, Harper Perennial, 2003; *Once You're Lucky, Twice You're Good: The Rebirth of Silicon Valley and the Rise of Web 2.0*, by Sarah Lacy, Gotham, 2008; *Stealing MySpace: The Battle to Control the Most Popular Website in America*, by Julia Angwin, Random House, 2009. "Me Media; How Hanging Out on the Internet Became Big Business," by John Cassidy, *The New Yorker*, May 15, 2006; "Facebook Goes off Campus," by Brad Stone, *New York Times*, May 25, 2007; "Facebook's Plan to Hook Up the World," by David Kirkpatrick, *Fortune*, May 29, 2007; "Facebook Grows Up," by Steven Levy, *Newsweek*, August 20, 2007; "How to Kill a Great Idea," by Max Chafkin, *Inc.*, June 2007; "Facebook Ignites Entrepreneurial Spirit at Harvard," by Vauhini Vara, *Wall Street Journal*, May 20, 2008; "The Battle For Facebook," by Clarie Hoffman, *Rolling Stone*, June 26, 2008; "How Chris Hughes Helped Launch Facebook and the Barack Obama Campaign," by Ellen McGirt, *Fast Company*, April 2009.

p. 204   noticed that traffic shot up: "How to Kill a Great Idea," by Max Chafkin, *Inc.*, June 2007.

p. 210   a typical approach is to create thousands of web pages: Interview with Dave Dittrich.

p. 210   cybercriminals have been borrowing black-hat SEO techniques: "Google Bombing and the IRS," by Adam L. Penenberg, *fastcompany .com*, March 30, 2009; "Search Google, Click to Massive Malware Attacks?" by Gregg Keizer, *Computerworld*, November 27, 2007.

p. 211   A 2009 report: "Tracking GhostNet: Investigating a Cyber Espionage Network," Information Warfare Monitoring, March 2009.

p. 213   the six degrees patent, *"probably the pioneer patent out there"*: "Idea for Online Networking Brings Two Entrepreneurs Together," by Teresa Riordan, *New York Times*, December 1, 2003.

p. 214–216   RockYou material: Interviews with Lance Tokuda, Jia Shen, and Sandi Sayama.

p. 216   Metrics for Viral Loop: Presentation by Lance Tokuda, RockYou, on using social networking platforms and applications for viral marketing distribution, at Startonomics workshop, San Francisco, 2008.

p. 216–219 Slide material: Interview with Max Levchin; *Once You're Lucky, Twice You're Good: The Rebirth of Silicon Valley and the Rise of Web 2.0*, by Sarah Lacy, Gotham, 2008; *Stealing MySpace: The Battle to Control the Most Popular Website in America*, by Julia Angwin, Random House, 2009; *Founders at Work: Stories of Startups' Early Days*, by Jessica Livingston (ed.), Apress, 2007.

p. 218 Click-through rate on banner ads on social networks is barely 0.02 percent: Interview with Seth Goldstein, founder of Social Media, an ad firm.

CHAPTER 12

p. 220 "electric toy" and "utterly out of the question": *Engines That Move Markets*, by Alasdair Nairn, John Wiley & Sons, 2002.

p. 220 At a conference in December 1996, "off their rocker," and "Bill has an extraordinary ability . . .": "Cable told to make 'digital money,'" by Harry A. Jessell, *Broadcasting & Cable*, December 16, 1996.

p. 221–224 Battle between marketers and consumers: Some of these issues were explored in "The Speed Squeeze," by Adam L. Penenberg, *Media*, September 22, 2006.

p. 222 "Long-tail marketing effect": Email exchange with Mark Cuban.

p. 222 "How many times have you gone home from a commute": Interview with David Schwartz.

p. 224 "Anything that causes the audience": Interview with Colby Atwood.

p. 224 "the right to be left alone": "The Right to Be Left Alone," by Mark Skousen, *Ideas on Liberty*, May 2002.

p. 224–229 The Privacy Shibboleth explored in previously published pieces: "Surveillance Nation," by Adam L. Penenberg, *Wired*, December 2001, and "Nowhere to Run," by Adam L. Penenberg, *Media*, April 1, 2008.

p. 225 more than five hundred surveillance cameras: The Surveillance Camera Players, http://www.notbored.org/nyu.html.

p. 225 "Moore's Law of cameras": Interview with David Brin.

p. 225 "privacy is the power to selectively reveal": "A Cypherpunk's Manifesto," by Eric Hughes, http://w2.eff.org/Privacy/Crypto/Crypto_misc/cypherpunk.manifesto.

p. 225 "You have no privacy": "On the Record: Scott McNeally," *San Francisco Chronicle*, September 14, 2003.

p. 226   CVS's ExtraCare program, which has signed up tens of millions: CVS CareMark History: http://info.cvscaremark.com/our-company/history.

p. 226   "no longer can mean anonymity": "Top Intelligence Official: Public Needs to Change Their Definition of Privacy," by Pamela Hess, Associated Press, November 11, 2007.

p. 226   127 million sensitive electronic and paper records were lost or pierced by hackers: "The Anonymity Experiment," Catherine Price, *Popular Science*, February 8, 2008.

p. 227   can't keep secret his home address: "Google Balances Privacy, Reach," by Elinor Mills, *CNET news.com*, July 14, 2005.

p. 229–231   Time, Not Clicks: The New Ad Unit material: Interview with Andy Monfried, CEO, Lotame.

p. 233   users should receive a commission: "Facebook's Beacon Coming Back? Sort Of*," by Vasanth Sridharan, *Business Insider (Silicon Alley Insider)*, August 20, 2008.

p. 233   Find the Viral Loop widget at viralloop.com.

EPILOGUE

p. 235–236   Population growth rate figures: "Year-by-Year World Population Estimates: 10,000 B.C. to 2007 A.D.," by Scott Manning, http://www.digitalsurvivors.com/archives/worldpopulation.php, January 12, 2008; Worldometers: http://www.worldometers.info/population; U.S. Census International Database, World Population Information, http://www.census.gov/ipc/www/idb/worldpopinfo.html.

Index